Springer Proceedings in Business and Economics

Springer Proceedings in Business and Economics brings the most current research presented at conferences and workshops to a global readership. The series features volumes (in electronic and print formats) of selected contributions from conferences in all areas of economics, business, management, and finance. In addition to an overall evaluation by the publisher of the topical interest, scientific quality, and timeliness of each volume, each contribution is refereed to standards comparable to those of leading journals, resulting in authoritative contributions to the respective fields. Springer's production and distribution infrastructure ensures rapid publication and wide circulation of the latest developments in the most compelling and promising areas of research today.

The editorial development of volumes may be managed using Springer Nature's innovative EquinOCS, a proven online conference proceedings submission, management and review system. This system is designed to ensure an efficient timeline for your publication, making Springer Proceedings in Business and Economics the premier series to publish your workshop or conference volume.

This book series is indexed in SCOPUS.

Eric Tsui · Montathar Faraon · Kari Rönkkö
Editors

Management Information Systems in a Digitalized AI World

Proceedings of 2024 International Conference on Management Information System

Springer

Editors
Eric Tsui
Educational Research Centre (ERC)
The Hong Kong Polytechnic University
Hong Kong, China

Montathar Faraon
Kristianstad University
Kristianstad, Sweden

Kari Rönkkö
Kristianstad University
Kristianstad, Sweden

ISSN 2198-7246 ISSN 2198-7254 (electronic)
Springer Proceedings in Business and Economics
ISBN 978-981-96-6525-9 ISBN 978-981-96-6526-6 (eBook)
https://doi.org/10.1007/978-981-96-6526-6

This Springer imprint is published by the registered company Springer Nature Singapore Pte Ltd.
The registered company address is: 152 Beach Road, #21-01/04 Gateway East, Singapore 189721, Singapore

Committees

Conference Advisory Committees

Piet Kommers, University of Twente, The Netherlands
Yong Jin Kim, Sogang University, South Korea

Conference Organizing Chair

Yoshifumi Manabe, Kogakuin University, Japan

Conference Organizing Co-Chair

Eric Tsui, The Hong Kong Polytechnic University, Hong Kong, China

Conference Program Chairs

Bob Fox, University of New South Wales Sydney, Australia
Yuji Iwahori, Chubu University, Japan
Zehui Zhan, South China Normal University, China

Conference Publicity Chairs

Xuebo Zhang, Northwest Normal University, China

Fang Yu, Jinan University, China

Conference Program Co-Chair

Yu-Mei Wang, University of Alabama at Birmingham, USA

Conference Local Organizing Committee

Akio Ishida, National Institute of Technology, Japan

Technical Program Committees

Cong Doan Truong, Vietnam National University, Vietnam
Raymond Li, University of Canberra, Australia
Wei Wang, Nanjing Normal University, China
Vilem Novak, The University of Ostrava, Czech Republic
Ka-Chun Wong, City University of Hong Kong, Hong Kong, China
Lee Chien Sing, Sunway University, Malaysia
Cheng Siong CHIN, Newcastle University in Singapore, Singapore
Chau Kien Tsong, Universiti Sains Malaysia, Malaysia
Ritthiwut Puwaphat, Princess of Naradhiwas University, Thailand
Prantosh Kumar Paul, Raiganj University, India
Thaweesak Yingthawornsuk, King Mongkut's University of Technology Thonburi, Thailand
Eunice B. Custodio, Bulacan State University, Philippines
Nursabillilah Binti Mohd Ali, Universiti Teknikal Malaysia Melaka, Malaysia
Sunghye Lee, Korea Advanced Institute of Science and Technology, South Korea
Gamal Alawi, Taiz University, Yemen

Preface

2024 2nd International Conference on Management Information System (ICMIS 2024) was held in Tokyo, Japan September 28–30, 2024. The Technical Program Committee put together an excellent program, which includes presentations from keynote speakers—Prof. Piet Kommers (University of Twente, The Netherlands), Prof. Bob Fox (University of New South Wales Sydney, Australia), Prof. Eric Tsui (The Hong Kong Polytechnic University, Hong Kong, China), and Prof. Yong Jin Kim (Sogang University, South Korea).

ICMIS is an annual event which aims at a key theme on management information system. It is aimed to provide a stimulating forum for researchers, scientists, engineers and practitioners to present their latest research findings, ideas, developments and applications in all aspects of management information system.

The proceedings of ICMIS 2024 cover a range of topics, including *(1) Technological Innovation and Marketing Strategies; (2) Management Informatization and Risk Management; (3) Machine Learning Models and Artificial Intelligence in Financial Market Forecasting and Decision Making; (4) Econometric Analysis and Financial Mathematics.*

Efforts taken by peer reviewers contributed to improving the quality of papers and provided constructive critical comments; improvements and corrections to the authors are gratefully appreciated. We are very grateful to the international/national advisory committee, session chairs, and administrative assistants who selflessly contributed to the success of this conference. Also, we are thankful to all the authors who submitted papers, because of them the conference became a story of success. It was the quality of their presentation and passion to communicate with other participants that made this conference a great success.

As you read these proceedings, you're very welcome to contribute a paper to the ICMIS 2025 conference, which is scheduled for September 27–29, 2025 in Yokohama, Japan. We look forward to seeing you at ICMIS 2025!

Hong Kong SAR, China

Warmest regards,
Prof. Eric Tsui
Conference Organizing Co-Chair,
ICMIS 2024

Contents

Technological Innovation and Marketing Strategies

Technology Path Way: Reframing with a New Perspective

Ahyun Kim, Jinwoo Kim, and Yong Jin Kim

Abstract The product life cycle has long been cited as a concept explaining the cycle of birth and extinction of products and technologies. However, according to our observation over patents and research papers, a technology after its inception did not extinct even though its original product faded out, but is often used or cited by other industries or research. To explain this phenomenon, this study proposes a concept of Technology Pathway instead of the Product Life Cycle. This study focuses on the characteristics of technology (multipurpose and transferability) as the factor that allows technologies to survive and grow even after its original product disappeared. To illustrate Technology Path Way, examined in detail are technologies used in the battery, printing, and memory industries.

Keywords Multipurpose · Technology Demand · Technology pathway · Transferability

1 Introduction

The product life cycle has long been cited as a concept describing the cycle of birth and extinction of products and technologies. While traditional product life cycles have generally been described at both the hardware level and technology, such broad approach can be seen as inadequate, as they do not consider products as aggregates of various levels of technologies. The product life cycle typically follows a gradual

A. Kim
Dongyang Mirae University, Seoul, Korea
e-mail: ahyunk@dongyang.ac.kr

J. Kim
Frism Investment Advisory Inc, Seoul, Korea
e-mail: jwkim@frism.io

Y. J. Kim (✉)
Sogang University, Seoul, Korea
e-mail: yongjkim@sogang.ac.kr

E. Tsui et al. (eds.), *Management Information Systems in a Digitalized AI World*,
Springer Proceedings in Business and Economics,
https://doi.org/10.1007/978-981-96-6526-6_1

S-curve, wherein products enter, grow, mature, and eventually decline in the market over time. As product life cycles have shortened compared to the past, various forms of life cycles have been studied [1].

When examining life cycles in which the S-curve repeats, it is challenging to explain product longevity solely through product-level factors, such as release dates. To accurately describe a product's life cycle in terms of its role or value, it is essential to consider technical aspects. For example, while recently released smartphones continue to provide the same value to customers, it is difficult to determine whether life cycle interpretations should rely strictly on the number of product releases. Comparing recent series of Samsung's Galaxy Z Flip, for instance, reveals that the architecture remains largely the same, with only component-level technologies or modules modified upon release. Rather than interpreting these changes solely within the product life cycle, a technology-based view that includes additional factors, such as technology advancement and complexity, is needed to describe these developments as part of a technology life cycle.

The technology life cycle follows an S-curve, characterized by an initial phase of investment and time devoted to development, followed by growth, maturity, and eventual decline. Like the product life cycle, the technology life cycle can generate a new S-curve when the previous one enters a decline phase [2]. Although previous studies have explored various forms of technology life cycles, questions about their validity remain [3]. This skepticism arises because traditional technology life cycles do not adequately capture the broader characteristics of technology (e.g., development speed, technological units). Consequently, there is a need to redefine the technology life cycle, not from the product perspective but from the technology perspective, and design a new technology life cycle. This study defines this cycle as the "Technology Pathway" and seeks to address it through three research questions to achieve a more detailed understanding.

RQ1: Does the Technology Pathway graph differ by technological units?
RQ2: What are the factors that determine the Technology Pathway?
RQ3: How do the characteristics of technology influence relationships among the factors that determine the Technology Pathway?

To address these three research questions, this study will examine various technologies to clarify the concept of the Technology Pathway and observe differences across technology levels. Building on prior research, we aim to identify the elements that determine the Technology Pathway and integrate relationships with technological characteristics into our research model.

2 Theoretical Background and Technology Cases

2.1 *Theory of Technology Pathway*

The Technology Pathway is a model that explains the non-linear characteristics of technology life cycle along with time and performance dimensions. The pathway of technology advancement can be broadly divided into four stages: the investment phase, growth phase, maturity phase, and decline phase. During the investment phase, the costs associated with technology investment negatively affect business performance. However, at the growth and maturity phases, as the technology becomes stabilized and integrated into various products, it generates positive returns. Eventually, due to factors like technological advancement, the usage of the technology decreases, leading to the decline phase. Traditionally, the technology life cycle has been interpreted primarily as a means of tracking performance over time from a corporate perspective [3]. This approach, however, does not account for the possibility of technological con(di)vergence, highlighting the need for a revised conceptualization that includes such considerations. Thus, it is preferable to specify the factors that shape the pathways from the perspective of technology itself.

Just as various components—from single parts to semi-finished products—are needed to complete a product, technology can be segmented by hardware and software, as well as by technological units. Previous studies have examined the technology life cycle through a software-centered approach, such as research focused solely on software [4]. Software-centered cycles encompass a range of functional updates, making it difficult to differentiate distinct stages, which is why this study emphasizes hardware-based technology. From a hardware perspective, previous studies have primarily examined the effectiveness of upgrades and advancements [5–7]. Given this study's aim to investigate differences between simple and complex technologies integrated into products, it revisits the cycle by focusing on technology units, which have been less explored in the prior research.

As technology advances, it becomes integrated and applied across diverse industries, warranting a market perspective in interpreting the Technology Pathway. When there is market demand for technology, R&D is often expanded to further develop the technology. Just like the previous research, this study identifies technology demand and the number of inventions as the key factors determining the graph of the technology pathway [8, 9]. This study aims to refine the concept of the technology pathway by specifically examining cases of rechargeable secondary batteries, printing technologies, and storage technologies.

2.2 *Technology Case 1 (Battery)*

Rechargeable batteries have undergone continuous development, starting with lead-acid batteries. Unlike traditional energy-consuming structures, lead-acid batteries can

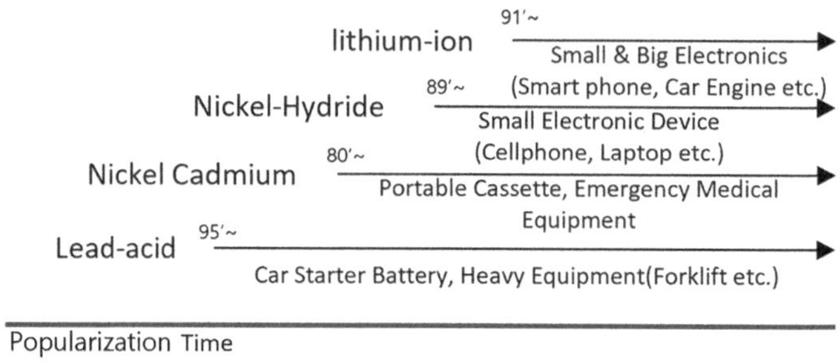

Fig. 1 Electronic energy—battery technology

return to their original state when an external current is supplied, enabling repeated recharging and reuse. Currently, lead-acid batteries are used in cars to start the engine or power accessories like brake lights. However, while these batteries are affordable and stable, they are also very heavy, making them unsuitable for smaller electronic devices. To address this limitation, cylindrical nickel–cadmium batteries were developed. Although lighter than lead-acid batteries and suitable for smaller electronics, nickel–cadmium batteries drain quickly, prompting the development of nickel-metal hydride (NiMH) batteries with higher energy density. NiMH batteries were initially used in early electric and hybrid vehicles but suffered from self-discharge, leading to the development of the lighter, higher-energy–density lithium-ion battery. Lithium-ion batteries have since evolved into three main forms. The cylindrical type, which had a high market share, faced limitations in reducing device thickness, driving the development of pouch-type batteries for slim, lightweight devices like mobile phones. Consequently, development of cylindrical and prismatic batteries slowed until the transition to electric vehicle (EV) engines renewed demand for these forms due to their high energy density and reasonable cost. In pursuit of even higher energy density and lower cost, ongoing research is focused on developing batteries utilizing lithium or sodium to enhance commercialization potential across various applications.

Rechargeable secondary battery technology now powers both small electronics and large devices. Key factors in the development of secondary batteries include the expanding market for portable batteries driven by increased demand for small electronics, the versatility of lithium-ion batteries, and the broad applicability of batteries across diverse industries. (see Fig. 1).

2.3 Technology Case 2 (Printer)

Printer technology is a representative product that encompasses the ability to print large volumes of information. The origins of printers date back to the 1980s with the advent of dot matrix printing, also known as mechanical printing or typewriting. In the early 1990s, black-and-white inkjet printers allowed for the rapid printing

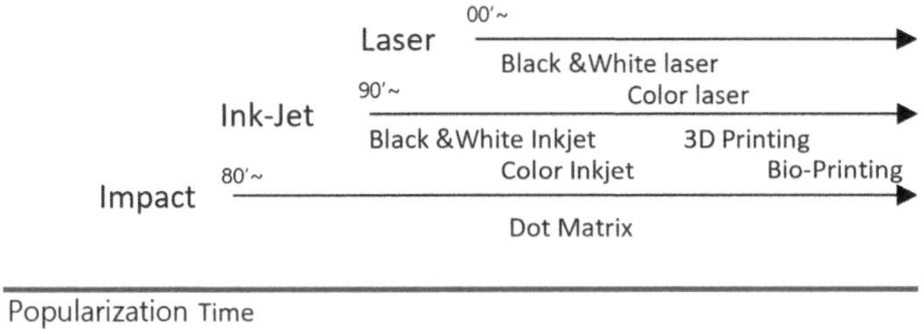

Fig. 2 Printing-output technology

of various documents; however, the high cost of ink made printing large quantities of information difficult. With the introduction of color inkjet printers, the ability to print high-quality color images in bulk became more accessible. However, one disadvantage of inkjet printers was that the ink did not dry instantly, leaving some risk of smudging. To address this, laser printers using heat and pressure were developed, enabling fast and precise printing of color images. These printer technologies are now widely used across various industries. For example, dot matrix printers are still used in the banking sector, where they are essential for printing on forms of varying thickness and size, such as bank passbooks. The spraying technology used in inkjet printers is now integrated into Material Jetting (MJ) 3D printing. Laser printers, which use dry powder, are capable of producing high-speed, precise outputs, making them ideal not only for basic document printing but also for high-resolution graphics and photos.

When viewed from the perspective of the evolution of printing technology, each of these methods can be described as developing over time. However, the core function of printing text onto paper continues to find new applications in emerging industries (see Fig. 2).

2.4 *Technology Case 3 (Data Storage)*

The method of data recording began with paper. Information was stored by punching holes in thick paper, with the holes representing the recorded data, a technique used before the development of computers. With the advent of magnetic tape, it became possible to store various types of information, such as audio and video, using computers. Magnetic tape stores data by utilizing magnetism to record information, and it was a key technology for recording audio and video content. Later, magnetic disk technology was integrated into hard disks and floppy disks, allowing for the storage of larger amounts of data. Similar to magnetic tape, this technology records information by focusing on changes in magnetism. The development of optical discs followed, which involves recording data on a thin layer, where a laser from a pickup device reflects off the surface, and the reflected light is detected to retrieve the information. This technology was applied in products like compact discs

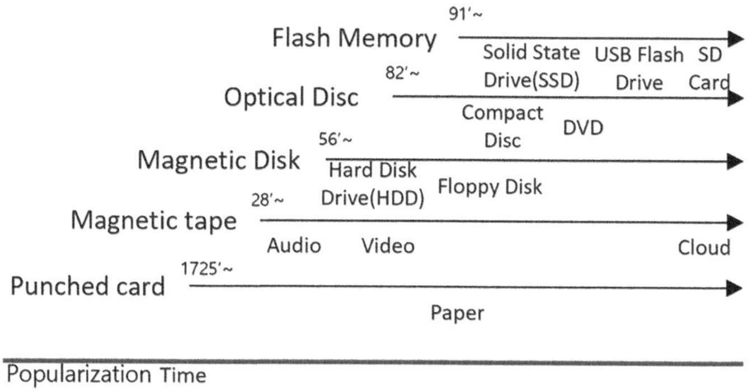

Fig. 3 Recording and storage—memory technology

(CDs) and DVDs, leading to widespread commercialization. Later, Flash memory, based on the arrangement of cells, emerged as a technology that could store even more data, and it has been used in devices such as SSDs, USB flash drives, and SD cards.

Today, all these technologies are used for data storage, but magnetic tape, in particular, is still actively used in industrial applications. Through continuous improvements in this technology, services like Cloud storage have become possible (see Fig. 3).

3 Proposed Research Model

Technology is also influenced by path dependence, meaning that once a technology is developed, it becomes difficult to reverse the process. While it may seem that a technology has disappeared, when examined from the perspective of the technology itself, it is not that the market has vanished; rather, it may have shrunk and, depending on the circumstances, could even experience a resurgence. To support this idea, concepts were derived and relationships were established based on the earlier explanations of battery technology and wheel technology.

This study established a total of five assumptions. The central assumption is that if the form of an existing technology is altered in a way that increases demand, there is a higher likelihood of investment and development in related technologies, leading to an increase in the number of inventions associated with them. Based on this assumption, two moderating variables were defined according to the characteristics of the technology. These technology characteristics were identified as factors that significantly influence market expansion or change, and were specifically defined as multipurpose and transferability. Accordingly, the model was specified as shown in Fig. 4.

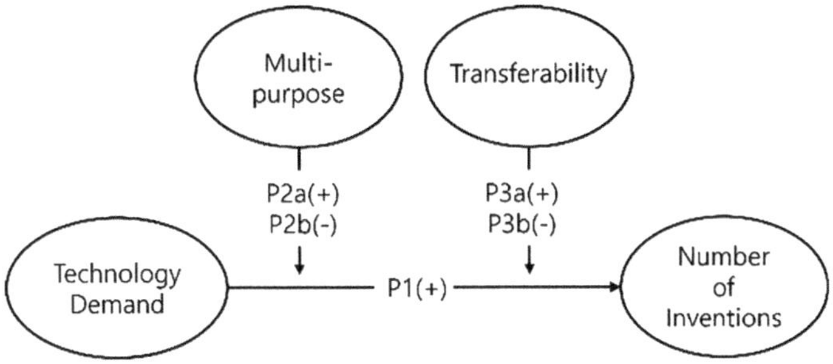

Fig. 4 Research Model

4 Proposition

4.1 Technology Demand and Number of Inventions

Solving customer demands can either open up attractive new markets or maintain the sustainability of existing markets [10]. As individual demands diversify through online platforms, companies have actively invested in technological R&D to solve problems [11]. In order to sustain a competitive market share, companies need to differentiate their resources for functional upgrades, going beyond simple changes to architecture [12]. Both major and minor technological innovations that significantly impact the market can deliver new value to customers. This value, as recognized by customers, is referred to as technology demand.

The situation of technology demand can be explained through three examples:

First, the demand for battery technology. While the energy density of batteries has increased enough to power cars, there is still a consumer need for higher single-charge capacity. In order to increase the driving range per charge, companies will seek to find technologies that offer higher energy density at a lower production cost through R&D. If hydrogen-based energy production methods prove superior to improved lithium-ion batteries, consumers will prefer hydrogen-powered engines, and related technologies will continue to be developed. Second, the demand for printing technology, which not only prints text but also photos and high-definition images on paper. The core of a printer is the nozzle for ink spraying, and to address the drawbacks of spraying methods, various inkjet technologies have emerged. Although inkjet printing offers fast production speed, it has the downside of ink not drying quickly, making it difficult to achieve sharp quality. To address this, technologies that use powder sprayed onto the nozzle and apply hot pressure were developed. Although laser printing is slower than inkjet printing, it can print high-quality photos directly from a camera, making innovation in this technology crucial for market advancement. Third, the demand for storage technology. With the development of computers, there was an increasing need for space to store various forms of data. Storage technologies have evolved from floppy disks, which could hold just one file, to CDs, USBs, SD cards, and, today, the Cloud, which allows for the storage of hundreds of long, high-definition videos without the need for physical storage devices. Each product has integrated technologies to increase storage memory, which can be explained by the growing demand for technology driven by the popularization of online electronic devices such as computers.

The increase in technology demand influences the development of technology. This study conceptualizes the development of technology in terms of the number of inventions related to that technology. Inventions that are continuously developed can be explained through a concept similar to patents. While inventions and patents are not fully interchangeable terms, previous research has explained that innovation is strongly correlated with invention (Sekhar & Dismukes, 2009). Therefore, in this study, invention will be used as a dependent variable to differentiate the characteristics of technology.

P1. The higher the Technology Demand, the more positive the effect on the Number of Inventions.

4.1.1 Multi-purpose and Transferability

Multipurpose refers to a technology that holds various values and can solve customer problems in multiple ways. The higher the multipurpose value, the more diverse the ways it can solve problems. The following examples explain technologies with high multipurpose:

First, the technology applied to batteries. Lithium-ion batteries, which have advantages in energy density and weight, dominate the current electric battery market. As the market demands, technologies that can increase the energy density of batteries to meet the continuous need for electrical energy in non-electric fields will help maintain a high market share. Unlike electric energy, hydrogen energy is a new way of producing energy, and since it is currently focused on the automotive industry, it will influence the technology demand and number of inventions related to automotive technologies. Second, the technology applied to printers. Laser printing technology offers the ability to print high-resolution images. This advantage has expanded the application of laser printing beyond just photo printing to various industries. It is used not only for printing text but also in industrial laser printers that serve sectors like electronics, precision instruments, food and pharmaceuticals, automotive parts, hardware products, plastic packaging, and other specialized applications. The printing market is projected to continue growing, reaching approximately $2.3 billion last year. Third, the technology applied to film. Cassette tapes, often referred to simply as tapes, use a technology where ferromagnetic powders such as iron oxide or chromium dioxide are applied to store and modify audio and video data. The technology that allows the recording of audio signals through magnetic information was expanded to store video as well, thus broadening its storage capabilities. This technology has evolved and is now used for cloud-based storage.

Based on these three technologies, the hypothesis is set that technologies with high multipurpose will positively influence the relationship between technology demand and the number of inventions, while technologies with low multipurpose will negatively impact this relationship.

P2a. *Technologies with higher Multipurpose will have a positive (+) effect on the relationship between Technology Demand and Number of Inventions.*

P2b. *Technologies with lower Multipurpose will have a negative (–) effect on the relationship between Technology Demand and Number of Inventions.*

Transferability refers to the potential for a technology to be used in new products or industries beyond its original application. A technology is considered to have high transferability if it can function effectively in different products or even in an upgraded form. Technologies with high transferability are more likely to be continuously upgraded and expanded to other products or product categories.

First, consider the case of batteries. While lithium-ion batteries are one type of battery, depending on the amount of energy stored, they play a crucial role in powering a wide variety of products. On a small scale, they can function as batteries to power small electronic devices, but when they can store more energy, they can serve as engines to power larger electronic devices, such as automobiles. Initially, batteries were designed to power only small electronic devices, but as the technology evolved to power large cars, the same technology was applied to new industries. The ability to improve energy storage in batteries has made it easy to apply the technology to various products and industries, increasing the likelihood of transferability. Second, consider the print nozzle used in printers. Inkjet printing technology sprays ink through a nozzle to print information. This core function has been adapted for use in 3D printing. With advancements in materials, alternatives to ink are now used in 3D printers, demonstrating how the same spray technology from printing can be applied in other products. The inkjet spraying technology has high transferability, making it easier to incorporate into other products, thereby increasing the number of inventions related to these products. hird, consider the memory used for recording data such as audio and video. One of the technologies for storing data, flash memory, was initially used in solid-state drives (SSDs), which were embedded within products rather than portable. This technology was then used to create portable USB drives, enabling the transport of large amounts of data. Even smaller SD cards, which are used not only in computers but also in small electronic devices (such as smartphones, digital cameras, and dash cams), show how the same technology can be transferred and adapted for different uses.

In summary, technologies with high transferability have the potential to expand beyond their original applications and contribute to innovations in new products and industries.

P3a. *Technologies with higher Transferability will have a positive (+) effect on the relationship between Technology Demand and the Number of Inventions.*

P3b. *Technologies with lower Transferability will have a negative (–) effect on the relationship between Technology Demand and the Number of Inventions.*

5 Conclusion

This study explained the concept of the technology pathway by drawing upon perspectives from existing research that utilizes the product life cycle. It outlined how the process of technology development and the level of technology influence the resulting graphs. By examining the technological development sequence in rechargeable batteries, printing, and the battery industry, the study concretized the technology life cycle through various interpretations. Based on this, three research questions were addressed.

RQ1: Does the Technology Pathway graph differ according to technological units?

Existing research aimed to generalize the pathway of all technologies, whether small or large. Therefore, even successful technologies, once they reach a certain level of growth, were interpreted as eventually becoming obsolete over time. However, through the examples examined in this study, it was discovered that technologies develop and extend in a sequential manner. Moreover, since the life cycle of a technology differs depending on whether its technical characteristics are at the component or module level, it cannot be said that the same graph applies to all technologies.

RQ2: What are the factors that determine the Technology Pathway?

The factors determining the traditional technology life cycle were based on management profits and time, with graphs drawn accordingly. However, instead of technologies being invested in and supplied to the market based on management profits, technologies are developed based on market demand. Therefore, it is more appropriate to conceptualize the technology life cycle graph based on Technology Demand and Number of Inventions. Looking at the examples explained in this study, even if a new technology is developed and it appears that the old technology disappears from the market, it can still be activated in other markets. Moreover, if the technology serves the same purpose, solutions to the demand for that technology can be interpreted in the same context.

RQ3: How do the characteristics of technology influence relationships among the factors that determine the Technology Pathway?

Since technology is not a product itself, elements that influence the relationship were selected based on the characteristics of technology, focusing on Multipurpose and Transferability. Multipurpose and Transferability are concepts that not only affect the demand for technology but also encompass the potential for technological advancement, making them crucial for explaining the technology pathway which is quite different from the concept of technology life cycle.

6 Additional Discussion

The graph of the technology lifecycle by technology type will be elaborated with a focus on the battery industry. By segmenting according to the size of the technology, it is possible to redesign the technology lifecycle.

First, at the element-level technology, the technology unit is the smallest, and even if there is a change in the technology, it is reflected minimally on the graph. Lithium-ion batteries, the most commonly used, are produced in cylindrical, pouch, and prismatic shapes. The chemicals required to produce lithium-ion batteries are similar, but the construction method slightly differs depending on the shape. For example, prismatic batteries have an outer material made of aluminum cans with an internal structure that is folded, while pouch-type batteries are made with soft film as the outer material and have a stacked internal structure. Cylindrical batteries have an outer material made of jelly roll, with an internal structure that is wound. Although the shapes differ, all types are being developed by gradually changing the outer and internal materials to accommodate more energy (see Fig. 5).

Second, at the module-level technology, it acts as a core technology and occupies a large range, which can be observed on the graph. In the case of batteries, various types are produced depending on the configuration of the cathode, anode, and electrolyte, such as lead-acid batteries, nickel–cadmium batteries, nickel-metal hydride batteries, and lithium-ion batteries. Among these, lithium-based batteries are currently being developed in various forms, such as lithium-sulfur and lithium-air batteries. These have advantages in that they can be manufactured with higher energy density and lower costs compared to the widely used lithium-ion batteries. Continuous development is underway for these batteries, and while their market share may temporarily decrease due to their properties being less developed than lithium-ion batteries, they have the potential to gain market share over time through further development of the same module technology (see Fig. 6).

Third, at the system-level technology, existing technologies combine with other smaller technologies, so the technology lifecycle appears as an S-curve on the graph, similar to what was described in earlier life cycles. While the earlier lifecycle graphs were drawn based on smaller technologies, at the system level, the technology

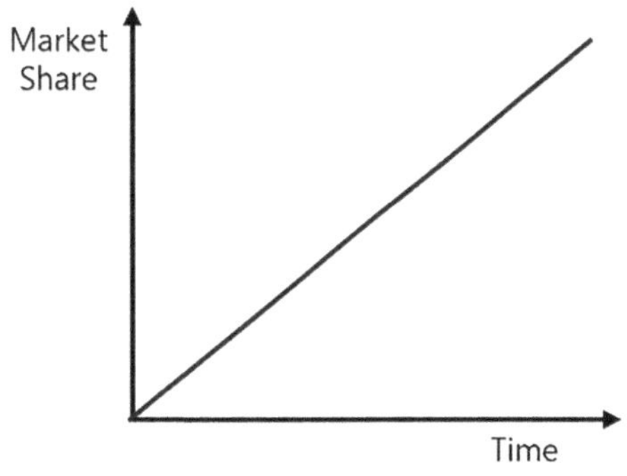

Fig. 5 Element-level pathway graph

Fig. 6 Module-level pathway graph

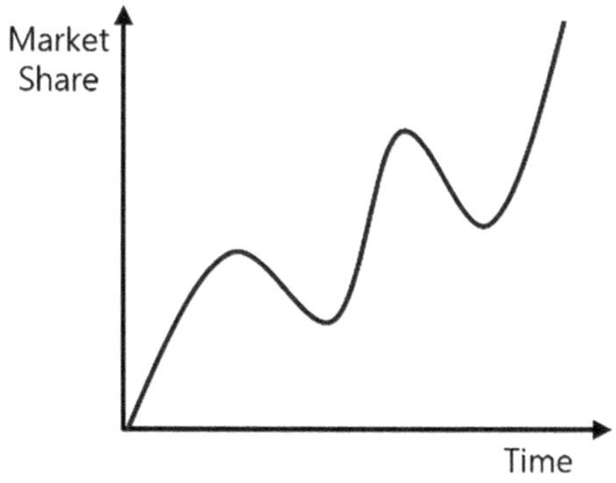

Fig. 7 System-level pathway graph

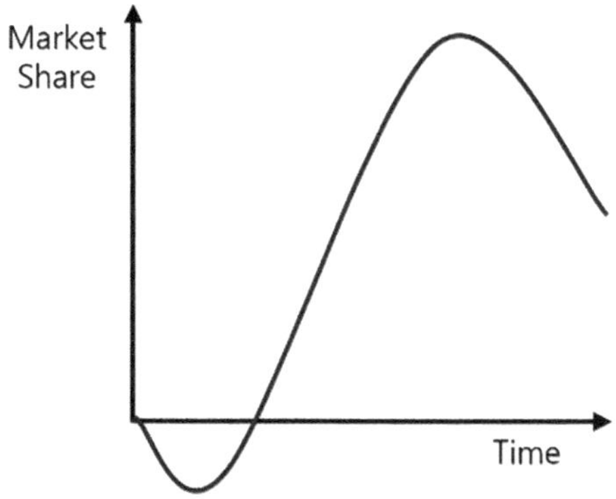

consists of various combined technologies, and its shape on the graph is expected to follow an S-curve as it evolves over time (see Fig. 7).

By categorizing technology into three levels, it can be seen that all technologies have a positive slope. The smaller the unit of technology, the less the variation, which suggests a stronger influence on the assumptions set in the research model described in this study.

References

1. Cao, H., Folan, P.: Product life cycle: the evolution of a paradigm and literature review from 1950–2009. Production Planning & Control 23, 641-662 (2012).
2. Christensen, C. M.: Exploring the limits of the technology S-curve. Part I: component technologies. Production and operations management 1, 334–357 (1992).
3. Taylor, M., Taylor, A.: The technology life cycle: Conceptualization and managerial implications. International journal of production economics 140, 541-553, (2012).
4. Bičevska, Z., Bičevskis, J.: Smart technologies in software life cycle. In Product-Focused Software Process Improvement: 8th International Conference, pp. 262–272, Springer, Berlin Heidelberg (2007).

5. Sandén, B. A.: Technology path assessment for sustainable technology development. Innovation 6, 316-330 (2004).
6. Marchal, P.: Bougard, B.: Katti, G.: Stucchi, M.: Dehaene, W.: Papanikolaou, A.: Verkest, D.: Beyne, E.: 3-D technology assessment: Path-finding the technology/design sweet-spot. Proceedings of the IEEE 97, 96–107 (2009).
7. Simmie, J.: Path dependence and new technological path creation in the Danish wind power industry. European Planning Studies 20, 753-772 (2012).
8. Adner, R.: A demand-based perspective on technology life cycles, In Business Strategy over the Industry Lifecycle. Emerald Group Publishing Limited, 25–43 (2004).
9. Kalthaus, M.: Knowledge recombination along the technology life cycle. Journal of Evolutionary Economics 30, 643-704, (2020).
10. Majava, J.: Nuottila, J.: Haapasalo, H.: Law, K. M.: Customer needs in market-driven product development: Product management and R&D standpoints. 5, 16–25 (2014).
11. Fabijan, A.: Olsson, H. H.: Bosch, J.: Customer feedback and data collection techniques in software R&D: a literature review. In Software Business: 6th International Conference, pp.139–153, Springer, Portugal (2015).
12. Qiu, Y.: Ortolano, L.: Wang, Y. D.: Factors influencing the technology upgrading and catch-up of Chinese wind turbine manufacturers: Technology acquisition mechanisms and government policies. Energy Policy 55, 305–316 (2013).

Sales Management in a Retail Chain of Non-food Stores

Sergei Semakov

Abstract We consider three problems related to the management of sales of goods in a retail chain of non-food stores. The first problem is related to the analysis and management of the remains of goods of the old (outgoing) season during the off-season. From the point of view of maximizing sales revenue during the off-season, we propose a scheme that, as a first approximation, can be used to solve this problem. The second problem is related to the cases of untimely replenishment of stores when goods arrive at stores behind schedule due to transport, customs, political, and other reasons. We propose an algorithm that allows us to adjust the planned volume of goods imported for the season depend on the mode of replenishment of stores. The third problem is the problem of finding the optimal distribution of retail space between the old (outgoing season) and new (coming season) collections of goods during the off-season. We propose a scheme that allows us to distribute the area in such a way that the total revenue from sales is maximum. Our proposed solutions to the described problems are successfully used in a large retail chain that includes several hundreds clothing stores. This article is practical in nature: the proposed solutions to the described problems are successfully used in a large retail chain that includes several hundreds clothing stores.

Keywords Seasonal goods · Sales revenue · Off-season sales · Replenishment of stores · Distribution of retail space

---

S. Semakov (✉)
HSE University, Moscow, Russia
e-mail: slsemakov@yandex.ru

Federal Research Center "Computer Science and Control" of Russian Academy of Siences, Moscow, Russia

Moscow Institute of Physics and Technology, Moscow, Russia

E. Tsui et al. (eds.), *Management Information Systems in a Digitalized AI World*, Springer Proceedings in Business and Economics,
https://doi.org/10.1007/978-981-96-6526-6_2

1 Introduction

When managing the sales process in any retail chain of stores, the central question is how to maximize sales at a profitable price for the company, minimize the costs of transporting and storing the goods and thereby get the greatest profit. When searching for an answer to this question, a number of problems arise related to the operational management of the sales process. These problems are discussed in many papers and relate to various types of goods and services (see, e.g., [1]–[6]).

One of the problems directly related to this question is the problem of rational management of price discounts for goods. Any reputable company plans sales for the coming season in advance. This plan defines the purchasing strategy of the company. If the actual sales lag behind the planned ones, then the company is forced to introduce additional (i.e., unplanned) price discounts in order to avoid overstocking of warehouses and to provide space for new collections of goods. In [7], we presented an original algorithm for managing price discounts. Since 2010, this algorithm is successfully used in a large retail network that includes several hundreds clothing stores.

Another problem is related to the analysis and management of the remains of goods of the old (outgoing) season during the off-season. The problem is that arrival of new season collections does not happen all at once, but over time. For this reason, shops should always have some reserve of old collections in order to prevent a situation where there is nothing to put on the trading floor of the store if the process of selling old collections will outstrip the process of new arrivals. In other words, during the off-season, there must be a certain balance between old collections remaining in the store and resoldering new ones. This problem is considered in Sect. 2.

When studying the sales process, it often turns out that the planned scenario is violated due to such a factor as untimely replenishment of stores. Untimely replenishment of stores can occur, for example, due to transport problems, customs delays, managerial errors, etc. We will try to quantify how some important sales parameters, namely (a) the projected balance of goods at the end of the season and (b) the planned volume of goods imported for the season depend on the mode of replenishment of stores. This problem is considered in Sect. 3.

In planning the sales of seasonal goods in large retail chains, an important problem is the problem of finding the optimal distribution of retail space between the old (outgoing season) and new (coming season) collections of goods during the off-season. It is required to distribute the area in such a way that the total revenue from sales is maximum. This problem is considered in Sect. 4.

2 Managing Good Balances During the Off-Season

2.1 Description of the Problem

Consider the process of selling a certain category of product in a particular store during two consecutive seasons, for example, during the transition from autumn-winter (AW) to spring-summer (SS). Let us denote by Δ the remainder of the AW collection by February 28, i.e., by the end of the AW season. We will be interested in the following question: what should be the value of Δ by February 28?

Let us denote by Δ_0 the nominal presentation, i.e., the quantity of goods that must be simultaneously on the trading floor. The restriction $\Delta_{\min}$ from below to Δ should be such that, by February 28, the remainder of the AW collection together with the SS collection (already partially received by the store) is enough to fill the value of Δ_0: $\Delta_{\min} \leq \Delta$. The restriction $\Delta_{\min}$ is set by experts based on the processing of statistical data. Numerical examples of estimations of $\Delta_{\min}$ are given in Sect. 2.3.

Let us now obtain an upper estimate for the value Δ. Let $P(\Delta)$ denote the cash loss by the end of the season due to the unsold remainder Δ. We assume that the function $P(\Delta)$ is known. Obviously, $P(\Delta)$ is a continuous and monotonically increasing function. We will impose a restriction:

$$P(\Delta) \leq P_{\max}, \tag{1}$$

where $P_{\max}$ is the maximum allowable cash loss by the end of the season due to the unsold remainder Δ. The $P_{\max}$ value is determined by experts. It follows from (1) that

$$\Delta \leq P^{-1}(P_{\max}). \tag{2}$$

Inequality (2) provides an upper estimate for Δ. Here P^{-1} denotes the function inverse to the function $P(\Delta)$.

Thus, for admissible values of Δ, we have the following two-sided estimate: $\Delta_{\min} \leq \Delta \leq P^{-1}(P_{\max})$. Now we must propose a criterion for choosing the best Δ from this range.

Let the moment t^* characterize the end of the season, i.e., in our case, it is February 28. Let $D(\Delta)$ be the income received from the sale of the remainder Δ after time t^*. If the entire remainder Δ is sold at the planned prices, then, obviously, $D(\Delta) = P(\Delta)$. But since, as a rule, the entire remainder Δ cannot be sold and selling prices at the end of the season are lower than planned prices, then $D(\Delta) \leq P(\Delta)$. We need to minimize the difference $P(\Delta) - D(\Delta)$, i.e., to find $\min_{\Delta_{\min} \leq \Delta \leq P^{-1}(P_{\max})} \Big(P(\Delta) - D(\Delta)\Big)$.

Note that both functions $P(\Delta)$ and $D(\Delta)$ are monotonically increasing. Function $P(\Delta)$ is easily determined, because all planned prices are known. The situation is more complicated with the function $D(\Delta)$. There is an element of uncertainty here, namely, we do not know how much of the remainder Δ we will be able to sell after the moment t^*. To resolve this issue, it is proposed to analyze the situations of past years and choose some average scenario.

2.2 Variant of the Approximate Solution of the Problem

We can propose the following solution to the problem. We will assume that

$$D(\Delta) = k_1 \cdot k_2 \cdot P(\Delta), \tag{3}$$

where k_1 and k_2 are two coefficients taking values from the interval (0,1). The meaning of the coefficients k_1 and k_2 is as follows.

Coefficient k_1 is a coefficient that takes into account that not all goods will be sold out after moment t^*. An analysis of long-term statistical data shows that if we are talking about a seasonal product, then the completeness of the sale of this product depends on the product category. For example, a seasonal product of the "Equipment" category is sold by about 40%, i.e., if at time t^* the balance is 100%, then by the time this product is removed from the trading floor (in order to free up retail space for goods of next season), its balance is approximately 60%. A seasonal product of the "Apparel" category is sold by about 60%. Therefore, in the case of the "Equipment" category, we should consider $k_1 = 0.6$, and in the case of the "Apparel" category, we should consider $k_1 = 0.4$.

The coefficient k_2 is a coefficient that takes into account that, after the moment t^*, the goods are usually sold at lower prices. For example, if an advertising campaign "Prices in half" is carried out, then $k_2 = 0.5$.

Taking into account (3), we get

$$\begin{aligned} &\min_{\Delta_{\min} \le \Delta \le P^{-1}(P_{\max})} \Big(P(\Delta) - D(\Delta)\Big) = \\ &= \min_{\Delta_{\min} \le \Delta \le P^{-1}(P_{\max})} \Big((1 - k_1 k_2) P(\Delta)\Big) \\ &= (1 - k_1 k_2) \min_{\Delta_{\min} \le \Delta \le P^{-1}(P_{\max})} P(\Delta). \end{aligned}$$

Due to the monotonic increase of the function $P(\Delta)$, the minimum $\min_{\Delta_{\min} \le \Delta \le P^{-1}(P_{\max})} P(\Delta)$ will be reached at $\Delta = \Delta_{\min}$.

2.3 Numerical Examples

Let's give examples of numerical values for Δ_0 and $\Delta_{\min}$. We will consider real stores of the same retail chain that was considered in [7].

Store No. 1: $\Delta_0 = 39056$ pieces of goods and $\Delta_{\min} = 16021$ pieces of goods.
Store No. 2: $\Delta_0 = 30593$ pieces of goods and $\Delta_{\min} = 9410$ pieces of goods.
Store No. 3: $\Delta_0 = 30316$ pieces of goods and $\Delta_{\min} = 18642$ pieces of goods.

If we introduce a dimensionless parameter $\rho = \Delta_{\min}/\Delta_0$, then for stores 1, 2, and 3 this parameter takes the values 0.4102, 0.3075, and 0.6149, respectively.

3 Influence of Untimely Replenishment of Stores on the Sales Process

3.1 Estimation of the Forecasted Remainder of Goods at the End of the Season Depending on the Replenishment Mode of the Store

Let the season last from moment $t = 0$ to moment $t = T$. Let's divide the interval $(0, T)$ into smaller time intervals (for example, weeks):

$$0 = t_0 < t_1 < t_2 < \ldots < t_i < \ldots < t_{n-1} < t_n = T.$$

Denote $\Delta t_i = t_{i+1} - t_i$, where $i = 0, 1, \ldots, n-1$. We introduce the following notation:

- ΔV_i is the quantity of goods in pieces sold for the i-th period of time, i.e., during the time from t_i to t_{i+1};
- W_i is the average number of goods (in pieces) in the trading floor for the i-th period of time.

Sales experience shows that, as a rule, we can use the following assumption (see, e.g., [8]): $\Delta V_i = k\sqrt{W_i}$, where k is some coefficient of proportionality. Then sales for the entire season are equal to $\sum\limits_i \Delta V_i = \sum\limits_i k\sqrt{W_i}$ and the remainder of goods at the end of the season will be $V_0 - \sum\limits_i k\sqrt{W_i}$, where V_0 is the total volume of goods brought in and intended for sale for the season in question. The remainder at the end of the season in fractions of a unit to the total volume V_0 will be

$$r = 1 - \frac{\sum\limits_i k\sqrt{W_i}}{V_0}. \tag{4}$$

We will now consider how the situation will change if we take into account not 100% replenishment of stores. We will take this circumstance into account using the *OutOfStock* parameter. In what follows, the parameter *OutOfStock* will be abbreviated as *OOS*. We will show, for example, how this parameter is calculated on a weekly time interval at the SKU/Day/Shop level (see Table 1). Here SKU is an abbreviation for

Stock Keeping Unit. The "+" sign in the cell of the table means that, on the corresponding day, the corresponding SKU was sold in the store, more precisely, it was available on the trading floor at the end of the working day. The sign "–" means that the corresponding SKU was absent at the end of the corresponding day. The fact of the absence of SKU is recorded only if there are at least two "–" signs in a row. In the example under consideration (see Table 1), this situation occurs only in one case, namely, for SKU 1 on Wednesday and Thursday. In the example under consideration, the value of the OOS parameter is OOS=2/28. Here, the denominator of the fraction is the total number of cells in Table 1, and the numerator of the fraction is the number of signs "–", which are located in a row in the amount of at least two pieces.

Let OOS_i be the value of the OOS parameter for the i-th time interval. Then the real average quantity of goods on the trading floor during this time interval will be equal to $\tilde{W}_i = W_i(1 - OOS_i)$, and the projected sales for this time interval will be equal to $\Delta\tilde{V}_i = k\sqrt{\tilde{W}_i} = k\sqrt{W_i(1 - OOS_i)}$. The projected sales for the full season will be equal to $\sum_i \Delta\tilde{V}_i = \sum_i k\sqrt{W_i}\sqrt{1 - OOS_i}$. Therefore the remainder at the end of the season will be equal to $V_0 - \sum_i k\sqrt{W_i}\sqrt{1 - OOS_i}$, or, in fractions of unit,

$$\tilde{r} = 1 - \frac{\sum_i k\sqrt{W_i}\sqrt{1 - OOS_i}}{V_0}. \tag{5}$$

We introduce the average value of the coefficient $\sqrt{1 - OOS}$ according to the formula

$$(\sqrt{1 - OOS})_{average} = \frac{\sum_i k\sqrt{W_i}\sqrt{1 - OOS_i}}{\sum_i k\sqrt{W_i}}.$$

Taking into account (4), expression (5) for $\tilde{r}$ can be rewritten as:

$$\tilde{r} = 1 - (1 - r)(\sqrt{1 - OOS})_{average}. \tag{6}$$

By formula (6), if (a) we know the projected remainder r at the end of the season with 100% store replenishment and (b) we know the average $(\sqrt{1 - OOS})_{average}$ over

Table 1 An example of calculating *OOS*

SKU	Monday	Tuesday	Wednesday	Thursday	Friday	Saturday	Sunday
SKU 1	+	+	–	–	+	+	+
SKU 2	+	+	–	+	–	+	+
SKU 3	–	+	+	+	+	+	+
SKU 4	+	+	+	–	+	+	+

the period under consideration, then we can estimate the projected remainder $\tilde{r}$ with actual store replenishment.

3.2 *Estimation of the Optimal Volume of Imported Goods Depending on the Mode of Replenishment of Stores*

Let's fix the store and the collection of goods. Let V be the volume of the imported collection and Δ be its balance at the end of the season. In Sect. 1, the problem of the most acceptable value of Δ was solved. It turned out that this value is $\Delta = \Delta_{\min}$. The value of $\Delta_{\min}$ is determined from the experience of experts and the analysis of statistical data. This value is represented as $\Delta_{\min} = \rho\Delta_0$, where Δ_0 is the nominal presentation, i.e., the quantity of goods that must be simultaneously on the trading floor, and ρ is is a coefficient that shows how much of Δ_0 is $\Delta_{\min}$, i.e., $\rho = \Delta_{\min}/\Delta_0$ (see Sect. 2). In this case, the required volume of the imported collection can be estimated as $V = \Delta_{\min} + V_{\text{plan}}$, where V_{plan} is the planned sales volume of the collection for the entire season.

During the sales process during the season, it may be that the actual sales fall behind the planned sales schedule. We will assume that the lag of actual sales from planned ones is caused by the presence of a non-zero value of the OOS parameter. We want to answer the following question: in this situation, how should the volume of imported goods be adjusted in order to reach the optimal balance $\Delta_{\min}$ by the end of the season?

In order to answer this question, we will use the previously derived formula $\tilde{r} = 1 - (1 - r)\sqrt{1 - OOS}$, where r is the predicted remainder in fractions of unit at $OOS = 0$ and $\tilde{r}$ is the remainder at actual $OOS \neq 0$. In our case, $r = \frac{\Delta_{\min}}{V}$. With a non-zero value of OOS, the remainder of goods by the end of the season will be equal to $\tilde{r}V = \left(1 - \left(1 - \frac{\Delta_{\min}}{V}\right)\sqrt{1 - OOS}\right)V$; this value is greater than $\Delta_{\min}$. Since the remainder should be $\Delta_{\min}$, the quantity of goods must be imported less by the quantity $\delta V = \left(1 - \left(1 - \frac{\Delta_{\min}}{V}\right)\sqrt{1 - OOS}\right)V - \Delta_{\min}$. Thus, the adjusted volume of imported goods should be equal to

$$V^* = V - \delta V = \Delta_{\min} + \left(1 - \frac{\Delta_{\min}}{V}\right)\sqrt{1 - OOS} \cdot V. \qquad (7)$$

3.3 Proposed Algorithm

Based on the results obtained, we propose the following algorithm for forming the volume of imported goods for the coming season and subsequent monitoring of the sales process.

1. At the beginning of the season, we calculate the value $V = \Delta_{\text{min}} + V_{\text{plan}}$.
2. Focusing on a similar past season, we determine the value OOS.
3. Using formula (7), we calculate the adjusted volume V^* that must be imported for the upcoming season.
4. We determine the adjusted sales plan for the upcoming season: $V^*_{\text{plan}} = V^* - \Delta_{\text{min}}$.
5. Further, when tracking sales in the current season, we focus on the plan $V^*_{\text{plan}} = V_{\text{plan}} \cdot k$, where $k = \frac{V^* - \Delta_{\text{min}}}{V - \Delta_{\text{min}}}$.

In particular, we introduce current discounts (see [7]) by comparing actual sales with V^*_{plan}, not with V_{plan}.

3.4 Numerical Example

We'll look at Store No. 1, which we already covered in Sect. 2.2. In this case, $\Delta_0 = 39056$ pieces of goods and $\Delta_{\text{min}} = 16021$ pieces of goods. Also, for this store, $V_{\text{plan}} = 144262$ pieces of goods and $OOS = 1{,}6\%$. We will find the values of V, V^*, and δV that appear in formula (7). We have: $V = \Delta_{\text{min}} + V_{\text{plan}} = 160283$ pieces of goods, $\delta V = \left(1 - \left(1 - \frac{\Delta_{\text{min}}}{V}\right)\sqrt{1 - OOS}\right) V - \Delta_{\text{min}} = \left(1 - \left(1 - \frac{16021}{160283}\right)\sqrt{1 - 0{,}016}\right) \cdot 160283 - 16021 = 1159$ pieces of goods, $V^* = V - \delta V = 160283 - 1159 = 159124$ pieces of goods. In this case, the value of the coefficient k is equal to

$$k = \frac{V^* - \Delta_{\text{min}}}{V - \Delta_{\text{min}}} = \frac{159124 - 16021}{160283 - 16021} = 0{,}991966\ldots \quad .$$

4 A Problem of the Optimal Distribution of Retail Space in Trading Networks Between Collections of Goods

4.1 Description of the Problem

Consider the process of selling a certain category of product in a particular store during two consecutive seasons, for example, during the transition from autumn-winter (AW) to spring-summer (SS). Let us introduce the following notation:

- t is time, independent variable;
- $S_{aw}(t)$ is the sales area occupied at the moment t by the AW collection;
- $S_{ss}(t)$ is the sales area occupied at the moment t by the SS collection;

Let the time interval from t^* to t^{**} be an off-season. For definiteness, we will assume that the moment t^* corresponds to the date February 1, and the moment t^{**} corresponds to the date March 30. For every t

$$S_{aw}(t) + S_{ss}(t) = S_0, \tag{8}$$

where S_0 is the entire available sales area for the AW and SS collections; S_0 is a constant value. We assume that

$$S_{aw}(t) = S_0 \text{ and } S_{ss}(t) = 0 \text{ as } t \le t^*, \tag{9}$$

$$S_{aw}(t) = 0 \text{ and } S_{ss}(t) = S_0 \text{ as } t \ge t^{**}, \tag{10}$$

i.e., until the moment t^*, the entire sales area is occupied by the AW collection, and, after the moment t^{**}, the entire sales area is occupied by the SS collection. The problem is to find functions $S_{aw}(t)$ and $S_{ss}(t)$ satisfying conditions (8–10) such that the revenue received from the sale of goods in the off-season is maximum.

4.2 Problem Statement

Let's divide the interval (t^*, t^{**}) into smaller time intervals (for example, weeks): $t^* = t_0 < t_1 < \ldots < t_{i-1} < t_i < \ldots < t_{n-1} < t_n = t^{**}$. Denote $\Delta t = t_i - t_{i-1}$, $i = 1, \ldots, n$. Let us introduce the following notation:

- $\Delta_- S^i_{aw}$ is the area freed from the sale of goods from the collection AW for the i-th period of time, i.e., during the time from t_{i-1} to t_i;
- $\Delta_- S^i_{ss}$ is the area freed from the sale of goods from the collection SS for the i-th period of time, i.e., during the time from t_{i-1} to t_i;
- $\Delta_+ S^i_{aw}$ is the area that was supplemented with the goods of the AW collection from the warehouse for the i-th period of time, i.e., during the time from t_{i-1} to t_i;

- $\Delta_+ S^i_{ss}$ is the area that was supplemented with the goods of the SS collection from the warehouse for the i-th period of time, i.e., during the time from t_{i-1} to t_i.

  Then

$$S_{aw}(t_{i+1}) = S_{aw}(t_i) + \Delta_+ S^i_{aw} - \Delta_- S^i_{aw} \tag{11}$$

and

$$S_{ss}(t_{i+1}) = S_{ss}(t_i) + \Delta_+ S^i_{ss} - \Delta_- S^i_{ss}. \tag{12}$$

We will consider the values

$$\Delta_+ S^i_{aw} \text{ and } \Delta_+ S^i_{ss} \tag{13}$$

as control actions. With the help of values (13) we will control the areas $S_{ss}(t)$ and $S_{aw}(t)$ at the control moments t_i.

Let us introduce the following notation:

- ΔV^i_{ss} is the quantity of goods in pieces of the SS collection sold for the i-th period of time, i.e., during the time from t_{i-1} to t_i;
- ΔV^i_{aw} is the quantity of goods in pieces of the AW collection sold for the i-th period of time, i.e., during the time from t_{i-1} to t_i;
- p^i_{ss} is the average price of a product in the SS collection sold for the i-th period of time, i.e., during the time from t_{i-1} to t_i;
- p^i_{aw} is the average price of a product in the AW collection sold for the i-th period of time, i.e., during the time from t_{i-1} to t_i.

Then the revenue received for the i-th period of time is $R^i = \Delta V^i_{ss} p^i_{ss} + \Delta V^i_{aw} p^i_{aw}$.

It is known that ΔV^i_{ss} is the greater, the more goods of the SS collection are on the counter, i.e., the more $S_{ss}(t_i)$ (all other things being equal). Denote by $V_{ss}(t_{i-1})$ the quantity of goods (in pieces) of the SS collection in the shopping room at the beginning of the i-th time interval, i.e., at the moment t_{i-1}. Taking into account [8], we will assume that $\Delta V^i_{ss} = k_{ss}\sqrt{V_{ss}(t_{i-1})}$, where k_{ss} is a certain coefficient of proportionality. If we take into account the directly proportional dependence between the amount of goods in the shopping room and the area occupied by these goods: $V = kS$; then we get $\Delta V^i_{ss} = k_{ss}\sqrt{k}\sqrt{S_{ss}(t_{i-1})}$, where $S_{ss}(t_{i-1})$ is the area occupied by goods of the SS collection at the beginning of the i-th time interval, i.e., at the moment t_{i-1}. Similarly, $\Delta V^i_{aw} = k_{aw}\sqrt{k}\sqrt{S_{aw}(t_{i-1})}$. As a result we get

$$\sum_{i=1}^{n} R^i = \sum_{i=1}^{n} \left(\sqrt{S_{ss}(t_{i-1})} k_{ss} \sqrt{k} p^i_{ss} + \sqrt{S_{aw}(t_{i-1})} k_{aw} \sqrt{k} p^i_{aw} \right),$$

where $S_{ss}(t_j) + S_{aw}(t_j) = S_0 = const$ for every t_j. We are to find the maximum

$$\max_{\Delta_+ S^i_{ss}, \Delta_+ S^i_{aw}} \sum_{i=1}^{n} R^i,$$

where $\Delta_+ S^i_{ss} \geq 0$, $\Delta_+ S^i_{aw} \geq 0$, $\Delta_+ S^i_{ss} + \Delta_+ S^i_{aw} \leq S_0$, $S_{ss}(t_{i+1}) = S_{ss}(t_i) + \Delta_+ S^i_{ss} - \Delta_- S^i_{ss}$, $S_{aw}(t_{i+1}) = S_{aw}(t_i) + \Delta_+ S^i_{aw} - \Delta_- S^i_{aw}$, i.e., the control variables are variables (13) associated with areas $S_{ss}(t_{i-1})$ and $S_{aw}(t_{i-1})$ by formulas (12) and (11).

4.3 Main Result

Consider first a two-period model, i.e., when the entire off-season segment (t^*, t^{**}) is divided into two elementary intervals: $t^* = t_0 < t_1 < t_2 = t^{**}$. We obtain $\sum_{i=1}^{2} R^i = \sqrt{S_{ss}(t_0)} k_{ss} \sqrt{k p^1_{ss}} + \sqrt{S_{aw}(t_0)} k_{aw} \sqrt{k p^1_{aw}} + \sqrt{S_{ss}(t_1)} k_{ss} \sqrt{k p^2_{ss}} + \sqrt{S_{aw}(t_1)} k_{aw} \sqrt{k p^2_{aw}}$. Taking into account the boundary conditions (9) and (10), we have $S_{ss}(t_0) = 0$ and $S_{aw}(t_0) = S_0$. Therefore $\sum_{i=1}^{2} R^i = \sqrt{S_0} k_{aw} \sqrt{k p^1_{aw}} + \sqrt{S_{ss}(t_1)} k_{ss} \sqrt{k p^2_{ss}} + \sqrt{S_{aw}(t_1)} k_{aw} \sqrt{k p^2_{aw}}$. Let us denote for brevity $S_{ss}(t_1) = x$ and $S_{aw}(t_1) = y$. Then the stated problem is reduced to maximizing the sum $\sqrt{x} k_{ss} \sqrt{k p^2_{ss}} + \sqrt{y} k_{aw} \sqrt{k p^2_{aw}}$ under condition $x + y = S_0$. Solving this simplest problem for a conditional extremum, we find that the maximum is achieved at $x = S_{ss}(t_1) = S_0 \Big/ \left(1 + \left(\frac{k_{aw} p^2_{aw}}{k_{ss} p^2_{ss}}\right)^2\right)$ and $y = S_{aw}(t_1) = S_0 - S_{ss}(t_1)$.

Now, considering the n-period model $t^* = t_0 < t_1 < \ldots < t_{i-1} < t_i < \ldots < t_{n-1} < t_n = t^{**}$ and arguing similarly, we obtain

$$S_{ss}(t_i) = S_0 \Big/ \left(1 + \left(\frac{k_{aw} p^{i+1}_{aw}}{k_{ss} p^{i+1}_{ss}}\right)^2\right), \quad S_{aw}(t_i) = S_0 - S_{ss}(t_i). \tag{14}$$

When attempting to use these formulas in practice, the following difficulty arises. When calculating the values of $S_{ss}(t_i)$ and $S_{aw}(t_i)$ according to formulas (14), the average prices p^{i+1}_{ss} and p^{i+1}_{aw} for the interval from t_i to t_{i+1} should be known. But, at time t_i, these prices are, of course, still unknown. For the practical application of formulas (14), it is proposed to replace the values p^{i+1}_{ss} and p^{i+1}_{aw} on the right side of these formulas with the values p^i_{ss} and p^i_{aw}, respectively.

4.4 Proposed Algorithm

Based on the results obtained, we propose the following scheme for deciding on the distribution of retail space during the off-season between the goods of the old (AW) and new (SS) collections.

1. The off-season period (t^*, t^{**}) is divided into n smaller time intervals (for example, weeks): $(t_0, t_1), (t_1, t_2), \ldots, (t_{n-2}, t_{n-1}), (t_{n-1}, t_n)$, where $t_0 = t^*$, $t_n = t^{**}$.
2. Experimentally, by computer processing of statistical data (see, e.g., [9, 10]) for the previous off-season, the coefficients of proportionality k_{aw} and k_{ss} are determined in accordance with formula $\Delta V = k\sqrt{V}$.
3. At the moment t_0, according to the decision of the manager, part of the area of the shopping room (occupied until the moment t_0 only by the goods of the AW collection) is released for the goods of the SS collection. According to the results of sales up to the moment t_1, the following values are calculated:

   - p^1_{aw}, i.e., the average price of the sold goods of the AW collection for the time interval (t_0, t_1);
   - p^1_{ss}, i.e., the average price of the sold goods of the SS collection for the time interval (t_0, t_1).

   After that, at the moment t_1, the following distribution of the area for the goods of the SS and AW collections is proposed: $S_{ss}(t_1) = S_0 \Big/ \left(1 + \left(\frac{k_{aw}p^1_{aw}}{k_{ss}p^1_{ss}}\right)^2\right)$, $S_{aw}(t_1) = S_0 - S_{ss}(t_1)$.
4. By the moment t_2, the average prices p^2_{aw} and p^2_{ss} are calculated for the time interval (t_1, t_2), and at the moment t_2 the following distribution of the area for the goods of the SS and AW collections is proposed: $S_{ss}(t_2) = S_0 \Big/ \left(1 + \left(\frac{k_{aw}p^2_{aw}}{k_{ss}p^2_{ss}}\right)^2\right)$, $S_{aw}(t_2) = S_0 - S_{ss}(t_2)$. And so on up to the moment t_{n-1}.
5. At the moment $t_n = t^{**}$, in accordance with the boundary conditions (10), we set $S_{ss}(t_n) = S_0$, $S_{aw}(t_n) = 0$.

4.5 Numerical Example

The described algorithm was implemented in a large (real-life) retail network[1] store selling sportswear in the February-March off-season. The week from February 7 to February 13 was taken as the calculation week for which the optimal distribution of the area was sought. The average price of a piece sold in this store for the previous

[1] Here we are talking about the same trading network that was considered in [7].

week (from January 31 to February 6) was $p_{ss} = 20.27$ dollars for summer assortment (SS collection) and $p_{aw} = 62.79$ dollars for winter assortment (AW collection). Taking into account the knowledge of the coefficients k_{ss} and k_{aw} for this store, this gave, according to formula (14), the following optimal distribution of the area for the week from February 7 to February 13:

$$S_{ss} = 0.12S_0, \quad S_{aw} = 0.88S_0,$$

where S_0 is the entire available sales area.

A comparison was made of the sales results obtained in this store with the sales results in an absolutely similar (by area, assortment, location, etc.) store for the same time period from February 7 to February 13, but in a situation where the distribution of the area was given to the discretion of the manager of the shopping room. Sales in the first store were 8% higher.

5 Conclusion

In this paper, we proposed a solution to

1. the problem of management of residues goods during the off-season;
2. the problem of calculating the planned volume of goods imported for the season depending on the mode of replenishment of stores;
3. the problem of the optimal distribution of retail space between the old (outgoing season) and new (coming season) collections of goods during the off-season.

The proposed solutions of these problems are successfully used in a large retail chain that includes several hundreds clothing stores.

References

1. Shakkottai, S., Ying, L., Sah, S.: Implicit learning for explicit discount targeting in online social networks. In: 49th IEEE Conference on Desicion and Control (CDC), pp. 647–654, Atlanta, GA, USA. IEEE Press (2010). https://doi.org/10.1109/CDC.2010.5717034.
2. Ramakrishnan, R.: Markdown management. In: Ö. Özer, R. Fhillips (eds.) The Oxford handbook of pricing management, pp. 620–654. Oxford University Press, Oxford, UK (2012).
3. Sano, N., Suzuki, T.: Evaluation of discount effects using Poisson regression based on interaction effects between bargain scale and product category. In: 13th International Conference on Data Mining Workshops, pp. 234–241, Dallas, TX, USA. IEEE Press (2013). https://doi.org/10.1109/ICDMW.2013.73.
4. Chen, M., Chen, Z.-L., Pundoor, G., Acharya, S.,Yi, J.: Markdown optimization at multiple stores. IIE Transactions. 47, pp. 84–108 (2015). https://doi.org/10.1080/0740817X.2014.916459.
5. Ferreira, K.J., Lee, B.H.A., Simchi-Levi, D.: Analytics for an online retailer: demand forecasting and price optimization. Manufacturing Service Operations Management. 18, pp. 69–88 (2016). https://doi.org/10.1287/msom.2015.0561.

6. Smith, S.A., Agrawal, N.: Optimal markdown pricing and inventory allocation for retail chains with inventory dependent demand. Manufacturing Service Operations Management. 19, pp. 290–304 (2017). https://doi.org/10.1287/msom.2016.0609.
7. Semakov, S.L., Semakov, A.S.: Management of price discounts in retail trade network. In: 6th IEEE Conference on Control Technology and Applications (CCTA), pp. 522–527, Trieste, Italy. IEEE Press (2022). https://doi.org/10.1109/CCTA49430.2022.9966111.
8. Oracle retail demand forecasting user guide, Release 13.0. http://www.oracle.com.
9. Box, G.E.P., Jenkins, G.M., Reinsel, G.C., Ljung, M.: Time series analysis: forecasting and control. 5th edn. Wiley, New Jersey (2016).
10. Bendat, J.S., Piersol, A.G.: Analysis and measurement procedures. Wiley, New York-Chichester-Brisbane-Toronto-Singapore (1986).

Exploring the Government's Incentives' Role in Overcoming Diffusion Barriers to Electric Motorcycle Adoption in Indonesia

Wawan Dhewanto, Eko Agus Prasetio, Aang Noviyana Umbara, and Tiffany Ar Rahim

Abstract Given the interesting switching behavior to the significant environmental impact of conventional motorcycles, transitioning to electric motorcycles (EMs) is critical. Despite government subsidies, the adoption rate remains low. This study investigates the role of government incentives in overcoming diffusion barriers to the adoption of electric motorcycles in Indonesia. Utilizing the Theory of Planned Behavior (TPB) and Diffusion of Innovation (DOI) theory, this research examines determinants factors, attitudes, and intentions toward EMs. The study employs a comprehensive model integrating psychological and technical factors to explore the mediating role of consumer attitudes. The study suggests that despite government incentives positively impacting adoption intentions, psychological and technical factors play crucial roles in shaping consumer attitudes. Ultimately, the study aims to offer a research agenda that encourages further investigation.

Keywords Electric motorcycles · Technology diffusion · Technology adoption · Theory of planned behavior · Diffusion on innovation

W. Dhewanto · E. A. Prasetio · A. N. Umbara · T. A. Rahim (✉)
School of Business and Management, Bandung Institute of Technology, Bandung, Indonesia
e-mail: tiffany_arrahim@sbm-itb.ac.id

W. Dhewanto
e-mail: w_dhewanto@sbm-itb.ac.id

E. A. Prasetio
e-mail: eko.prasetio@sbm-itb.ac.id

A. N. Umbara
e-mail: aang.noviyana@sbm-itb.ac.id

E. Tsui et al. (eds.), *Management Information Systems in a Digitalized AI World*,
Springer Proceedings in Business and Economics,
https://doi.org/10.1007/978-981-96-6526-6_3

1 Introduction

The landmark Paris Agreement, established during COP21 in 2015, exemplifies international cooperation among nations in addressing climate change and committing to ambitious targets for reducing greenhouse gas emissions. This agreement encompasses 17 goals and 169 targets, integrating sustainable development into economic, environmental, and social frameworks [1]. To stay within the maximum temperature increase of 1.5 °C, analysis indicates that Indonesia should only produce around 449 $MtCO_2e$ by 2030. This means Indonesia falls short of ambition by about 1,212 $MtCO_2e$ (excluding emissions from changes in land use and forestry). To achieve this target, Indonesia needs to strengthen its commitment and take more stringent measures to reduce greenhouse gas emissions in its national contribution plan [2].

Indonesia is the second highest country with motorcycle users. In 2020, as noted it reached 125.305.332 motorcycle users in Indonesia, and it is predicted will increase over the year [3]. Besides, motorcycles also constitute a significant portion of this air pollution burden in Indonesia, with an annual emission load recorded at 14,510,395.9 tons, where motorcycles alone contribute 69 percent, equivalent to 9,982,769.16 tons per year. Moreover, in terms of greenhouse gas emissions, motorcycles account for approximately 41%, totaling 104,267,147 tons per year [4]. Among these studies, one conducted study contributes to this discourse by underscoring the various benefits associated with the adoption of electric vehicles [5]. Their research emphasizes not only the cost-effectiveness of electric vehicles but also the significant reductions in energy consumption and carbon footprint compared to traditional gasoline-powered vehicles. By elucidating these advantages, they provide valuable insights into the potential of electric vehicles to mitigate environmental impacts and enhance sustainability in the transportation sector [5].

Conversely, Indonesia boasts the world's largest nickel reserves, a crucial element in lithium batteries used in electric vehicles. This positions Indonesia to potentially become a leading global producer of battery materials and batteries. Therefore, with such abundant resources, the government needs to capitalize on this opportunity, not only by advancing the battery industry but also by addressing environmental concerns. One example is promoting the use of electric motorcycles, which are widely popular among the public (Fig. 1).

To address this disparity and encourage the adoption of electric motorcycles, the Indonesian government has introduced incentives and subsidies. Each unit of a brand-new electric two-wheeler, as well as a converted e-motorbike that originally ran on combustion engines, is eligible for a subsidy of Rp 7 million for 200 thousand electric motorcycles in March 2023. This initiative aims to make electric motorcycles more accessible and affordable for consumers, thereby stimulating demand and accelerating the transition towards more sustainable transportation alternatives.

Conversely, as of March 2023, the number of electric motorcycles in circulation remains significantly low, with just 40,312 units on the road. Despite the incentives provided by the government, by October 2023, the number of electric motorcycles increased to only 74,988 units, falling short of the government's target [7]. The

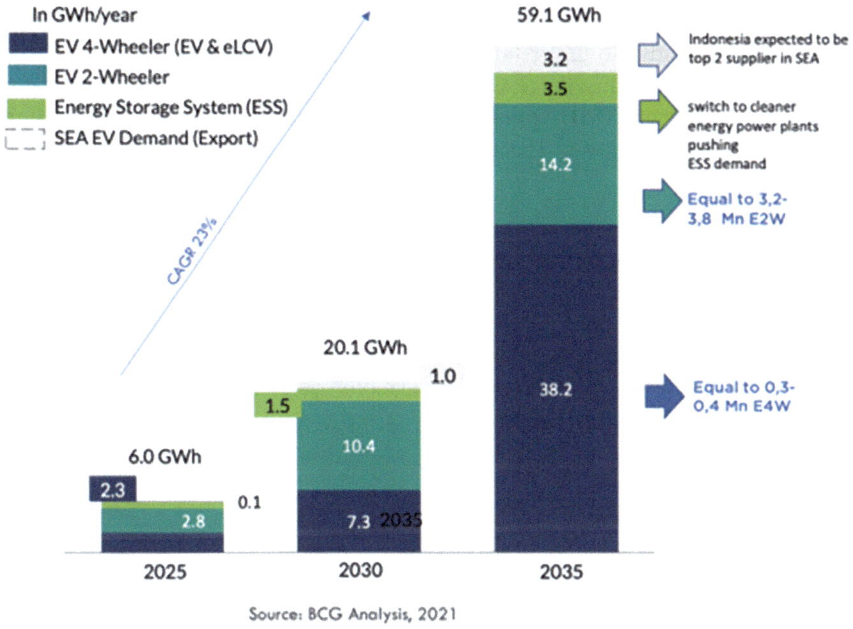

Fig. 1 Total domestic battery demand until 2035. *Source* [6]

increase in electric motorcycles in 2023 shows little improvement compared to the growth from 2021 to 2022 when the numbers rose from 5,485 to 25,782 units without any incentives [8].

In contrast, sales of conventional motorcycles (CMs) continue to dominate, averaging around 5 million units annually [3]. Despite the potential benefits of electric motorcycles for Indonesia's environment, their adoption rate remains low compared to conventional gasoline models. This limited diffusion presents a significant challenge. The key issue lies in the diffusion barriers that hinder the widespread adoption of e-motorcycles in Indonesia. These barriers prevent a smooth transition from traditional motorcycles to their electric counterparts.

The complete realization of electric vehicle (EV) diffusion programs and the comprehensive decarbonization of the transportation sector hinges upon social acceptance [9]. Therefore to gain a more comprehensive understanding of consumers' behavioral intentions towards electric motorcycles, this study investigates the mediating effect of consumer attitudes between psychological, technical factors, and behavioral intentions, while also considering government incentives. Given the dynamic nature of the electric motorcycle market, characterized by rapid technological advancements, such mediation analysis is crucial for elucidating how consumer attitudes intervene in the relationship between various factors and behavioral intentions.

This study intends to fill this gap in the literature by examining consumers' behavioral intentions to use electric motorcycles within a comprehensive model. Provides a new perspective by integrating psychological factors and technical factors with government incentive to understand electric motorcycle usage intention especially Indonesia. To achieve this, the research model is developed by combining the theory of planned behavior (TPB) with the diffusion of innovation theory (DOI) along with government incentives. Specifically, it seeks to answer the following research questions:

- RQ1: How do perceive behavioral control, subjective norms, complexity and triability impact consumers' behavioral intention to use electric motorcycles?
- RQ2: What is the role of government incentives regarding consumers' behavioral intention to use electric motorcycles?
- RQ3: How do consumer attitudes mediate the relationship between the psychological and technical attributes of electric motorcycles and consumers' behavioral intention to use electric motorcycles?

2 Literature Review

2.1 Switching Behavior Intention to Use Electric Motorcycles

In many Southeast Asian countries with low to moderate incomes, motorcycles typically make up the majority of vehicles in mixed traffic flow [10]. Several studies on customers' intentions to use EM have been conducted to achieve varying results depending on the location.

The switching intention of Vietnamese, particularly influenced by environmental concerns and global motives [11]. Later on, the study of Vietnamese intention to use EM was continued, finding that the intention is also influenced by subjective knowledge of EM [10]. In Lome, Africa, adoption was shown to depend on suppliers' ability to demonstrate that EM is superior to gasoline-powered motorcycles, potentially increasing early adopters' satisfaction [12]. Similarly, in Ecuador, the increasing use of EM is driven by awareness, concern, and ecological values among the population [13].

A study conducted in Vietnam delves into the intention of Generation Z individuals to utilize electric motorcycles (EMs), examining the impact of factors such as the frequency of energy replenishment and governmental policies on their decision-making process [14]. Research conducted in Pakistan discovered that factors such as perceived ease of use, perceived usefulness, environmental concerns, and perceived value significantly influence the intention to adopt electric motorcycles (EMs) [15].

Individuals' intentions regarding the intention to use electric motorcycles (EMs) are shaped by a blend of demographic, situational, contextual, and psychological determinants [16]. Psychological factors and demographic profiles have been identified as exerting a positive influence on the intention to purchase electric vehicles [17, 18]. Conversely, situational and contextual factors are contingent upon consumers' readiness to adopt change or switch, alongside numerous other variables.

2.2 Theoretical Background

The Theory of Planned Behavior (TPB) was developed out of the Theory of Reasoned Action (TRA), a theory first proposed by Ajzen [19], offers a comprehensive framework for understanding human behavior and decision-making processes. Central to the TPB are three main constructs: attitudes (ATT), subjective norms (SN), and perceived behavioral control (PBC), which collectively shape individuals' intentions and subsequent behaviors.

TPB has been applied across intensive behavioral contexts [20]. For example, predict consumer acceptance of AI-based intelligent products by integrating TPB, the Technology acceptance model, and the Value-based adoption model [21]. On the basis of TPB, a study uses TPB along with environmental risk perception and behavioral willingness to explain citizens' plastic reduction behavior. [22]. Further, TPB, expectation-confirmation model, and consumption values explore the individual continuing intention with social media experience as a moderating variable [23].

According to TPB, as outlined by researchers, intentions stand out as the primary predictor of actual behavior within the model. These intentions are shaped by individuals' attitudes toward the behavior, adherence to social norms, and perceived control over engaging in the behavior and further elaborates that if an individual holds a more favorable attitude toward a specific behavior, perceives greater social pressure or external norms, and feels a stronger sense of control over performing the behavior, they are more likely to exhibit a heightened determination to adopt that behavior [24].

In the context of this study, the intention to utilize electric motorcycles (EMs) is bolstered by perceived behavioral control (PBC), reflecting one's perceived control over the decision to adopt EM based on available opportunities and optimistic attitudes regarding EM benefits.

On the other hand, According to Rogers' DOI (Diffusion of Innovations) theory in 1995, the adoption of a new product or service is mainly influenced by its perceived advantages compared to existing alternatives. Relative advantages encompass various technological aspects of a product, such as its compatibility, complexity, testability, and visibility. The Diffusion of Innovation theory is a well-known framework that examines how and at what pace new innovations or technologies are adopted by end-users over a particular period [25].

In recent years, researchers have increasingly employed the DOI theory to investigate technology product initiatives [26]. The latest research on 2024 uncovered significant associations between dimensions of the DOI theory and enterprise metaverse usage intention [27]. Furthermore, numerous researchers have utilized DOI theory to examine adoption intentions across various emerging technologies, including social media intention in SMEs [28], augmented reality mobile applications [26], autonomous vehicles [29], driving intention based on gender [30], pick up point services [31]. Furthermore, the DOI theory is used in conjunction with the TPB to predict consumer adoption and behavior [32]. Researchers utilized the DOI theory to explore factors influencing the adoption of electric vehicles (EVs) from economic, functional, and social [33]. Moreover, they used DOI and the moderate role of lifestyle to predict the purchase intention of electric vehicles. This comprehensive approach underscores the versatility and effectiveness of the DOI theory in understanding and predicting adoption behaviors across a wide range of contexts.

In the study on electric motorcycle (EM) intention to use, researchers have also applied DOI theory to examine adoption intentions in this domain.

3 Methodology

Maintaining academic rigor was reinforced by following the PRISMA Statement. PRISMA was chosen to ensure a systematic and transparent review process. Furthermore, PRISMA also allows clear and comprehensive reporting, which is a crucial aspect of solid research, as it enables readers to assess important factors related to the research's execution and reliability, and it is vital for ensuring a study's replicability (Fig. 2):

1. Identification:

   The goal is to gather as many relevant articles as possible, including empirical studies, reviews, and theoretical papers that discuss electric motorcycle adoption and the role of government incentives. The Scopus database was initiated on August 15th, 2024. The terms "electric motorcycle*", "electric scooter", "electric motorbike*", "Electric bike", "E-motorcycle", "Electric two-wheeler", "Battery-powered motorcycle", "Zero-emission motorcycle", "Green motorcycle" was employed to target titles, abstracts, and keywords yielding an initial expansive pool of 2,970 articles. To narrow down the research objectives, extra search terms were included using the connector "AND" for the "Adoption" term and the connector "OR" for the "usage" "OR" for the "government" term to explore the adoption of electric motorcycles factors. By incorporating these extra search terms, the number of articles was reduced to 340, enabling a more precise study of the subject matter.
2. Screening

   To refine this vast collection, strategic and well-defined parameters were set:

   - Inclusion criteria: Only articles that:
     (1) Were published within the past decade (2014–2024).
     (2) Were authored in English.
     (3) Were Source from Journal in the realms of business, management, and accounting & social sciences
   - Exclusion criteria: Articles were discarded if they:
     (1) Deviated from the core research theme.
     (2) Were not authored in English.
     (3) Were published prior to our defined ten-year window.

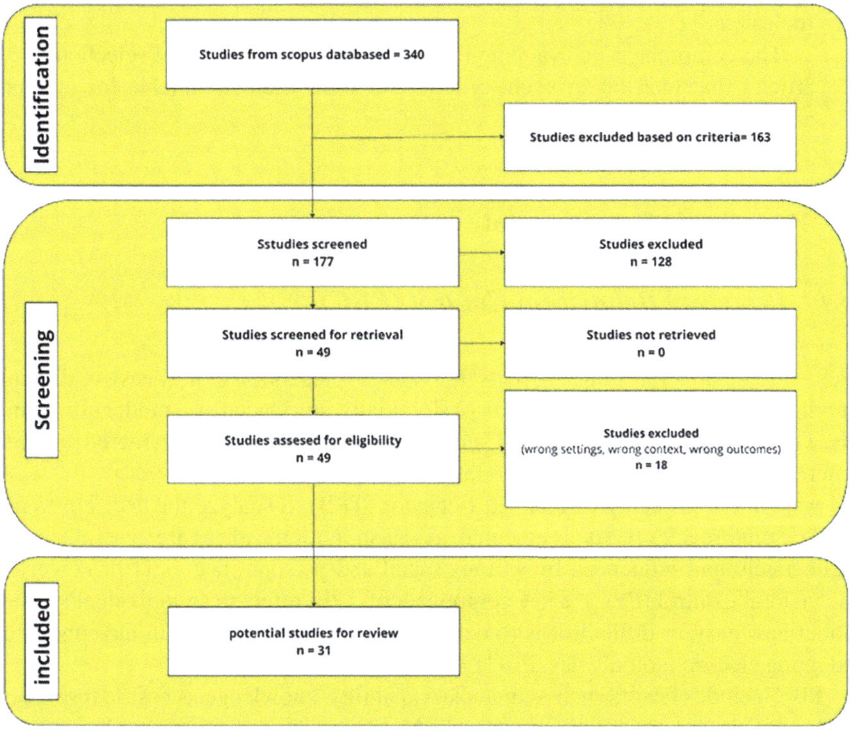

Fig. 2 Papers quality assessment and screening based on the Preferred Reporting Items for Systematic Reviews and Meta-Analyses (PRISMA) Statement for transparent reporting

(4) Were not Source from Journal in the realms of business, management, and accounting or & social sciences.

After applying those filters, the articles were reduced to 177 articles and was procured for further assessment.

3. Eligibility

The remaining studies undergo a more detailed evaluation to determine their eligibility for inclusion in the review. This involves assessing the quality of the studies, their methodologies, and their relevance to the research question. The assessment were guiding by research questions:

Articles were deemed out of scope if they focused solely on Electric motorcycles without addressing any of the variables mentioned in the research question, or vice versa. This stringent screening process ensured that only articles closely aligned with our research objectives progressed to the next stage. When reviewers had differing opinions on an article's relevance, a structured discussion was conducted to reach a consensus.

4. Inclusion

   The comprehensive evaluation process culminated in a final selection of 31 articles that met the stringent criteria and were deemed suitable for in-depth analysis.

4 Hypothesis Development

4.1 Perceived Behavioral Control (PBC)

Perceived behavioral control reflects individuals' perception of how easy or difficult it will be to use electric motorcycles [24]. Initially introduced as a moderator within the TPB framework [19], perceived behavioral control has recently garnered renewed interest as a moderator of various relationships within the TPB [34].

Applying the Theory of Planned Behavior (TPB) to analyze the decision to use electric motorcycles (EMs) is essential, as transportation choices are generally made deliberately and influenced by various social and personal factors [10]. Perceived Behavioral Control (PBC), a key component of TPB, refers to an individual's belief about how easy or difficult it is to perform a particular behavior. In the context of adopting electric motorcycles, PBC plays a significant role.

PBC includes factors such as financial capability, knowledge, access to resources, and confidence in one's ability to use an EM. For instance, individuals who perceive themselves as having greater control over these factors are more inclined to consider using an electric motorcycle in the future [10]. This sense of control not only influences their intention to adopt green mobility solutions but also shapes their overall attitude toward these choices.

Research has shown that PBC significantly impacts consumer intentions to engage with various green products and services. For example, when considering the recycling of lead-acid batteries from e-bikes, those who believe they have the necessary resources and conditions are more likely to engage in the behavior [35]. Similarly, consumers who feel they have full control over their purchasing decisions, including financial independence and ease of purchase, are more likely to intend to buy an electric motorcycle [36].

Therefore, we proposed:

H1: Perceived behavioral control positively influences consumers' attitude

4.2 Subjective Norms

Subjective norms, which reflect the social pressure individuals experience when deciding whether to engage in a particular behavior, significantly shape consumer attitudes toward using electric motorcycles (EMs). These norms represent the influence of important people in an individual's life, such as family, friends, and colleagues, on their decision-making process.

For example, the opinions and recommendations of close contacts can heavily influence whether a person develops a positive attitude toward adopting an EM. If key figures in someone's social circle express support for EM use or hold favorable views toward it, this social pressure can lead the individual to align their own attitudes with those of their peers [10]. This effect is particularly evident when purchasing hybrid or electric vehicles, where social norms and attitudes (ATT) play a significant role in shaping consumer intentions [38].

Additionally, subjective norms include the broader social image associated with adopting EMs. For instance, the desire to be seen as environmentally responsible or to stay current with modern trends can motivate individuals to choose EMs, as the need to maintain or enhance one's social image is a strong behavioral driver [39]. Consequently, social influence not only impacts the decision to use EMs but also influences attitudes toward this behavior by reinforcing the perceived advantages of EM adoption within a social setting [40]. This dynamic underscore the strong connection between subjective norms and attitudes, as people adjust their views based on the perceived expectations and behaviors of those around them. Therefore, we propose:

H2: Subjective norms positively influence consumers' attitude

4.3 Triability

Consumers' hesitation towards new technologies often stems from a lack of firsthand experience [42]. To address this, we propose that the triability of electric motorcycles, the ease with which people can try them, has a positive influence on consumer attitudes. This hypothesis is supported by established theories like the Diffusion of Innovation, which emphasizes the importance of triability in reducing uncertainty and promoting adoption [43]. Similarly, the Theory of Planned Behavior suggests that triability can improve perceived ease of use, a key factor influencing attitudes [44]. By enabling potential users to experience electric motorcycles directly, triability can alleviate concerns, enhance perceived ease of use, and ultimately lead to a more favorable disposition towards this sustainable transportation option.

Trialability, or the ability to test and experiment with a new technology before fully committing to it, significantly affects consumer attitudes toward electric motorcycles (EMs). When users have the chance to test EMs, they can directly experience their usability and advantages, which enhances their perception of the technology's practicality and value [11].

The idea of trialability implies that innovations that can be tested before purchase are more likely to be adopted compared to those that cannot be. Personal testing of an EM reduces the uncertainty potential users might feel about the technology. Experiencing the performance, functionality, and convenience of EMs firsthand allows users to develop a more positive attitude toward the technology. This trial experience provides concrete evidence of the EMs' benefits, such as ease of use and effectiveness, which are crucial for decision-making [45]. Therefore, we propose:

H3: Triability of using electric motorcycles positively influences consumers' attitude

4.4 Complexity

Complexity, as reflected in the implementation difficulty, arises when operationalizing new knowledge into practice [46]. It is the degree to which an innovation is challenging to comprehend and use [47]. In other words, Innovations that are difficult to understand or require significant cognitive effort are usually not accepted [48].

The complexity associated with electric motorcycles has a notable impact on users' attitudes toward their adoption. Key obstacles include issues with battery performance—such as driving range, charging time, and replacement costs—as well as the availability of charging infrastructure and technical support. These factors are crucial in determining how users perceive the complexity of using electric motorcycles [49]

The ease of use is a major factor in the adoption of technology, particularly for those who are not technologically savvy. Technologies that are easy to understand and operate are more likely to be accepted. Therefore, electric motorcycles that are straightforward and user-friendly tend to be adopted more quickly than those requiring complex learning processes [50].

Complexity involves various functional aspects, such as maintenance, battery charging, and repairs. The extent to which users find these aspects easy or difficult affects their perception of the technology's usefulness and ease of use. Electric vehicles (EVs) with intuitive designs and user-friendly features are likely to see faster adoption, as users generally have more positive attitudes towards them and integrate them into their daily lives more readily [11]. Therefore, we propose:

H4: The complexity of using electric motorcycles positively influences consumers' attitude

4.5 Attitude

Drawing on the preceding hypotheses, it is reasonable to assume that a positive attitude towards electric motorcycles correlates with a heightened intention to use them. This linkage is firmly supported by theories such as TPB, which asserts that a favorable attitude directly impacts behavioral intention [24]. Attitude plays a pivotal role in shaping the intention to use electric motorcycles (EMs), making it a primary focus for strategies aimed at increasing adoption. Evidence shows that attitude is the most influential factor in determining whether individuals will decide to use EMs, emphasizing its critical role in adoption efforts [10].

Their environmental concerns and knowledge significantly influence a person's attitude towards EMs. Positive attitudes towards eco-friendly products, such as EMs, act as a mediator between environmental concerns and the willingness to purchase green technologies. This indicates that a favorable attitude towards green products enhances the likelihood of their adoption [54]. Attitudes reflect individuals' positive or negative evaluations of behaviors related to EM use. These evaluations are crucial in determining whether users will engage in specific practices, such as recycling batteries through formal channels [41]

Furthermore, attitudes is essential in shaping consumer values and influencing behavior. A positive attitude towards EMs strengthens the intention to use them, underscoring the importance of attitude in the decision-making process [55].

A positive attitude towards electric motorcycles is strongly correlated with a higher intention to use them. Research shows that consumers who hold a favorable attitude towards e-bikes are more likely to intend to adopt them [56]. Additionally, attitudes mediate the influence of perceived usefulness on the intention to use e-scooters, highlighting how perceptions of the technology's utility affect adoption decisions [57].

Fostering a positive attitude towards EMs can significantly boost purchase intentions. Given that attitudes heavily influence the intention to adopt electric motorcycles, enhancing these attitudes is crucial for increasing adoption rates [11, 40, 52]. Therefore, we propose:

H5: Consumers' attitude positively influences behavioral intention towards electric motorcycles.

4.6 Government Incentive

Electric vehicles are still in the infancy stage; hence, the government should offer some incentives, such as tax credits and subsidies to electric vehicles [29]. Customers usually purchase electric vehicles when the government offers incentives [58]. Other study proof that financial incentives given by the Chinese government impact the intention to adopt electric vehicles [59]. Similarly, showed that customers' perceived tax and subsidy policy attractiveness positively influences their intentions to adopt autonomous vehicles [60].

Furthermore, safety concerns, such as battery explosions, can affect attitudes towards EMs. Financial incentives can address these safety concerns by enhancing the perceived value and reliability of electric motorcycles making them a more attractive option compared to traditional vehicles. Safety features combined with financial support contribute to more positive attitudes towards electric motorcycles [61]. These incentives lower the perceived financial risks associated with purchasing electric motorcycles, which positively influences consumer attitudes [35, 37]. However, sustaining these incentives can be challenging, especially in developing economies where cost considerations are prominent. Therefore, policymakers need to explore sustainable approaches that extend support beyond initial subsidies [35] which,

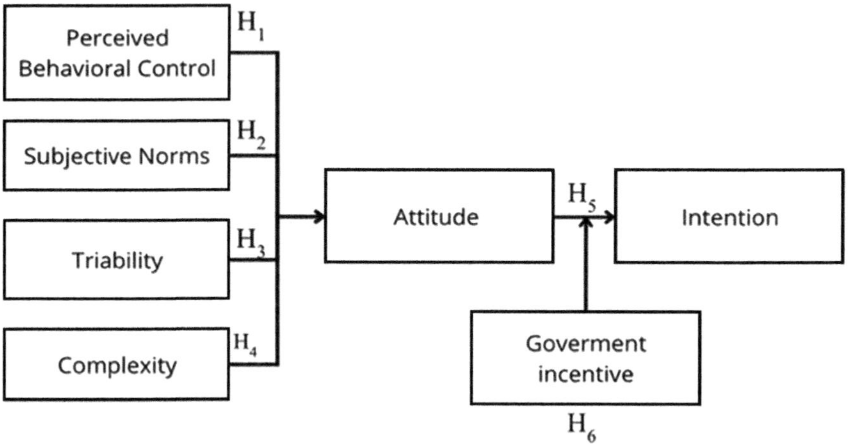

Fig. 3 Proposed conceptual framework

address ongoing costs and are more effective in encouraging adoption than one-time purchase discounts. This indicates that continuous support is vital for sustaining positive attitudes and increasing electric motorcycle usage [62]

Strategic, long-term incentive policies are essential for moderating the relationship between attitudes and the intention to adopt EMs, making them a key factor in driving higher adoption rates [36]. The reduction or elimination of government subsidies could significantly lower the intention to purchase EMs, underscoring the importance of maintaining effective incentive policies. Local governments can further support adoption by offering tax reductions and exemptions from road user charges, which help lower the overall cost of EM ownership [51, 63]. Therefore, we propose:

H6: Government incentives toward the intention to use electric motorcycles positively strengthen the relationships between attitude and intention (Fig. 3).

5 Conclusion

This study aimed to thoroughly investigate how to Overcome Diffusion Barriers to Electric Motorcycle Adoption by examining the factors using TPB theory and DOI theory. Using the PRISMA Statement, a detailed Systematic Literature Review (SLR) was performed for the years 2014 to 2024. Through a meticulous process of screening and filtering with the Covidence web-based tool, 31 pertinent papers were selected from an initial set of 177 papers in the Scopus database.

RQ1: How do perceive behavioral control, Subjective norms, complexity and triability impact consumers' behavioral intention to use electric motorcycles?

In response to RQ1, the findings consistently support the positive impact of perceived behavioral control, Subjective norms, complexity, and triability to influence intention to use electric motorcycles through positive attitude [10, 36, 37, 54]. The literature reveals that Perceived Behavioral Control, which includes financial capability, access to information, and social influences, plays a critical role in shaping positive attitudes toward using electric motorcycles. As consumers feel more empowered to make informed and autonomous choices, their likelihood of adopting EMs increases, highlighting the broader influence of PBC on their attitudes and intentions. Subjective norms have a significant impact on attitudes toward using electric motorcycles by exerting social pressure that encourages individuals to adopt behaviors deemed favorable by their peers. Whether through direct support from close contacts or the broader desire to conform to social trends, these norms shape how individuals perceive and ultimately decide to engage with Ems. Trialability positively impacts attitudes toward electric motorcycles by allowing users to reduce uncertainties and directly evaluate the technology's benefits. Hands-on experience fosters greater confidence and commitment, leading to more favorable attitudes and higher adoption rates. The complexity is vital to simplify the user experience. Features that enhance ease of use—such as intuitive controls, straightforward charging solutions, and clear information on battery status and range—can make electric motorcycles more accessible and user-friendly. Simplifying the technology and providing easy-to-understand guidance can help demystify electric motorcycles for new users and reduce perceived complexity.

RQ2: How is the role of government incentives regarding consumers' behavioral intention to use electric motorcycles?

In response to RQ2, government incentives play a moderator construct between a person's attitude and intention to use. Previous literature has often highlighted that government incentives have a direct impact on consumers' intentions to use electric motorcycles. These incentives, such as tax credits, rebates, or subsidies, can make electric motorcycles more financially attractive, thereby directly influencing consumer decision-making. Retraction of government incentives or subsidies could significantly lower the intention to purchase EMs, underscoring the importance of maintaining effective incentive policies, but for success in achieving goals, it must also be supported by regulation for sustainable approaches that extend support beyond initial subsidies.

RQ3: How do consumer attitudes mediate the relationship between the psychological and technical attributes of electric motorcycles and consumers' behavioral intention to use electric motorcycles?

The consistent result provided in this paper that attitude positively influence intention to use electric motorcycles [10, 11, 38, 40, 41, 52, 54–57]. A positive attitude towards electric motorcycles (EMs) is strongly linked to a higher intention to use them. This connection is supported by theories such as the Theory of Planned Behavior (TPB), which highlights that a favorable attitude directly impacts behavioral intention. Evidence suggests that attitude is a critical factor in adoption decisions, as environmental concerns and knowledge influence it. Positive attitudes towards eco-friendly products mediate the relationship between environmental concerns and the willingness to adopt green technologies, such as EMs. Additionally, attitudes shape consumer values and behaviors, such as recycling practices. Research shows that consumers with favorable attitudes towards EMs are more likely to intend to adopt them, and attitudes also mediate the impact of perceived usefulness on adoption decisions. Therefore, enhancing positive attitudes towards EMs is essential for boosting adoption rates.

In summary, the presented SLR offers insights into overcoming diffusion barriers for electric motorcycle adoption by examining factors such as perceived behavioral control, subjective norms, complexity, and trialability, as well as the role of government incentives and consumer attitudes.

6 Limitation and Future Directions

One potential limitation of this study is the dependence on a literature review as the main data source. While an extensive review of scholarly articles is a robust method for developing a conceptual model, it may not fully capture the intricacies and complexities of actual behaviors related to the intention to use EMs in specific contexts. Additionally, the study introduces a conceptual model without empirical validation, which may limit the applicability of its findings. Furthermore, the study centers on constructs from the TPB and DOI models, such as perceived behavioral control, subjective norms, triability, complexity, attitude, and government incentives. While these factors are important, other variables might also play a critical role in shaping the intention to use EMs.

The following research hypotheses were proposed on this paper:

H1: Perceived behavioral control positively influences consumers' attitude
H2: Subjective norms positively influence consumers' attitude
H3: The triability of using electric motorcycles positively influences consumers' attitude
H4: The complexity of using electric motorcycles positively influences consumers' attitude
H5: Consumers' attitude positively influences behavioral intention towards electric motorcycles.
H6: Government incentives toward the intention to use electric motorcycles positively strengthen the relationships between attitude and intention to use electric motorcycles

These hypotheses highlight potential directions for future empirical research, underscoring the complex relationships between electric motorcycles, adoption rates, diffusion processes, and broader cultural and contextual factors. Furthermore, further research could address these limitations by incorporating empirical testing and employing a mixed-methods approach to collect data from both current and prospective users. Moreover, expanding the conceptual model to include a more comprehensive set of variables could provide a deeper understanding of the factors influencing EM adoption.

References

1. A. L. Salvia, W. Leal Filho, L. L. Brandli, and J. S. Griebeler, "Assessing research trends related to Sustainable Development Goals: local and global issues," *J Clean Prod*, vol. 208, pp. 841–849, Jan. 2019, https://doi.org/10.1016/j.jclepro.2018.09.242.
2. Climate Transparency, "Climate Transparency Report: Comparing G20 Climate Action," 2023.
3. BPS, "Perkembangan Jumlah Kendaraan Bermotor Menurut Jenis (Unit), 2021–2022," BPS.
4. Kompas, "Sepeda Motor Sumbang Polusi Udara Terbesar di Indonesia," Kompas.
5. Q. Dong, S. Liang, J. Li, H. C. Kim, W. Shen, and T. J. Wallington, "iScience Cost, energy, and carbon footprint benefits of second-life electric vehicle battery use", https://doi.org/10.1016/j.isci.
6. BCG, "Electrifying Indonesia's Two-Wheeler Industry," Nov. 2022.
7. PLN, "Kaleidoskop 2023 Dorong Pertumbuhan EV di Tanah Air, PLN Bangun Lebih Dari 624 SPKLU Hingga Tahun 2023," Word Press.
8. Deloitte and Foundry, "An electric revolution: The rise of Indonesia's e-motorcycle," 2023.
9. C. Deka, M. K. Dutta, M. Yazdanpanah, and N. Komendantova, "Can gain motivation induce Indians to adopt electric vehicles? Application of an extended theory of Planned Behavior to map EV adoption intention," *Energy Policy*, vol. 182, Nov. 2023, https://doi.org/10.1016/j.enpol.2023.113724.
10. D. Q. Nguyen-Phuoc, T. M. Truong, M. H. Nguyen, H. G. Pham, Z. C. Li, and O. Oviedo-Trespalacios, "What factors influence the intention to use electric motorcycles in motorcycle-dominated countries? An empirical study in Vietnam," *Transp Policy (Oxf)*, vol. 146, pp. 193–204, Feb. 2024, https://doi.org/10.1016/j.tranpol.2023.11.013.
11. D. Ngoc Su, D. Quy Nguyen-Phuoc, P. Thi Kim Tran, T. Van Nguyen, T. Trong Luu, and H. G. Pham, "Identifying must-have factors and should-have factors affecting the adoption of electric motorcycles—A combined use of PLS-SEM and NCA approach," *Travel Behav Soc*, vol. 33, Oct. 2023, https://doi.org/10.1016/j.tbs.2023.100633.
12. Y. T. Amedokpo, "Tracking early adoption of electric motorcycles: The mototaxi riders' experience in Lomé," *Transp Res D Transp Environ*, vol. 131, Jun. 2024, https://doi.org/10.1016/j.trd.2024.104184.
13. L. Bonisoli and R. A. Blacio Guañuna, "Going green in Ecuador: Unpacking the motivations behind brand loyalty for organic products," *J Clean Prod*, vol. 418, Sep. 2023, https://doi.org/10.1016/j.jclepro.2023.138116.
14. N. T. Van Anh, T. T. Tuyet, L. C. Kiet, N. P. Trang, N. Thi, and K. Yen, "Factors Affecting the Electric Motorbikes Demand of Gen Z in Vietnam", https://doi.org/10.56472/25835238/IRJEMS-V2I3P152.
15. S. Shaikh, M. A. H. Talpur, F. Baig, F. Tariq, and S. H. Khahro, "Adoption of Electric Motorcycles in Pakistan: A Technology Acceptance Model Perspective," *World Electric Vehicle Journal*, vol. 14, no. 10, Oct. 2023, https://doi.org/10.3390/wevj14100278.
16. I. Gunawan, A. A. N. P. Redi, A. A. Santosa, M. F. N. Maghfiroh, A. H. Pandyaswargo, and A. C. Kurniawan, "Determinants of Customer Intentions to Use Electric Vehicle in Indonesia: An Integrated Model Analysis," *Sustainability (Switzerland)*, vol. 14, no. 4, Feb. 2022, https://doi.org/10.3390/su14041972.
17. A. Priessner, R. Sposato, and N. Hampl, "Predictors of electric vehicle adoption: An analysis of potential electric vehicle drivers in Austria," *Energy Policy*, vol. 122, pp. 701–714, Nov. 2018, https://doi.org/10.1016/j.enpol.2018.07.058.

18. A. Nayum, C. A. Klöckner, and M. Mehmetoglu, "Comparison of socio-psychological characteristics of conventional and battery electric car buyers," *Travel Behav Soc*, vol. 3, pp. 8–20, Jan. 2016, https://doi.org/10.1016/j.tbs.2015.03.005.
19. I. Ajzen, "From intentions to actions: A theory of planned behavior," *Springer*, pp. 11–39, Jan. 1985.
20. H. Joyram, K. Govindan, and R. Nunkoo, "Development of a novel psychological model to predict the eco-block building adoption in Mauritius," *Cleaner and Responsible Consumption*, vol. 12, Mar. 2024, https://doi.org/10.1016/j.clrc.2024.100172.
21. K. Sohn and O. Kwon, "Technology acceptance theories and factors influencing artificial Intelligence-based intelligent products," *Telematics and Informatics*, vol. 47, Apr. 2020, https://doi.org/10.1016/j.tele.2019.101324.
22. B. Wang, T. Tang, E. Kaspar, and Y. Li, "Explaining citizens' plastic reduction behavior with an extended theory of planned behavior model: An empirical study in Switzerland," *J Environ Manage*, vol. 358, May 2024, https://doi.org/10.1016/j.jenvman.2024.120869.
23. M. Mehrabioun, "A multi-theoretical view on social media continuance intention: Combining theory of planned behavior, expectation-confirmation model and consumption values," *Digital Business*, vol. 4, no. 1, Jun. 2024, https://doi.org/10.1016/j.digbus.2023.100070.
24. Ajzen Icek, "The theory of planned behavior," *Organ Behav Hum Decis Process*, vol. 50, no. 2, pp. 179–211, Dec. 1991.
25. S. Hutajulu, W. Dhewanto, E. A. Prasetio, and P. Rudito, "Key Success Factors for 5G Technology Commercialization in Telecommunication Company Case Study of an Established XYZ Company in Indonesia," *The Asian Journal of Technology Management (AJTM)*, vol. 13, no. 1, pp. 16–34, 2020, https://doi.org/10.12695/ajtm.2020.13.1.2.
26. K. Y. Lin and T. K. Huang, "Shopping in the digital world: How augmented reality mobile applications trigger customer engagement," *Technol Soc*, vol. 77, Jun. 2024, https://doi.org/10.1016/j.techsoc.2024.102540.
27. A. Kumar, A. Shankar, R. Agarwal, V. Agarwal, and E. A. Alzeiby, "With enterprise metaverse comes great possibilities! Understanding metaverse usage intention from an employee perspective," *Journal of Retailing and Consumer Services*, vol. 78, May 2024, https://doi.org/10.1016/j.jretconser.2024.103767.
28. W. S. Kwon, H. Woo, A. Sadachar, and X. Huang, "External pressure or internal culture? An innovation diffusion theory account of small retail businesses' social media use," *Journal of Retailing and Consumer Services*, vol. 62, Sep. 2021, https://doi.org/10.1016/j.jretconser.2021.102616.
29. J. Heo, H. Lee, S. Yoon, and K. Kim, "Responses to Take-Over Request in Autonomous Vehicles: Effects of Environmental Conditions and Cues," *IEEE Transactions on Intelligent Transportation Systems*, vol. 23, no. 12, pp. 23573–23582, Dec. 2022, https://doi.org/10.1109/TITS.2022.3201074.
30. M. Al-Razgan, A. Alrowily, R. N. Al-Matham, K. M. Alghamdi, M. Shaabi, and L. Alssum, "Using diffusion of innovation theory and sentiment analysis to analyze attitudes toward driving adoption by Saudi women," *Technol Soc*, vol. 65, May 2021, https://doi.org/10.1016/j.techsoc.2021.101558.
31. L. Guarino Neto and J. Geraldo Vidal Vieira, "An investigation of consumer intention to use pick-up point services for last-mile distribution in a developing country," *Journal of Retailing and Consumer Services*, vol. 74, Sep. 2023, https://doi.org/10.1016/j.jretconser.2023.103425.
32. F. Acikgoz, A. Elwalda, and M. J. De Oliveira, "Curiosity on Cutting-Edge Technology via Theory of Planned Behavior and Diffusion of Innovation Theory," *International Journal of Information Management Data Insights*, vol. 3, no. 1, Apr. 2023, https://doi.org/10.1016/j.jjimei.2022.100152.
33. R. Xie, L. An, and N. Yasir, "How Innovative Characteristics Influence Consumers' Intention to Purchase Electric Vehicle: A Moderating Role of Lifestyle," *Sustainability (Switzerland)*, vol. 14, no. 8, Apr. 2022, https://doi.org/10.3390/su14084467.
34. F. Govaerts and S. Ottar Olsen, "Consumers' values, attitudes and behaviours towards consuming seaweed food products: The effects of perceived naturalness, uniqueness, and

behavioural control," *Food Research International*, vol. 165, Mar. 2023, https://doi.org/10.1016/j.foodres.2022.112417.
35. F. A. Bhat and A. Verma, "Electric two-wheeler adoption in India—A discrete choice analysis of motivators and barriers affecting the potential electric two-wheeler buyers," *Transp Policy (Oxf)*, vol. 152, pp. 118–131, Jun. 2024, https://doi.org/10.1016/j.tranpol.2024.05.004.
36. A. D. Murtiningrum, A. Darmawan, and H. Wong, "The adoption of electric motorcycles: A survey of public perception in Indonesia," *J Clean Prod*, vol. 379, Dec. 2022, https://doi.org/10.1016/j.jclepro.2022.134737.
37. N. T. Trung and T. Urmee, "Electrifying Vietnam's streets: Identifying the determinants of electric two-wheelers uptake," *Transp Res D Transp Environ*, vol. 129, Apr. 2024, https://doi.org/10.1016/j.trd.2024.104116.
38. K. Ravishankar, A. K. Subramani, N. Akbar Jan, and C. Ramkumar, "Examining the Factors Influencing the Intention to Use Electric Bikes by Young Adults: Using Extended Theory of Planned Behavior Model," *Asian Journal of Business Research*, vol. 13, no. 2, pp. 65–85, 2023, https://doi.org/10.14707/ajbr.230150.
39. F. A. Bhat and A. Verma, "Consumer intention to accept electric two-wheelers in India: a valence theory approach to unveil the role of identity and utility," *Transportation (Amst)*, 2023, https://doi.org/10.1007/s11116-023-10430-z.
40. S. Jayasingh, T. Girija, and S. Arunkumar, "Factors influencing consumers' purchase intention towards electric two-wheelers," *Sustainability (Switzerland)*, vol. 13, no. 22, Nov. 2021, https://doi.org/10.3390/su132212851.
41. S. Seebauer, "Why early adopters engage in interpersonal diffusion of technological innovations: An empirical study on electric bicycles and electric scooters," *Transp Res Part A Policy Pract*, vol. 78, pp. 146–160, Aug. 2015, https://doi.org/10.1016/j.tra.2015.04.017.
42. O. Egbue and S. Long, "Barriers to widespread adoption of electric vehicles: An analysis of consumer attitudes and perceptions," *Energy Policy*, vol. 48, pp. 717–729, Sep. 2012, https://doi.org/10.1016/j.enpol.2012.06.009.
43. S. S. Alam, M. Masukujjaman, S. Susmit, S. Susmit, and H. A. Aziz, "Augmented reality adoption intention among travel and tour operators in Malaysia: mediation effect of value alignment," *Journal of Tourism Futures*, 2022, https://doi.org/10.1108/JTF-03-2021-0072.
44. S. Davoodi, L. Akbarpour, and E. Hadopour, "Effect of Psychological Factors on EFL Teachers' Attitude about Technology Use: Perceived ease of use, trialability, and subjective norms in focus DOR: 20.1001.1.23223898.2021.9.37.5.3," *International Journal of Foreign Language Teaching and Research*, vol. 9, no. 37, pp. 83–93, Dec. 2021, https://doi.org/10.52547/jfl.9.37.83.
45. 47. S. Synek and J. Koenigstorfer, "Exploring adoption determinants of tax-subsidized company-leasing bicycles from the perspective of German employers and employees," *Transp Res Part A Policy Pract*, vol. 117, pp. 238–260, Nov. 2018, https://doi.org/10.1016/j.tra.2018.08.011.
46. K. D. Dryden-Palmer, C. S. Parshuram, and W. B. Berta, "Context, complexity and process in the implementation of evidence-based innovation: A realist informed review," *BMC Health Serv Res*, vol. 20, no. 1, Feb. 2020, https://doi.org/10.1186/s12913-020-4935-y.
47. E. M. , S. A. , & Q. M. M. Rogers, "Diffusion of innovations," *In An integrated approach to communication theory and research*, pp. 432–448, Apr. 2014.
48. C. Makanyeza, "Determinants of consumers' intention to adopt mobile banking services in Zimbabwe," *International Journal of Bank Marketing*, vol. 35, no. 6, pp. 997–1017, 2017, https://doi.org/10.1108/IJBM-07-2016-0099.
49. N. Truong, G. Trencher, M. Yarime, B. Barrett, and K. Matsubae, "Barriers to the adoption of electric cars and electric motorcycles in Vietnam," *Transp Res D Transp Environ*, vol. 131, Jun. 2024, https://doi.org/10.1016/j.trd.2024.104204.
50. L. Bonisoli, A. M. Velepucha Cruz, and D. K. Rogel Elizalde, "Revving towards sustainability: Environmentalism impact on electric motorcycle adoption," *J Clean Prod*, vol. 435, Jan. 2024, https://doi.org/10.1016/j.jclepro.2023.140262.

51. C. Balijepalli, S. Shepherd, R. Crastes Dit Sourd, M. Farda, T. Praesha, and H. A. R. Lubis, "Preferences for electric motorcycle adoption in Bandung, Indonesia," *Urban Plan Transp Res*, vol. 11, no. 1, 2023, https://doi.org/10.1080/21650020.2023.2238033.
52. M. Patil and B. B. Majumdar, "An investigation on the key determinants influencing electric two-wheeler usage in urban Indian context," *Research in Transportation Business and Management*, vol. 43, Jun. 2022, https://doi.org/10.1016/j.rtbm.2021.100693.
53. M. Patil and B. B. Majumdar, "Prioritizing key attributes influencing electric two-wheeler usage: A multi criteria decision making (MCDM) approach—A case study of Hyderabad, India," *Case Stud Transp Policy*, vol. 9, no. 2, pp. 913–929, Jun. 2021, https://doi.org/10.1016/j.cstp.2021.04.011.
54. A. Al Mamun, N. R. Zainol, and N. Hayat, "Electric scooter—intention and adoption of alternative mode of transportation for Malaysian youth," *Environ Dev Sustain*, 2024, https://doi.org/10.1007/s10668-024-05131-1.
55. T. S. Rahmawati, Yuniaristanto, W. Sutopo, and M. Hisjam, "Development of a Model of Intention to Adopt Electric Motorcycles in Indonesia," *Automotive Experiences*, vol. 5, no. 3, pp. 494–506, Apr. 2022, https://doi.org/10.31603/ae.7344.
56. E. Arı and V. Yılmaz, "Investigating the factors affecting electric scooter usage behavior with a proposed structural model," *Research in Transportation Business and Management*, vol. 56, Oct. 2024, https://doi.org/10.1016/j.rtbm.2024.101164.
57. M. Samadzad, H. Nosratzadeh, H. Karami, and A. Karami, "What are the factors affecting the adoption and use of electric scooter sharing systems from the end user's perspective?" *Transp Policy (Oxf)*, vol. 136, pp. 70–82, Jun. 2023, https://doi.org/10.1016/j.tranpol.2023.03.006.
58. J. H. M. Langbroek, J. P. Franklin, and Y. O. Susilo, "The effect of policy incentives on electric vehicle adoption," *Energy Policy*, vol. 94, pp. 94–103, Jul. 2016, https://doi.org/10.1016/j.enpol.2016.03.050.
59. S. U. Rehman, S. Bresciani, D. Yahiaoui, and T. Kliestik, "Customer satisfaction leading the intention to adopt battery electric vehicles with the moderating role of government support and status symbol," *J Clean Prod*, vol. 456, Jun. 2024, https://doi.org/10.1016/j.jclepro.2024.142371.
60. F. Wang, Z. Zhang, and S. Lin, "Purchase intention of Autonomous vehicles and industrial Policies: Evidence from a national survey in China," *Transp Res Part A Policy Pract*, vol. 173, Jul. 2023, https://doi.org/10.1016/j.tra.2023.103719.
61. V. Vishwakarma, "Corporate Social Responsibility (A Literature Review)," *Shanlax International Journal of Management*, vol. 7, no. 1, pp. 36–42, Jul. 2019, https://doi.org/10.34293/management. v7i1.554.
62. T. T. M. Truong, "Effectiveness of policy incentives on electric motorcycles acceptance in Hanoi, Vietnam," *Case Stud Transp Policy*, vol. 13, Sep. 2023, https://doi.org/10.1016/j.cstp.2023.101020.
63. X. Zhang and M. Chang, "Applying the Extended Technology Acceptance Model to Explore Taiwan's Generation Z's Behavioral Intentions toward Using Electric Motorcycles," *Sustainability (Switzerland)*, vol. 15, no. 4, Feb. 2023, https://doi.org/10.3390/su15043787.

Technology Innovation Paradox: The Causes and Solutions

Taeyeon Kim, Jinwoo Kim, and Yong Jin Kim

Abstract Technology innovation is one of the primary drivers of economic growth and wealth creation and a source of sustainable competitive advantage. Most innovations involve the recombination of existing knowledge. Previous studies on technology innovation have highlighted the importance of cross-industry technology transfer to drive innovation. However, there is lack of research on the situation where innovative technology developed in an industry, fails to significantly impact the industry while having a substantial influence when applied in another industry. This situation is defined in this study as the Technology Innovation Paradox. This study investigates the "Technology Innovation Paradox" by analyzing patent data to identify cases where technologies considered outdated and ineffective in one industry bring forth an extensive growth in other industries when transferred.

The root cause of this paradox lies in the tendency of established industries to focus on constrained technology for product differentiation or premium features rather than on marginal technology, while other industries identify and adopt the marginal technologies developed through such investments, integrating them into their products. Since these industries are utilizing already-developed innovations, they can achieve significant growth with relatively low investment. This study contributes to literature by conceptualizing the paradoxical situation for future research.

Keywords Technology Innovation Paradox · Technology Innovation transfer · Cross-Industry Innovation

T. Kim · Y. J. Kim (✉)
Sogang University, Seoul, Republic of Korea
e-mail: yongjkim@sogang.ac.kr

T. Kim
e-mail: taeyeon30@sogang.ac.kr

J. Kim
Frism Investment Adnisory Inc., Seoul, Republic of Korea
e-mail: jwkim@frism.io

E. Tsui et al. (eds.), *Management Information Systems in a Digitalized AI World*, Springer Proceedings in Business and Economics,
https://doi.org/10.1007/978-981-96-6526-6_4

1 Introduction

Technology innovation is one of the key factors driving social change, as new technologies are applied to products, fostering the development of new products, influencing corporate performance, and ultimately contributing to the growth and advancement of industries.

Companies may develop innovative products through the creation of new technologies, but they also bring forth industrial development by utilizing technologies developed in other industries to create new, groundbreaking products.

This type of innovation aligns with Schumpeter's concept of "creative destruction," and most innovations involve recombining existing knowledge [1]. By creatively imitating and applying existing solutions to meet current market needs or product demands [2], companies also influence industry growth.

Historically, many industries have seen successful examples of such technological spillover effects. For instance, BMW's iDrive system was derived from the gaming industry, and Nike's shock-absorption technology was adapted from Formula One racing [2]. Additionally, the disk brake technology from mountain bikes and single-wheel suspension structures from automotive design have been transferred to the baby product industry, leading to the development of high-quality strollers [3].

Meanwhile, some companies may succeed in developing innovative products with new technologies but fail to achieve sustained growth in their industry. These technologies may instead be utilized in other industries, where they lead to innovative products and substantial industry development.

In other words, companies make significant investments in technological innovation and product development, but their industry may decline, while companies in other industries that adopt these technologies achieve success with lesser degree of investment compared to the original industry, driving substantial industry growth. This paradoxical situation is defined in this study as the "Technology Innovation Paradox."

While prior research has highlighted the need for cross-industry technology transfer to drive innovation for corporate survival and growth, there is limited research on the causes and solutions for the paradoxical situation where innovative technologies developed within an industry have little impact on the originated industry but significant influence on others.

This study aims to identify cases where technologies considered obsolete in one industry were transferred to another, resulting in radical innovation. By analyzing patent data, this study will confirm the Technology Innovation Paradox, investigate its causes, and explore solutions to address it.

2 Theoretical Background

2.1 Technology Innovation Paradox

For a company to survive and grow, it must continually invest in technology development, which requires significant time and financial investment.

When a company successfully develops a product through technological advancement, this can also contribute to industry progress.

However, situations can arise where the industry fails to grow continuously and even declines, leaving both the company and the industry enjoying little benefit from its extensive time and financial investment.

In some cases, the technology developed in one industry is transferred to another, where it is used to develop products and in turn lead to explosive industry growth. The companies that receive the transferred technology succeed in product development with minimal investment to affect the company success and the industry growth.

The "Technology Innovation Paradox" describes this paradoxical situation, where industries that invest heavily in technology development see minimal benefit (input > output), while other industries reap substantial growth benefits with limited investment (input < output).

2.2 Marginal Technology Versus Constrained Technology

Technological A product is composed of various technologies integrated according to its functions. There are two types of technology in terms of adaptability to market conditions: marginal technology and constrained technology. Marginal technology is a type of technology that is actually influenced by even small changes in demand [4]. Therefore, it has a high potential for transition to new industries or uses, playing a crucial role in technology transfer. In other words, it is a technology that may no longer have a significant impact in its original industry but holds the potential to be newly applied in other industries.

Constrained technology, on the other hand, is technology that operates only under specific conditions or restrictions, making it difficult to respond immediately to demand fluctuations [4]. Due to its limited applicability, it is challenging for it to be utilized across various industries or effectively transferred to other industries.

3 Research Methodology

3.1 *Case Selection Criteria*

I have selected examples of outdated technologies to examine the Technology Innovation Paradox. These examples include the telegraph, vacuum tube, and bicycle, each developed in the 1800s. While initially successful in developing innovative products, these technologies are from industries that have not continued to grow or have declined.

3.2 *Research Methodology*

In this study, I analyzed the selected examples using market size data and patent data to verify the paradox where a technology was developed and applied to products, but the originating industry declined while the technology transferred to other industries and spurred their growth. By examining the types of technologies that were transferred and contributed to the development of other industries, I identified the causes behind this paradox.

For market size, it was challenging to obtain quantitative data for the selected examples, as these technologies were developed in the 1800s and belong to industries that subsequently declined, with no measurable statistics from that period. Therefore, I observed market size through changes in each example's market over time.

I collected and analyzed patent data using The Lens, focusing on the examples selected within the research scope. The data collection range covered patents from January 1, 1984, to December 31, 2023, and included patent filing volume, citation counts, IPC codes, and applicants. To track the ripple effect of each technology, I used backward citations, and to track technology transfer across industries, I limited applicants to corporations.

4 Results and Analysis

4.1 *Telegraph*

Market Size

The market size is difficult to quantify for outdated technologies, so the market size is assessed through analyzing the trends and shifts within the market.

The telegraph led to a communications revolution from the mid-nineteenth century to the early twentieth century, but its significance began to decline in the mid-twentieth century with the advent of new communication technologies such as the telephone and the inter-net.

In the early 1900s, during the initial emergence of the telegraph, telegraph technology became the primary means of communication. The telegraph industry developed across various sectors, including railroads, finance, and the press, and in the United States, the telegraph network expanded nationwide during this period.

From the 1920s, the development of telephone technology led to a decrease in the importance of the telegraph. The market size for the telegraph declined, especially during the Great Depression in the 1930s and World War II, as new communication means such as the telephone and radio emerged.

After the 1950s, as the adoption of telephones accelerated, the use of the telegraph continued to decrease. In the 1960s, the introduction of the fax machine further reduced the market share of the telegraph.

By the 1980s, with the rise of digital communication tools such as the internet and email, the telegraph was almost entirely phased out. Western Union ended its last telegraph service in 2006, and in 2013, India terminated its final telegraph service. With the onset of the digital age, the telegraph's primary role as a communication technology was effectively replaced.

Number of Telegraph Patents and Citations

The number of patents increased following the introduction of the telegraph but sharply declined from the mid-twentieth century onward. This trend mirrors the market pattern where, after initial growth from product applications, the industry declined as new technologies emerged to replace it.

Citation counts, however, surged starting in the 1970s. Given the sharp drop in patent numbers around that time, this increase in citations suggests that the technology had transferred to other industries and influenced the development of new technologies in those sectors (see Table 1 and Fig. 1).

The IPC count in the 2010s increased approximately 700-fold compared to the 1900s (see Table 2). This continuous growth since the development of the telegraph indicates that the technology has been utilized across various fields, rather than being limited to a specific sector.

Over time, the IPC count has shown an increasing trend, with a particularly dramatic rise beginning around 15 years ago (see Fig. 2). This trend suggests that, through technology transfer, the telegraph has continued to merge with products in other industries, contributing to their development and growth.

Examining the trend of inventions by applicant over time reveals that, while companies involved in invention were primarily in the telecommunications industry until the early twentieth century, this has now shifted to the lithium-ion battery industry (see Table 3).

The telegraph operates by receiving power from a battery and using that power to send and receive data. Its transfer to the lithium-ion battery industry can be attributed to power supply-related technologies within the telegraph, which are classified as

Table 1 Number of Telegraph patents and citations

Publication year	Patent	FWCitation
1900s	470	116
1910s	407	208
1920s	647	304
1930s	1,601	1,022
1940s	1,310	834
1950s	938	1,244
1960s	599	719
1970s	686	6,811
1980s	1,075	10,300
1990s	1,209	21,059
2020s	2,112	30,018
2010s	4,995	23,478
2020s	3,080	1,665
Total	19,129	97,778

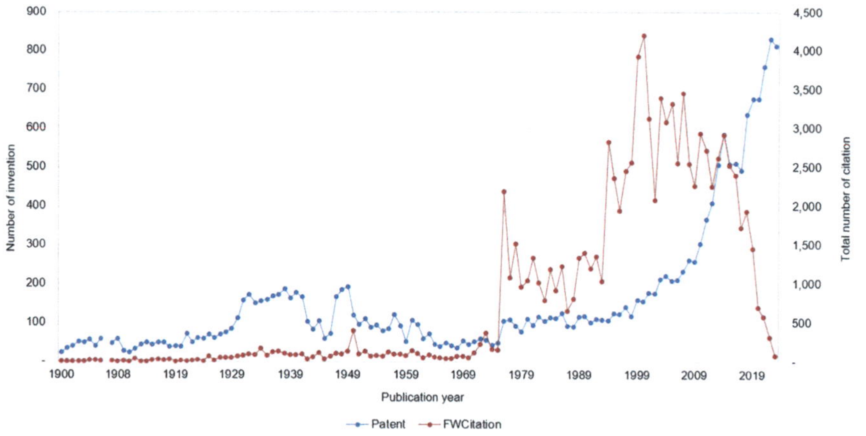

Fig. 1 The trend of patents and forward citations for telegraph

marginal technology. This type of technology, being sensitive to demand changes, is well-suited for adaptation and application in new industries, such as lithium-ion batteries.

Table 2 The number of IPC (International Patent Classification) codes for Telegraph

Publication year	IPC count
1900s	11
1910s	240
1920s	615
1930s	1,500
1940s	1,470
1950s	1,310
1960s	1,044
1970s	1,385
1980s	2,020
1990s	3,041
2020s	5,044
2010s	7,986
2020s	5,279
Total	30,945

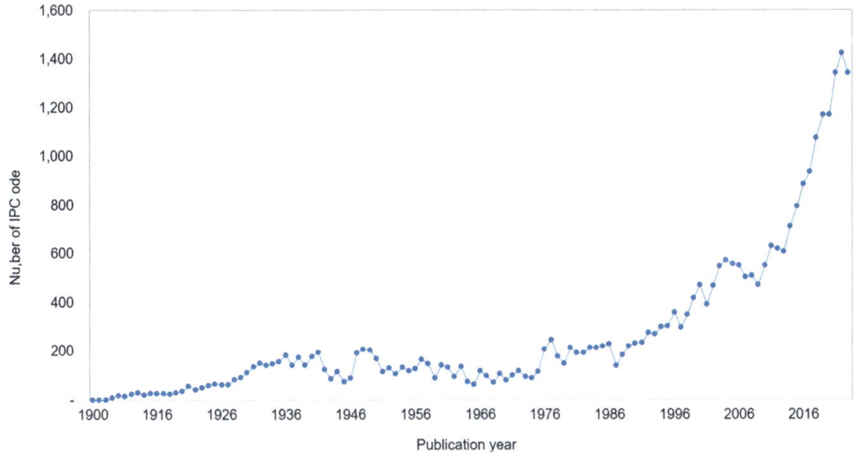

Fig. 2 Number of IPC codes for telegraph

4.2 *Vacuum Tube*

Market Size

In the 1900s, vacuum tubes were an essential component of radio technology and were widely used in radio broadcasting and communication systems. During the mid-twentieth century, vacuum tubes played a significant role in military communication and radar systems, especially during World War II. Following the war, as the

Table 3 Comparison of Telegraph Applicant Industries: Past and Present

Past		Present	
Industry	Corporate Name	Industry	Corporate Name
Telecommunication	Marconi Wireless Telegraph Co	Lithium-ion battery	Gillette Co
	Creed & Co Ltd		Mitsui Mining & Smelting Co
	General Electric Co Ltd		Hitachi Ltd
	Federal Telegraph Co		Samsung SDI Co Ltd
	Charles Samuel Franklin		Toshiba Battery
	Western Union Telegraph Co		IBM
	Standard Telephones & Cables Ltd		Samsung Electronics Co Ltd

consumer electronics market rapidly expanded, vacuum tubes reached peak usage in televisions, radios, and audio amplifiers. However, after the invention of the transistor and semiconductors in 1947, vacuum tubes were gradually replaced in most consumer electronics throughout the 1970s and 1980s, leading to a decline in the vacuum tube market. While vacuum tubes have largely disappeared from commercial and consumer electronics, a niche market persists, as vacuum tube amplifiers remain popular among audiophiles who prefer high-quality sound.

Number of Telegraph Patents and Citations

The number of patents for vacuum tubes rose significantly following their introduction, peaking by the mid-twentieth century but showing a decline from the 1960s onward. This period, particularly from the 1920s to the 1940s, aligns with the peak activity in the vacuum tube market (see Table 4 and Fig. 3).

Citation counts, however, increased notably from the 1970s, which coincides with the period when vacuum tubes were largely replaced in consumer electronics. The rise in citations from 1970 onward suggests that vacuum tube technology was repurposed and utilized in other industries, facilitating growth in those areas.

The number of technologies mirrors market changes. With the emergence of vacuum tube technology, the number of related technologies increased, but from the 1950s to the 1980s, as transistors began to replace vacuum tubes, this number sharply declined.

However, starting in the 1990s, the IPC count began to rise again. Considering the low patent activity at that time, this increase suggests that vacuum tube technology had been transferred to and utilized in various fields, leading to the development of new technologies across different sectors (see Table 5 and Fig. 4).

Vacuum tubes operate by applying heat to enable the flow of electrons in a vacuum, thereby amplifying electronic signals and transmitting them.

Table 4 Number of Vacuum tube patents and citations

Publication year	Patent	FWCitation
1900s	144	22
1910s	138	22
1920s	2,049	1078
1930s	2,212	1842
1940s	1,290	1494
1950s	1,134	1083
1960s	578	425
1970s	261	1759
1980s	298	2600
1990s	499	6273
2020s	767	8047
2010s	2,226	6114
2020s	777	404
Total	12,373	31,163

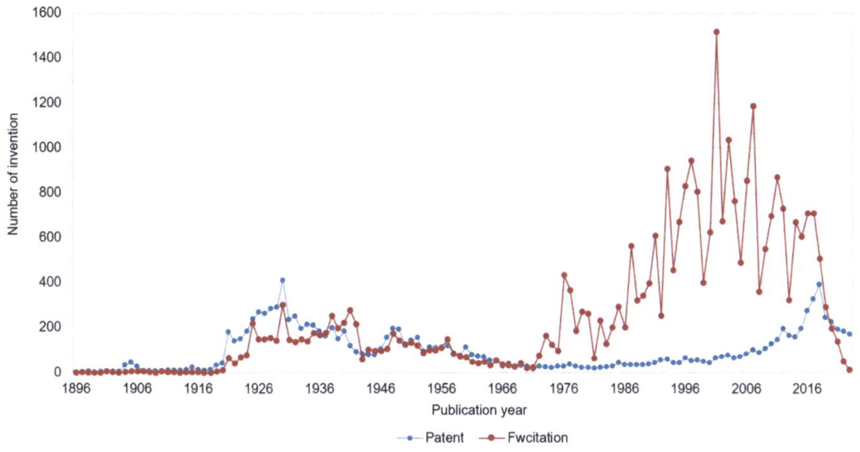

Fig. 3 The trend of patents and forward citations for Vacuum tube

Initially, the primary market for vacuum tubes was the telecommunications equipment industry, which dominated until the late twentieth century. However, this technology has since transferred to medical devices and high-quality audio industries (see Table 6).

The active invention in the medical and high-quality audio sectors today indicates that the amplification function within vacuum tube technology is a marginal technology, rediscovered for its value and re-applied in new contexts.

Table 5 The number of IPC (International Patent Classification) codes for Vacuum tube

Publication year	IPC count
1900s	0
1910s	150
1920s	1,440
1930s	1,653
1940s	1,230
1950s	1,138
1960s	780
1970s	554
1980s	740
1990s	1,224
2020s	1,565
2010s	3,497
2020s	1,854
Total	15,825

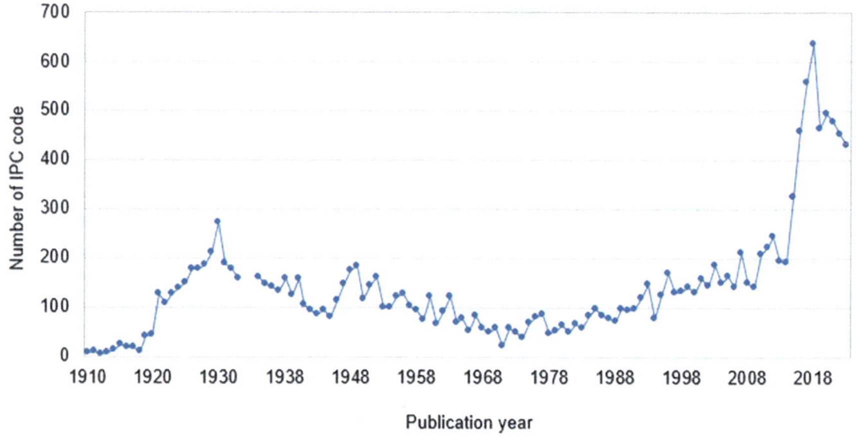

Fig. 4 Number of IPC codes for vacuum tube

4.3 Bicycle

Market Size

The bicycle was one of the main modes of transportation from the late nineteenth century to the early twentieth century. Its market expanded significantly, particularly in Europe and North America, where bicycles gained widespread popularity. However, from the mid-twentieth century, the demand for bicycles as a primary means of transportation declined as automobiles became more widely available. Since the

Table 6 Comparison of Vacuum Tube Applicant Industries: Past and Present

Past		Present	
Industry	Corporate Name	Industry	Corporate Name
Communication equipment	Standard Telephones & Cables Ltd	Medical devices	Buffalo Filter LLC
	British Thomson-Houston Co Ltd		Toshiba Corp
	Marconi Co Canada		Shimadzu Corp
	Telefunken GmbH		Hitachi Ltd
	Western Electric Co		Shimadzu Corp
	Bell Telephone Labor Inc	High-quality audio	Western Electric Co
	Ericsson Telefon AB L M		Philips Electrical Ind Ltd
	Plessey Co Ltd		Matsushita Electric Ind Co Ltd
	Raytheon Mfg Co		Loewe Opta GmbH

1960s, as interest in health and recreational activities grew, bicycles began to attract attention for leisure and sports purposes. In 2023, the global bicycle market size was estimated at approximately 11.137 billion USD [5].

Number of Telegraph Patents and Citations

Examining the trend of bicycle patent and citation counts (see Table 7 and Fig. 5), both metrics show an increase starting in the 1970s, with citations rising significantly during this period.

This trend aligns with shifts in the bicycle market around the same time, indicating that other industries began utilizing bicycle technology from the 1970s onward.

The IPC count for bicycles also shows a significant increase starting in the 1970s. This aligns with the period when citation counts surged, suggesting that bicycle technology had transferred to other industries, driving the rise in IPC count. This trend indicates that bicycle technology has continued to support growth and expansion in various industries over time (see Table 8 and Fig. 6).

A bicycle operates by transferring the rider's pedal force through a chain to drive the wheels and enable movement.

Initially, the primary market for bicycles consisted of bicycle and component manufacturers, but today, gear and transmission companies dominate (see Table 9).

Examining recent active inventions in related industries suggests that gear and transmission technology, which facilitates smoother riding, functions as a marginal technology. This technology has found renewed value, playing a pivotal role in enhancing ease of use and driving innovation in related fields.

Table 7 Number of Bicycle patents and citations

Publication year	Patent	FWCitation
1900s	5,069	4,640
1910s	508	1,105
1920s	524	1,419
1930s	510	1,576
1940s	775	2,513
1950s	1,094	3,686
1960s	664	3,729
1970s	2,654	32,712
1980s	7,358	62,309
1990s	20,179	156,214
2020s	30,382	184,339
2010s	69,294	192,228
2020s	31,661	15,096
Total	170,672	661,566

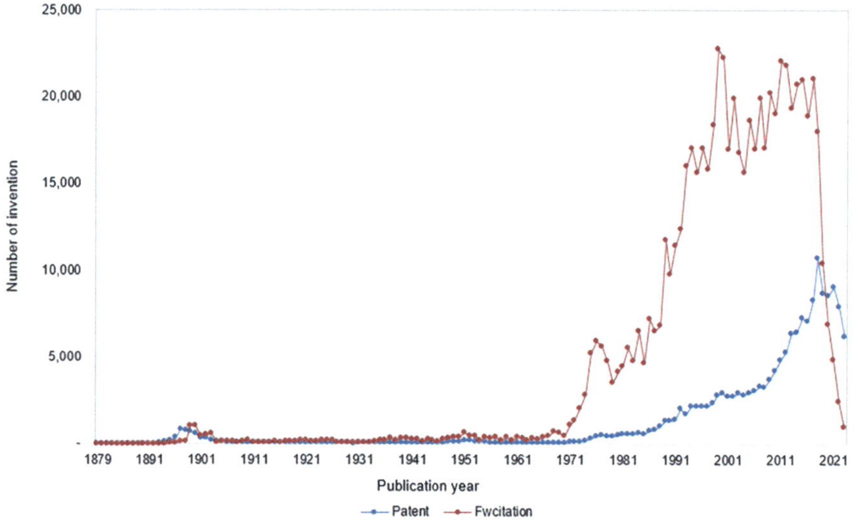

Fig. 5 The trend of patents and forward citations for Bicycle

5 Conclusion and Implication

We identified a paradoxical situation where a particular technology initially was developed with much investment to contribute to the growth of an industry but transferred to another industry to help expedite its growth dramatically even with lesser degree of investment.

Table 8 The number of IPC (International Patent Classification) codes for Bicycle

Publication year	IPC count
1900s	44
1910s	234
1920s	413
1930s	404
1940s	405
1950s	587
1960s	541
1970s	2,349
1980s	5,357
1990s	9,679
2020s	14,498
2010s	27,362
2020s	12,504
Total	74,377

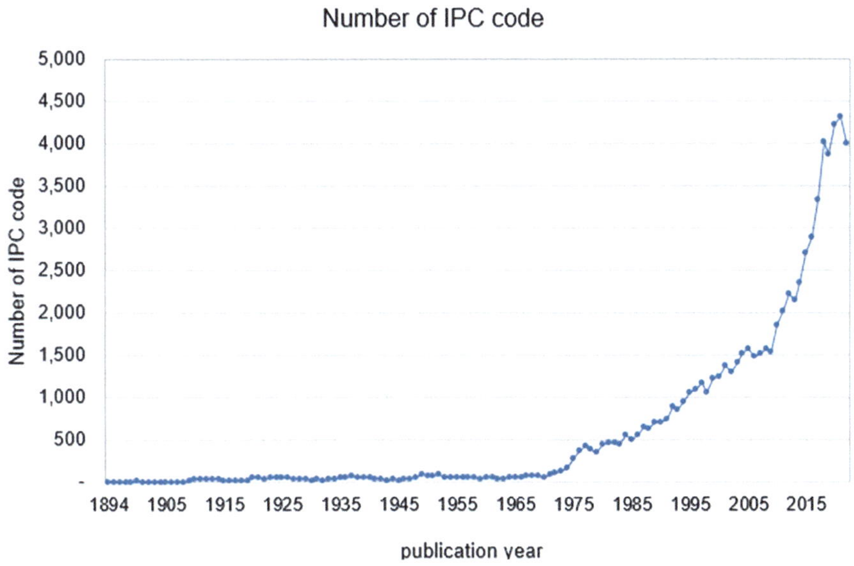

Fig. 6 Number of IPC codes for bicycle

In most cases, the industry where technological innovation occurred invested heavily in the technologies used in its products, but it eventually declined. Conversely, another industry, using these already invented and invested technologies, developed new products and achieved substantial output with minimal input, confirming the technology innovation paradox.

Table 9 Comparison of Bicycle Applicant Industries: Past and Present

Past		Present	
Industry	Corporate Name	Industry	Corporate Name
Bicycle manufacturing and components	Schwinn Bicycle Co	Gears and shifting	Shimano KK
	Beistegui Hermanos SA		Campagnolo SpA
	Raleigh Industries Ltd		Shimano Industrial Co
	Fichtel & Sachs AG		SRAM DE GmbH
	Maeda Ind		SRAM LLC
	Miyata Ind		Fichtel & Sachs AG
	Union Sils van de Loo & Co		Magenwirth GmbH & Co KG Gustav
	Akebono Brake Ind		DT Swiss Inc
	Yoshigai Kikai Kinzoku Co Ltd		Chosen Co Ltd
	Suzuki Motor Co		VP Components Co Ltd

The root cause of this paradox lies in the tendency of established industries to focus on constrained technology for product differentiation or premium features rather than on marginal technology. As companies in mature industries invest heavily in constrained technology, which has limited flexibility, this results in high input costs without proportionate industry growth, ultimately leading to decline with substantial sunk costs.

Meanwhile, other industries identify and adopt the marginal technologies developed through such investments, integrating them into their products. Since these industries are utilizing already-developed innovations, they can achieve significant growth with relatively low investment.

As this study confirms, marginal technology, due to its flexibility, allows other industries to achieve explosive growth with minimal effort when they adopt it. Therefore, companies are desired to prioritize investing in marginal rather than constrained technology to ensure sustainable growth and development.

This study establishes the concept of the technology innovation paradox and examines its causes and solutions.

The research is based on a limited set of cases and explores historical and current industrial shifts. Future research could benefit from examining a broader range of cases over time to deepen understanding of technology transfer across industries and foster further insights into this phenomenon.

References

1. Schumpeter, J.A.: Business Cycles: A Theoretical, Historical and Statistical Analysis of the Capitalist Process. New York: McGraw-Hill (1939).
2. Ellen Enkel and Oliver Gassmann.: Creative imitation: exploring the case of cross-industry innovation. R & D Management Vol 40, No 3, pp.256–270 (2010).
3. Kalogerakis, K., Lu, C., Herstatt, C.: Developing innovations based on analogies: experience from design and engineering consultants. Journal of Product Innovation Management 27 (3), 418–436 (2010).
4. Bo. P. Weidema, Niels Frees, Anne-Merete Nielsen,: Marginal production Technologies for Life Cycle Inventories. International Journal of Life Cycle Assessment 4(1), pp 48–56, (1999).
5. Bicycle Market Size, Share & Industry Analysis, By Technology (Electric and Conventional), By Type (Mountain, Road, Hybrid, Cargo, and Others), By End User (Men, Women, and Kids), By Design (Folding and Regular), By Distribution Channel (Offline and Online), and Regional Forecast, 2024–2032, Last Updated: October 28, 2024.

Management Informatization and Risk Management

Integrated Production Site and Network Planning

Tanya Jahangirkhani and Matthias Schmidt

Abstract Globalization and the rise of uncertainty have significantly impacted the competitiveness of producing companies. These changes have shifted the paradigm from localized production to globally dispersed supply chains, with many European manufacturers now sourcing components internationally. Small and medium-sized enterprises and global manufacturing companies face unique challenges due to globalization and increasing planning uncertainties. A crucial long-term task for companies is searching for and planning manufacturing plant sites. This involves identifying potential sites, evaluating them based on various factors, and selecting the optimal site. Internal and external factors drive this process, and companies often lack the expertise to manage and evaluate the necessary data systematically. Additionally, companies view themselves as global production networks, making planning and optimizing these networks complex. Integrating geoinformation and information management systems can aid in informed decision-making, though it presents challenges. This article explores the current state of integrated production and network planning and proposes a methodological approach for its development.

Keywords Production network · Site planning · Information management model · Geoinformation system · Integrative approach

1 Introduction

In the ages of globalization, different drivers for change challenge producing companies in their competitiveness [1]. A significant change is the globalization of sourcing, manufacturing and selling products. Whereas at the beginning of industrialization, production according to a local-for-local business was the standard, nowadays this

T. Jahangirkhani (✉) · M. Schmidt
Institute of Production Systems and Logistics, Leibniz Universität Hannover, Garbsen, Germany
e-mail: jahangirkhani@ifa.uni-hannover.de

M. Schmidt
e-mail: schmidt@ifa.uni-hannover.de

E. Tsui et al. (eds.), *Management Information Systems in a Digitalized AI World*,
Springer Proceedings in Business and Economics,
https://doi.org/10.1007/978-981-96-6526-6_5

is overhauled [2]. For example, 60% of all German producing companies have at least one piece of their supply chain in another country [3]. Next to globalization, another big change driver is the rising volatility, uncertainty, complexity and ambiguity (VUCA) [4] of the environment in which businesses operate. This means that it is far more likely that future events are not foreseeable, which makes strategic and mid- to long-term decisions complex.

Small and medium-sized companies (SMEs) and global manufacturing companies advancing globalization and increasing planning uncertainty due to the VUCA world can pose a challenge.

A long-term, strategic task for companies is the site search and planning for their manufacturing plants. The main tasks are the target-oriented search for possible alternative sites, their assessment based on the respective location conditions about the relevant site factors, and the selection of the best possible site [1]. This process can be triggered by various internal (weakness of being able to fulfill strategic goals) and external factors (technologies, market, environment, economics and legal) [1]. In the context of site selection, many production, market and performance factors [1] influence the optimal site choice. Companies often lack the expertise to procure and evaluate site factors systematically. Information management and geoinformation systems often contain all the information required to make a well-founded and transparent decision. However, using and instrumentalizing this information often presents companies with challenges.

Companies increasingly see themselves as global production networks (GPN) [2]. Planning, coordinating and continuously optimizing a production network is another strategic long-term task. Developing a new site in the production network automatically impacts the GPN. The interactions involved make site selection a complex task. Figure 1 shows the problem visually.

In practice, site selection is often based on a subjective decision that can be influenced by personal experience or the media [1]. It is, therefore, a subjective snapshot that cannot be reproduced.

Due to these reasons, a stand-alone site-planning approach is not enough. Ideally, integrated site and network planning should be carried out to account for possible independence between site and network planning. This article examines the state of the art of such an approach and presents a work plan for developing an integrated approach with methodological support.

2 Method

According to Tranfield et al. [5], a systematic literature review is conducted to gain insights into the current state of the art. A systematic literature review is a structured method of synthesizing research findings by comprehensively searching, selecting, and analyzing relevant studies based on predetermined criteria. This approach ensures a thorough, unbiased, and reproducible assessment of existing literature to address the topic of integrated site and network planning. According to TRANFIELD

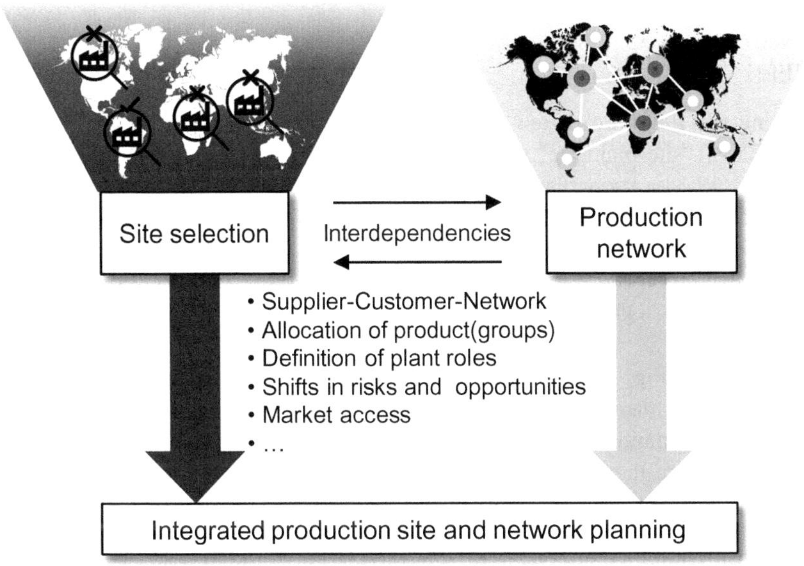

Fig. 1 Problem statement

ET AL., the systematic literature review method is a meticulous and structured approach to ensuring transparency, replicability, and comprehensiveness [5]. First, a review protocol outlines the objective and scope to ensure clarity and consistency. Next, studies are identified and chosen through thorough searches across multiple databases, using specific keywords and exclusion criteria. The selected studies then undergo systematic data extraction, focusing on key variables and findings. The findings are analyzed and reported in a structured format, highlighting key themes, gaps, and implications for future research and practice [5]. This method ensures transparency, replicability, and thoroughness.

3 Literature Review

A systematic literature review is necessary to gain insight into the current state of the art and understand existing approaches in integrated production site and network planning research. The review adopts the successful approach of TRANFIELD ET AL. [5]. For this reason, the following research question was defined: 'What existing approaches exist for integrative site and network planning in the industrial context?'.

To ensure a broad range of hits, the following academic databases were utilized to perform the systematic literature review:

- 'Scopus'
- 'Web of Science'
- 'IEEE Xplore'

During the literature review the following search string was applied: TITLE-ABS-KEY '((“site planning” OR “site search” OR “site selection” OR “location planning” OR “location search” OR “location selection”) AND (“network planning” OR “network optimization” OR “network configuration” OR “network alignment” OR “network strategy” OR “network footprint” OR “production footprint” OR “industrial footprint”) AND (“approach” OR “method” OR “solution” OR “concept” OR “model” OR “application”) AND (“production” OR “manufacturing” OR “industrial”))'.

As shown in Fig. 2, the search resulted in 23 hits on Scopus, 14 hits on Web of Science and 5 hits on IEEE Explore. After identifying and removing 9 duplicate publications, 33 unique publications remained for further review. These remaining publications were then filtered and excluded based on several exclusion criteria, which were as follows:

- No consideration of site planning
- No consideration of network planning
- No application in an industrial context

After completing this step, 13 articles were selected for full-text screening. However, four of the remaining articles did not contain context-relevant information in the full text, so they were excluded. Nine publications were added through a backward integration, bringing the total to 18.

Throughout the detailed review of the publications, five requirements were identified for an integrated approach to site and network planning:

- R1: Objectivity
- R2: Interactions
- R3: Long-term risks & opportunities
- R4: Data from IMS and GIS
- R5: Practice-oriented

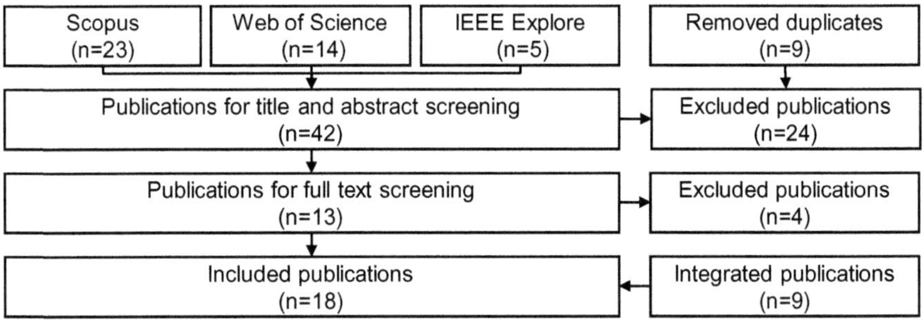

Fig. 2 Flowchart of the systematic literature search according to [5]

On the one hand, an approach should ensure that the results are as objective as possible. This ensures that it is also possible to retrace the decision later in time and to identify which decision-triggering variable may have changed. Therefore, reproducibility is guaranteed. Overall, objectivity in decision models enhances their utility, credibility, and effectiveness, making it a cornerstone of robust decision-making practices [6].

Furthermore, the approach should consider interactions based on a site decision on the production network and vice versa. Decisions on the allocation of products (groups), for example, not only influence the choice of site but also impact a company's overall production network structure. The same applies to positioning in the holistic supply chain, including suppliers and customers. The interaction between the site search process and the production network configuration is dynamic and interdependent. Decisions made in one area directly impact the other, requiring a holistic approach to ensure that the new site and the overall network are optimized for performance, cost-efficiency, and strategic alignment [7].

In addition to the interactions, the approach is intended to identify long-term opportunities and risks for individual site options and grid configurations and integrate them into the decision-making support. Anticipating future regulatory changes or long-term talent acquisition and retention planning is essential for overall business success. Incorporating long-term risks and opportunities into the site search process and production network configuration is essential for creating a resilient, sustainable, and competitive business [1]. This strategic approach ensures that companies are well-prepared to navigate future challenges and capitalize on emerging opportunities, securing their position in the market over the long term.

Information Management Systems (IMS) and Geoinformation Systems (GIS) enhance the site search process and production network configuration by providing comprehensive, actionable insights. IMS integrates and analyzes data for scenario planning, compliance, and historical performance [8]. GIS offers spatial analysis, risk assessment, and logistics optimization [9]. These systems enable enhanced decision-making, real-time monitoring, and strategic planning. They help identify optimal sites by evaluating cost, logistics, market access, and environmental risks, ensuring informed, data-driven decisions that optimize operations, reduce risks, and improve competitiveness.

A practice-oriented process model for integrated site search and production network planning is crucial for usability and adoption, ensuring it aligns with real-world conditions and daily operations. This relevance enhances efficiency, effectiveness, and risk mitigation while facilitating more accessible training, implementation, and customization. Such models support continuous improvement through user feedback and secure stakeholder buy-in, leading to better decision-making and operational success [1]. In essence, a practical approach ensures the model is user-friendly, actionable, and adaptable, ultimately improving the overall effectiveness and resilience of the production network.

Table 1 presents an overview of the 18 identified publications assessed according to the derived requirements.

Table 1 Literature Review

		Rating				
		R1	R2	R3	R4	R5
		Objectivity	Interdependencies	Long-term risks and opportunities	Data from IMS and GIS	Practice-oriented
L1	**LIN A. CHEN** (2006) [10]	●	◑	○	◑	●
L2	**MEYER** (2006) [11]	◑	○	◑	◑	◑
L3	**ACKERMANN A. MÜLLER** (2007) [12]	○	○	○	◑	●
L4	**WALTHER ET AL.** (2011) [13]	◑	○	●	◑	●
L5	**LANZA ET AL.** (2012) [14]	●	○	○	○	●
L6	**HÄNTSCH A. HUCHZERMEIER** (2016) [15]	◑	○	●	●	◑
L7	**MOSER ET AL.** (2016) [16]	●	◑	●	○	◑
L8	**CLAUSEN ET AL.** (2017) [17]	◑	◑	○	◑	◑
L9	**MOSER ET AL.** (2017) [18]	●	◑	●	○	●
L10	**LANZA ET AL.** (2019) [19]	◑	○	●	◑	●
L11	**SCHUH ET AL.** (2019) [20]	◑	○	●	◑	●
L12	**TIMPERIO ET AL.** (2019) [21]	◑	○	○	◑	●
L13	**WENZEL ET AL.** (2019) [22]	◑	◑	◑	○	●
L14	**CONSTANTINESCU ET AL.** (2021) [23]	◑	○	◑	●	●
L15	**HOOK ET AL.** (2023) [24]	◑	○	○	●	◑
L16	**SCHMIDT ET AL.** (2023) [25]	●	○	◑	○	◑

(continued)

Table 1 (continued)

		Rating				
		R1	R2	R3	R4	R5
		Objectivity	Interdependencies	Long-term risks and opportunities	Data from IMS and GIS	Practice-oriented
L17	STEIER ET AL. (2023) [26]	◑	○	◑	◑	◑
L18	STEIER ET AL. (2024) [27]	◑	◑	○	◑	●

● = Requirement fulfilled
◑ = Requirement partially fulfilled
○ = Requirement very low / not fulfilled

LIN AND CHEN (2006) propose a monolithic model for multi-stage and multi-site production planning. The model combines monthly and daily time scales and addresses practical constraints like capacity and inventory. Optimization yields production and procurement insights. The model is illustrated with a practical example from a TFT-LCD manufacturer in Taiwan [10]. The approach does not consider the long-term risks and opportunities regarding the decision options.

MEYER (2006) presents a systematic site selection procedure. The procedure model works as a funnel, starting with a global preselection and ending with the local choice, where the possible site choices shrink with each step [11]. The approach does not consider independencies between the network and site factors.

ACKERMANN AND MÜLLER (2007) present a Competence Cell (CC) concept. It offers a scientific approach, aiding small and medium-sized enterprises to adapt to economic changes. CC-based networks impact logistics structures, suggesting the need for suitable modeling and planning. Various logistics scenarios can be generated using basic structure types like point, line, and net alongside a three-layer model. It limits its analysis of logistic structures in the context of production networks [12]. The approach does not consider the independencies between the network and site factors or the long-term risks and opportunities regarding a decision option. The objectivity of the results is also compromised due to the broad spectrum of built scenarios.

WALTHER ET AL. (2011) conducted a case study on integrated planning for synthetic biodiesel production. The study assessed centralized and decentralized plant concepts while taking into account future uncertainties through scenario analysis. By addressing various risk attitudes and uncertainties, the study provides a valuable approach to planning [13]. However, it does not consider budget constraints, sustainability, global scale analysis, and disaster-related uncertainties, which would require specific solution procedures. Additionally, the approach does not consider independencies between the network and site factors.

LANZA ET AL. (2012) present an approach for strategically planning global changeable production networks based on future scenarios and multi-objective optimization to identify the most favorable network configuration. It aims to configure a production network that can be changed into network alternatives to control dynamics and positively utilize globalization [14]. The presented approach fails to consider the interdependencies between network and site factors and the long-term risks and opportunities linked to a decision option. Furthermore, it does not utilize geoinformation or information management systems data.

HÄNTSCH A. HUCHZERMEIER (2016) developed a multi-objective optimization model that addresses both qualitative and quantitative risks in strategic production and site planning. The model incorporates demand, exchange rate, and transport cost fluctuations and enhances site risk assessment using an ε-constraint approach, balancing profit and security. Validated through an automotive case study, the model demonstrates that considering qualitative risks can reduce profit by prioritizing secure, costly sites [15]. The model fails to consider the independence between the network and site factors.

MOSER ET AL. (2016) present a method for risk-efficient migration strategies for global production networks. They combine a stochastic, dynamic optimization model with a portfolio theory approach. The method considers both financial and time expenses for adapting the network configuration. It aims to recommend strategies for proactive adaptations of the network configuration, considering the decision maker's risk aversion [16]. The approach does not utilize data from geoinformation systems or information management systems.

CLAUSEN ET AL. (2017) propose decentralized production networks using innovative modular concepts instead of central ones. They develop a method for arranging mobile production units and allocating customers that is adaptable to market changes [17]. The approach does not consider dynamic effects and network structure details over time. Additionally, the approach does not consider the independencies between the network and site factors or the long-term risks and opportunities regarding a decision option.

MOSER ET AL. (2017) developed a method to monetarize the time expenses during planning, implementation, and ramp-up activities for migrating the network configuration. Based on the principles of modern portfolio theory, bundles of enablers and accelerators are built in the last step to minimize the risk of misinvestments and establish an efficient and tailor-made implementation plan based on the decision maker's risk preferences [18]. The approach does not incorporate data from geoinformation systems or information management systems.

LANZA ET AL. (2019) introduce a framework for designing and operating global production networks, which structures influencing factors, challenges, and enablers and outlines the need for decision support systems [19]. The framework fulfills most of the defined requirements. However, it does not consider the interactions between network and site planning. Linked to this, no data from GIS is included either. The approach does not consider the interdependencies between network and site factors.

SCHUH ET AL. (2019) propose an approach to systematically consider uncertainty, distinguishing between internal and external factors, applied to automotive supplier site selection. By prioritizing relevant factors and employing sensitivity analysis, informed decisions can be made swiftly [20]. However, the approach does not consider the interdependencies between network and site factors.

TIMPERIO ET AL. (2019) obtained a study that proposes a decision support framework integrating Multiple-criteria decision analysis, network optimization, and simulation for distribution network design and transport optimization. The framework was applied to PT Pos Indonesia, resulting in significant cost savings and CO_2 emission reductions without compromising service levels [21]. The framework does not consider the independencies between the network and site factors or the long-term risks and opportunities regarding a decision option.

WENZEL ET AL. (2019) focus on modeling and optimizing production plant operations interconnected through distribution networks, illustrated with a case study from INEOS in Köln, Germany. The problem was formulated as a mixed-integer linear problem to generate monthly plans considering technical constraints, production targets, and transportation schedules. The optimization considered energy prices, ambient temperature effects, and inventory management, showing significant potential for energy savings. The study proposed improvements for better coordination in process industry production through optimal site planning [22]. However, the approach did not incorporate data from geoinformation systems or information management systems.

CONSTANTINESCU ET AL. (2021) present a reference model that innovates through two continuously integrated Core and Factory Affective Loops. These loops enable human-driven system self-configuration based on required embodied intelligence at two levels: the first loop at the workplace (human-machine) level and the second at all factory scales, from micro to production network [23]. The approach does not consider the independence between the network and site factors.

HOOK ET AL. (2023) present the necessary fundamentals for factory site planning with GIS and explain which factory planning information can support site planning using GIS [24]. The approach does not consider the independencies between the network and site factors. It also does not consider the long-term risks and opportunities regarding the decision options.

SCHMIDT ET AL. (2023) introduce an algorithmic approach to optimize distributed additive manufacturing networks. The approach takes into account costs, pollution, and resilience. They used a two-level uncapacitated facility site problem solved by k-means clustering to identify the optimal number of factories, suppliers, and customers. The method evaluates factory distributions based on site-dependent pollution, costs, and resilience. The study found that focusing on pollution and resilience leads to highly distributed networks, while cost optimization favors centralization [25]. However, the study did not include delivery times, site-dependent costs, or a capacitated approach. It also did not consider the interdependencies between the network and site factors and did not utilize data from geoinformation systems or information management systems.

STEIER ET AL. (2023) propose a model deriving an optimal network configuration aligned with production strategy and strategic capabilities, comprising six steps including as-is analysis and target derivation using fuzzy inference and evaluation models [26]. However, the approach does not consider independencies between the network and site factors.

STEIER ET AL. (2024) present a fuzzy inference-based approach for the holistic evaluation of production networks. Two practical case studies could test the approach and yield results and implications [27]. However, the approach does not consider the long-term risks and opportunities of a decision option.

The systematic literature review of the state-of-the-art shows that several research approaches already exist for integrated site and network planning. However, no approach exists to date that fully meets the identified requirements R1–R5 and is therefore considered sufficient.

4 Result

The methodological approach was used to develop a conceptual work plan. This can be seen in Fig. 3.

The first step is to create a description model. For this purpose, a holistic site factor catalog and a network factor catalog are to be determined through structured literature research. Subsequently, the factors relevant to site and network planning will be identified. For this purpose, the two catalogs can be checked for duplications to create a third list with the factors relevant to both plans. Finally, the identified factors from the three catalogs should be categorized based on previously defined criteria.

The second step aims to develop an impact model between the site and network factors. For this purpose, asymmetric design structure matrices (DSM) are used to identify and evaluate the mutual interactions between the factors (e.g., reinforcing,

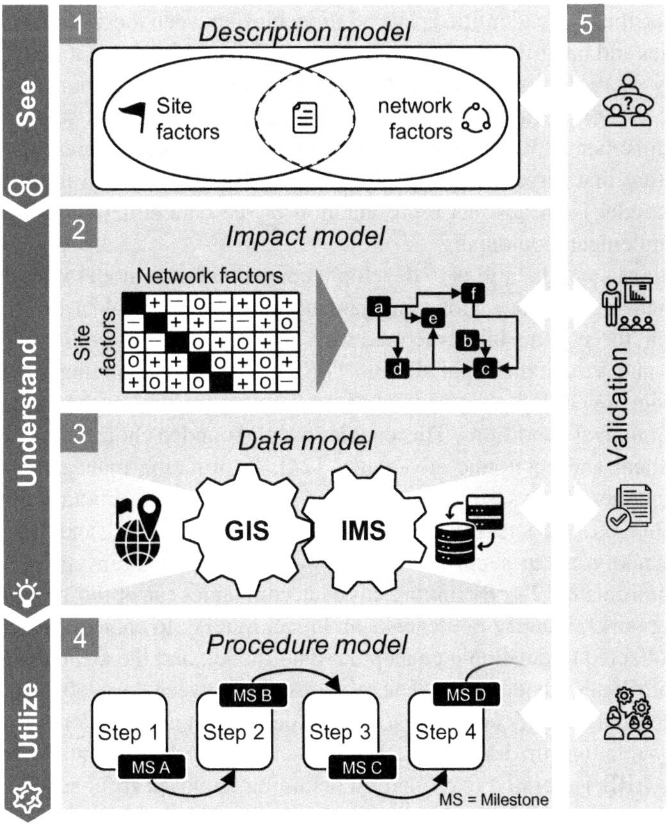

Fig. 3 Conceptual work plan to develop an integrated production site and network planning approach

weakening, neutral) [28]. This makes it possible to identify the intensity of influence per factor. The fundamental understanding of the interactions forms the basis for an integrated planning approach.

In the third step, the aim is to develop a conceptual data model with the help of geoinformation and information management systems that enable users to use information from the systems in a structured way. GIS offers the possibility of recording, analyzing and visualizing spatial data. GIS supports site planning by evaluating potential sites regarding geographical features, infrastructure, resource availability, and environmental conditions. This enables a well-founded choice of site that offers both logistical and economic advantages [24]. Information management systems complement these analyses by managing and integrating large amounts of data from different sources. IMS supports network planning by centralizing and making accessible information about supply chains, production capacities, inventory levels and market requirements [29]. By linking this data, companies can optimize the efficiency of their networks, identify bottlenecks and react quickly to changes. Requirements are first collected to develop a conceptual data model, and the critical data objects and their attributes are identified. The relationships between these objects, including cardinalities and integrity conditions, are then defined. This information is visualized in an entity-relationship diagram (ERD) representing entities, attributes and relationships. The ERD is iteratively refined by obtaining feedback from stakeholders and making adjustments [30]. The aim is to create a clear, abstract representation of the data structure that serves as the basis for the subsequent physical implementation. The data model is an abstract representation of the data structure independent of specific implementation details.

In the third step, the aim is to develop a conceptual data model with the help of geoinformation and information management systems that enable users to use information from the systems in a structured way. GIS offers the possibility of recording, analyzing and visualizing spatial data. GIS supports site planning by evaluating potential sites regarding geographical features, infrastructure, resource availability, and environmental conditions. This enables a well-founded choice of site that offers both logistical and economic advantages [24]. Information management systems complement these analyses by managing and integrating large amounts of data from different sources. IMS supports network planning by centralizing and making accessible information about supply chains, production capacities, inventory levels and market requirements [29]. By linking this data, companies can optimize the efficiency of their networks, identify bottlenecks and react quickly to changes. Requirements are first collected to develop a conceptual data model, and the critical data objects and their attributes are identified. The relationships between these objects, including cardinalities and integrity conditions, are then defined. This information is visualized in an entity-relationship diagram (ERD) representing entities, attributes and relationships. The ERD is iteratively refined by obtaining feedback from stakeholders and making adjustments [30]. The aim is to create a clear, abstract representation of the data structure that serves as the basis for the subsequent physical implementation. The data model is an abstract representation of the data structure independent of specific implementation details.

The fourth step aims to transfer the results and findings from the description, impact and data model into a holistic procedure model. As part of this, the description of the coordinated process for integrative site and network planning is presented. To this end, input and output variables required for each process step to complete the activities and results are defined as milestones. Milestones are essential events or stages in a planning project that track progress. They mark important points in the schedule and help monitor the course of the project, celebrate successes, and identify and address problems at an early stage. An exemplary milestone could be finalizing the decision for a global pre-selection of countries, products and production steps.

The fifth step runs parallel to steps 1–4 and aims to validate all partial results. The iterative validation of the description, active, data and process models is crucial to ensure they fulfill the previously defined requirements R1–R5. The description model must be checked for completeness. This can be done, for example, through workshops with technical experts or a survey with potential users. The defined impact relationships and directions must be checked in the impact model. This can be checked using a dynamic simulation model, for example, by testing the model's behavior under various conditions. The data model must then be checked for accuracy and consistency. This includes checking the structure to ensure that the fundamental relationships between entities are correctly represented. This includes checking the entities, attributes and relationships for completeness, correctness and consistency with the system's requirements. In addition, technical experts can check the model for consistency and clarification of relationships. Using scenarios and case studies can also help uncover potential vulnerabilities. Further validation can be performed by creating test data and simulating database queries to ensure that the ERD supports the desired queries and maintains data integrity. Validation of a process model involves reviewing its structure and processes to ensure that it effectively supports the project objectives. This can be achieved through expert interviews and stakeholder workshops to check the model for completeness, consistency and appropriateness. Checking compliance with industry standards and best practices can also help assess the process model's quality. Ultimately, continuous validation and adaptation of the planning approach during the development is crucial to ensure it meets the requirements.

5 Conclusion

Globalization presents various challenges for manufacturing companies, impacting their competitiveness. Notably, the ongoing globalization affects sourcing, manufacturing, and selling practices, contrasting with the localized approach of the industrialization era. This shift underscores the need for companies to adapt to global supply chains, with a substantial percentage of European companies now sourcing from other continents. Additionally, the business environment is characterized by volatility, uncertainty, complexity, and ambiguity, making long-term strategic decisions intricate. Small and medium-sized enterprises and global manufacturing companies are vulnerable to the complexities of globalization and VUCA, facing challenges in site planning and network optimization. The process involves systematically evaluating various internal and external factors, such as market trends and technological advancements, to identify optimal sites and network configurations. However, companies often lack the expertise to conduct this evaluation effectively. Information management and geoinformation systems can enhance decision-making by providing comprehensive insights into cost, logistics, and environmental risks. This integrative approach promotes companies' flexibility and adaptability by considering both spatial and operational aspects, thereby increasing competitiveness. Ultimately, GIS and IMS lead to better-informed, strategic decisions that ensure the long-term success of companies. Integrating production and network planning is crucial for optimizing operations and enhancing resilience in the face of future challenges.

A systematic literature review using a method by TRANFIELD ET AL. identified existing approaches to integrated site and network planning. The review revealed several requirements for an integrated approach, including objectivity, consideration of site-network interactions, long-term opportunities and risks, and using IMS and GIS data. However, no existing approach fully meets these requirements.

As a result, a conceptual work plan was proposed to develop an integrated production site and network planning approach. The work plan involves creating a description model, an impact model, a conceptual data model, and a holistic procedure model. These models are designed to comprehensively integrate site and network planning. Iterative validation of these models ensures that they meet the specified requirements. The procedure model for integrated site and network planning ultimately improves efficiency, effectiveness, and adaptability, helping companies to remain competitive in dynamic global markets. In future research, the aim is to develop integrated site and network planning with the assistance of the presented conceptual work plan.

References

1. H.-P. Wiendahl, J. Reichardt, and P. Nyhuis, Handbook Factory Planning and Design. Berlin, Heidelberg: Springer Berlin Heidelberg, 2015, ch. 1, 4.
2. S. Dreher, "Betriebswirtschaftliche Grundlagen globaler Produktionsnetzwerke und des Produktionsanlaufs," in mir-Edition, Koordination des Produktionsanlaufs in globalen Produktionsnetzwerken, S. Dreher, Ed., Wiesbaden: Springer Fachmedien Wiesbaden, 2024, pp. 23–110.
3. Statistisches Bundesamt, Globale Wertschöpfungsketten von Unternehmen in Deutschland: Pilotstudie zeigt internationale Verflechtung der deutschen Wirtschaft. [Online]. Available: https://www.destatis.de/DE/Presse/Pressemitteilungen/2022/11/PD22_498_52931.html (accessed: May 19 2024).
4. N. Bennett and G. J. Lemoine, "What a difference a word makes: Understanding threats to performance in a VUCA world," Business horizons, no. 57, pp. 311–317, 2014.
5. D. Tranfield, D. Denyer, and P. Smart, "Towards a Methodology for Developing Evidence-Informed Management Knowledge by Means of Systematic Review," British J of Management, vol. 14, no. 3, pp. 207–222, 2003, https://doi.org/10.1111/1467-8551.00375.

6. J. T. Buchanan, E. J. Henig, and M. I. Henig, "Objectivity and Subjectivity in the Decision Making Process," Annals of Operations Research, vol. 80, pp. 333–346, 1998, https://doi.org/10.1023/A:1018980318183.
7. E. Abele, T. Meyer, U. Näher, G. Strube, and R. Sykes, Eds., Global Production: A Handbook for Strategy and Implementation. Berlin, Heidelberg: Springer-Verlag Berlin Heidelberg, 2008. [Online]. Available: http://nbn-resolving.org/urn:nbn:de:bsz:31-epflicht-1618029, ch. 4.
8. M. Zhou, Y. Huang, K. Li, Z. Li, and J. Wei, "Design of Intelligent Power Material Storage Information Management System Based on Blockchain Technology," in 37th Annual Conference on Power System and Automation in Chinese Universities, pp. 479–485.
9. N. Mevenkamp, Geographie, Raum und geographische Informationssysteme: Univ. Bremen, 1999.
10. J. T. Lin and Y.-Y. Chen, "A multi-site supply network planning problem considering variable time buckets– A TFT-LCD industry case," Int J Adv Manuf Technol, vol. 33, 9–10, pp. 1031–1044, 2007, https://doi.org/10.1007/s00170-006-0537-z, .
11. E. Abele, T. Meyer, U. Näher, G. Strube, and R. Sykes, Handbuch globale Produktion. München: Hanser, 2006, ch. 4.
12. J. Ackermann and E. Müller, "Modelling, planning and designing of logistics structures of regional competence-cell-based networks with structure types," Robotics and Computer-Integrated Manufacturing, vol. 23, no. 6, pp. 601–607, 2007, https://doi.org/10.1016/j.rcim.2007.02.010.
13. G. Walther, A. Schatka, and T. S. Spengler, "Design of regional production networks for second generation synthetic bio-fuel – A case study in Northern Germany," European Journal of Operational Research, vol. 218, no. 1, pp. 280–292, 2011, https://doi.org/10.1016/j.ejor.2011.09.050.
14. G. Lanza and R. Moser, "Strategic Planning of Global Changeable Production Networks," Procedia CIRP, vol. 3, pp. 257–262, 2012, https://doi.org/10.1016/j.procir.2012.07.045.
15. M. Häntsch and A. Huchzermeier, "Transparency of risk for global and complex network decisions in the automotive industry," International Journal of Production Economics, vol. 175, pp. 81–95, 2016, https://doi.org/10.1016/j.ijpe.2016.02.010.
16. E. Moser, N. Stricker, and G. Lanza, "Risk Efficient Migration Strategies for Global Production Networks," Procedia CIRP, vol. 57, pp. 104–109, 2016, https://doi.org/10.1016/j.procir.2016.11.019.
17. U. Clausen, S. Langkau, I. Goedicke, and S. Lier, "Location and Network Planning for Modular Container Plants in the Process Industry," Chem Eng & Technol, 2017, https://doi.org/10.1002/ceat.201600735.
18. E. Moser, A. K. Huss, C. Liebrecht, and G. Lanza, "A Portfolio Theory Approach to Identify Risk-efficient Enablers of Change in Global Production Networks," Procedia CIRP, vol. 63, pp. 768–773, 2017, https://doi.org/10.1016/j.procir.2017.03.273.
19. G. Lanza et al., "Global production networks: Design and operation," CIRP Annals, vol. 68, no. 2, pp. 823–841, 2019, https://doi.org/10.1016/j.cirp.2019.05.008.
20. G. Schuh, J.-P. Prote, A. Gützlaff, and S. Henk, "Handling Uncertainties in Production Network Design," in IFIP Advances in Information and Communication Technology, Advances in production management systems: Towards smart production management systems: IFIP WG 5. 7 International Conference, APMS 2019, Austin, TX, USA, September 1–5, 2019, Proceedings, F. Ameri, K. E. Stecke, G. von Cieminski, and D. Kiritsis, Eds., Cham, Switzerland: Springer, 2019, pp. 43–50.
21. G. Timperio, S. Tiwari, J. M. Gaspar Sánchez, R. A. García Martín, and R. de Souza, "Integrated decision support framework for distribution network design," International Journal of Production Research, vol. 58, no. 8, pp. 2490–2509, 2019, https://doi.org/10.1080/00207543.2019.1680894.
22. S. Wenzel, Y.-N. Misz, K. Rahimi-Adli, B. Beisheim, R. Gesthuisen, and S. Engell, "An optimization model for site-wide scheduling of coupled production plants with an application to the ammonia network of a petrochemical site," Optim Eng, vol. 20, no. 4, pp. 969–999, 2019, https://doi.org/10.1007/s11081-019-09429-2.

23. C. Constantinescu, B. Pokorni, and J. Wimmer, "Affective Production Systems: Foundations, Reference Model and Roadmap for Implementation and Validation," Procedia CIRP, vol. 104, pp. 1783–1786, 2021, https://doi.org/10.1016/j.procir.2021.11.300.
24. J. Hook, C. Macdonald, and P. Nyhuis, Towards Factory location planning using GIS: Hannover: publish-Ing, 2023, pp. 221–228.
25. C. Schmidt, F. Finsterwalder, R. Griesbaum, and J. T. Sehrt, "Determination of factory locations for distributed additive manufacturing, considering pollution, resilience and costs," CIRP Journal of Manufacturing Science and Technology, vol. 43, pp. 115–128, 2023, https://doi.org/10.1016/j.cirpj.2023.03.005.
26. G. L. Steier, M.-C. Jaspers, S. Peukert, M. Benfer, and G. Lanza, "Strategic fit in global production networks – A decision support model for strategic configuration of global production networks," Procedia CIRP, vol. 120, pp. 1059–1064, 2023, https://doi.org/10.1016/j.procir.2023.09.125.
27. G. L. Steier, K. Gleich, and G. Lanza, "Strategic Manufacturing Network Performance Assessment Tool," Zeitschrift für wirtschaftlichen Fabrikbetrieb, vol. 119, 1–2, pp. 12–16, 2024, https://doi.org/10.1515/zwf-2024-1002.
28. D. V. Steward, "DSM Foundations and Applications, and an Update on the Explainer," in Risk and change management in complex systems, M. Maurer, D. M. Schmidt, and U. Lindemann, Eds., München: Carl Hanser Verlag GmbH & Co. KG, 2015, pp. 1–8.
29. T. Weimer, R. Kapp, P. Klemm, and E. Westkämper, "Integrated Data Management in Factory Planning and Factory Operation. An Information Model and its Implementation," in Manufacturing Systems and Technologies for the New Frontier, M. Mitsuishi, K. Ueda, and F. Kimura, Eds., London: Springer London, 2008, pp. 229–234.
30. Q. Li and Y.-L. Chen, "Entity-Relationship Diagram," in Modeling and Analysis of Enterprise and Information Systems, Q. Li and Y.-L. Chen, Eds., Berlin, Heidelberg: Springer Berlin Heidelberg, 2009, pp. 125–139.

Predicting Fire Incidents in Industrial Facilities and Developing Customized Fire Insurance Products Using Data Mining

SeokCheol Lee and Yong Jin Kim

Abstract The recent increase in large-scale fires has led to significant loss of life and property, posing a serious threat to social safety. This study aims to analyze the factors and patterns of fire incidents in industrial facilities using data mining techniques to offer some insight to the development of customized fire insurance products. In particular, this study focuses on fire grades (fireproof structures and non-combustible materials), crucial factors in fire insurance design. Fire incidents at industrial facilities were analyzed using annual fire statistics (2019–2022) provided by the National Fire Agency of South Korea. Additionally, fire insurance subscription data from Korea Statistical Information Service was referenced to analyze current fire insurance enrollment status. For data analysis, predictive models such as Decision Tree (C5.0), CART (Gini), CHAID, and Random Forest were used, with Mean Absolute Error (MAE) and classification accuracy employed to verify prediction accuracy. While previous studies on fire prediction that primarily focused on time, place, and climate factors, this study set building structure and fire grade as primary factors in fire insurance design. This study contributes to the literature on fire risk prediction and fire insurance studies by providing an essential theoretical basis for fire prevention and risk management in industrial facilities.

Keywords Accident Prediction · Data Mining · Fire incident · Fire insurance · Fire insurance building grade · Risk management

S. Lee (✉) · Y. J. Kim
Sogang University, Seoul, South Korea
e-mail: mjmusician@naver.com

Y. J. Kim
e-mail: yongjkim@sogang.ac.kr

E. Tsui et al. (eds.), *Management Information Systems in a Digitalized AI World*, Springer Proceedings in Business and Economics,
https://doi.org/10.1007/978-981-96-6526-6_6

1 Introduction

In recent years, large-scale industrial fires in South Korea have surged, increasing casualties and property damage. In 2023, 40,114 fire incidents resulted in 342 fatalities, 2,327 injuries, and $900 million in damage. Industrial fires alone accounted for 5,293 incidents, 16 deaths, 291 injuries, and $560 million in losses, highlighting the importance of tailored fire insurance for financial protection and fire prevention in industrial facilities.

Existing studies have developed fire risk prediction models by analyzing various factors such as fire occurrence frequency, regional characteristics, and building types. For example, Lee et al. (2020) examined the correlation between fire frequency and key factors like building age and area, while the National 119 Rescue Headquarters (2016) proposed a model assessing fire risk by building use type. Other studies, such as those by Lee et al. (2010) and Seo et al. (2021), analyzed regional fire data to identify major factors influencing fire occurrences. However, previous studies often faced limitations in prediction reliability due to data accuracy and insufficient analytical information.

For example, the correlation between fire frequency and key factors like building age and area was examined [1], while a model assessing fire risk by building use type was proposed (National 119 Rescue Headquarters, 2016). Other studies analyzed regional fire data to identify major factors influencing fire occurrences [1, 2]. However, previous studies often faced limitations in prediction reliability due to data accuracy and insufficient analytical information.

This study analyzes 23,127 industrial fire incidents from 2019 to 2022, using National Fire Agency data. Key variables include day/night (time), reason, factors, case, human life damage, deaths, injuries, property damage, place, and building structure grade. Additionally, KOSIS fire insurance data, including premium assessment standards, were referenced to enhance data reliability and applicability [3].

In this study, machine learning-based classification techniques such as C5.0, C4.5, CART(Gini), CHAID, and Random Forest (RF) were used to obtain more accurate results in fire prediction based on various data. These algorithms have higher predictive accuracy than traditional statistical methods and can effectively analyze the complex factors that contribute to fire behavior. And checked the accuracy of fire prediction with MAE and Classification accuracy.

This study aims to analyze fire occurrence trends in domestic industrial facilities and develop a predictive model to support customized fire insurance design. By examining building grades, particularly through fireproof structures and non-combustible materials, this research distinguishes itself from prior studies, establishing a basis for insurance design that effectively reflects industrial facility risks and aids in fire loss prevention. In addition, we propose a precise fire prediction model using machine learning and data mining to enhance the practical applicability of fire insurance and contribute to fire prevention and response in industrial facilities.

2 Literature Review

2.1 *Fire Occurrence Pattern Analysis*

Statistical analysis of fire occurrences examines factors like frequency, geographic distribution, population density, and damage to identify patterns and trends, using techniques such as correlation, regression, and Poisson regression to assess the impact of specific factors. These studies inform fire risk assessment, community safety management, and urban disaster risk analysis, which considers factors like population density, building use, and social vulnerability to guide prevention policies and resource allocation (Table 1).

2.2 *Fire Occurrence Prediction Analysis*

Research on fire occurrence prediction analysis has recently advanced toward more sophisticated methods to predict the likelihood of fire incidents, driven by the development of machine learning and artificial intelligence technologies. Prediction algorithms, primarily Random Forests, Neural Networks, and k-Nearest Neighbors (kNN), are used to learn and predict key factors contributing to fire occurrences. These techniques integrate a variety of environmental variables, such as climate information, fire source, location, and building characteristics, into models that predict fire occurrence probability. This approach supports real-time risk monitoring and early warning systems, while also predicting potential loss of life and property, allowing for more systematic fire response planning, and improve prediction accuracy by using variables such as weather conditions, time of day, and building condition. (Table 2).

2.3 *Fire-Resistant Structure and Materials*

Customized fire insurance for industrial facilities contributes to minimizing financial losses and creating a stable management environment by providing tailored coverage that reflects the unique fire risk factors of each industry. In customized fire insurance for industrial facilities, premiums and claim payments are calculated by comprehensively considering the building structure, fire risk level, and amount of loss.

The building grade, indicating fire risk level, and the K-value (risk loading factor) play crucial roles in determining insurance premiums. Buildings are graded from Level 1 to Level 4 based on fire risk, and the K-value, as a safety or risk loading factor, becomes more significant as the building grade increases, reflecting a higher likelihood of fire and influencing premium calculations accordingly [19, 20], (1), (2), (3), (Table 3).

Table 1 A study on the statistical analysis of fire occurrence pattern

Auth	Title	Analysis method	Scope of the study	Derived factors
Chris et al. (2016) [4]	Socioeconomic and demographic predictors of accidental dwelling fire rates	Principal component analysis, least squares regression analysis	The whole of the United Kingdom	Race composition, unemployment rate
Donna (2006) [5]	Income, housing and fire injuries: a census tract analysis public health reports	Multiple regression analysis	Philadelphia, U.S.A	Vacant housing rates, low-income, non-English speaking populations
Hwang et al. (2001) [6]	A Study on the Urban Disaster Risk Assessment Model—The Case of Cheongju City with the Focus on Fire, Facility, and Evacuation Risk-	Basic Statistics	Cheongju in South Korea	Fire hazard, facility hazard, and evacuation hazard
Kang (2003) [7]	The Current State of the Anti-Fire Zone and the Guidelines to Improve It	Correlation analysis, regression analysis	Daegu in South Korea	Number of fire occurrence, opulation, and use of buildings
Kim & Um (2007) [8]	The Urban Fire Prediction Mapping Technique based on GIS Spatial Statistics	Correlation analysis, Poisson rate distribution analysis	Daegu in South Korea	Fire burning, building density, population density, furniture density
Min (2018) [9]	Analysis of the Correlation between Fire Occurrence Status and Damage Factors in Seoul Using SPSS	Correlation analysis	Seoul in South Korea	Number of fires, casualties, property damage, type of fire
Paulo & Vitor (2014) [10]	The choices of fire—Debating socioeconomic determinants of the fires observed at Portuguese municipalities	Classification, regression tree analysis	Portuguese municipality	Regional aging index
Prem (2010) [11]	Modelling potential socioeconomic determinants of building fires in South East Queensland	Multiple regression, ANOVA	South Queensland, Australia	The number of unemployed and indigenous people, and single-parent families with children

Table 2 A study on the preditive analysis of fire occurrence pattern

Auth	Title	Analysis method	Scope of the study	Derived factors
Hong et al. (2018) [12]	Data-driven Fire Accident Analysis and Developing Prediction and Corrsponding System using Artificial Intelligence	Correlation Analysis Classification Regression	The whole of the South Korea	Weather, date and time, and regional information
Kim (2014) [13]	A Study on Fire Prediction Model Development Using Data Mining	Data mining	The whole of the South Korea	Time Variables, meteorological variables
Kim (2013) [14]	Prediction of Fire Risk Using Weather Information	Bayesian network, logistic regression	The whole of the South Korea	Weather information, number of fires
Kim (2021) [15]	A Study on the Development of Fire Prediction Model Using Big Data	Statistical analysis, one-way ANOVA Multiple regression analysis	The whole of the South Korea	Utterance reason, Factor, Time, Type, Days, Place etc
Lee (2020) [16]	Prediction and Analysis of Fire Risk by Building: Based on Property Damage and Fire Occurrence	Random forest	Seoul in South Korea	Building characteristics, access to fire fighting facilities
Lim (2022) [17]	Development of city-level fire prediction model through analysis of factors affecting fire damage	Correlation analysis, multiple regression analysis	The whole of the South Korea	Fire occurrence number, area of use area, population, household & housing factors
Park (2020) [18]	A Study on the Development of Fire Prediction Platform by Analyzing Fire Occurrence Characteristics	Correlation analysis, NN neural network	The whole of the South Korea	Fire areas, ignition factors, month, electricity/gas usage, building age, non-smoking areas

Table 3 Building classification criteria by grade

Grade/primary material	Columns/beams/floor	Roof	Exterior wall
Grade 1	Fireproof Structure	Fireproof Structure	Fireproof Structure
Grade 2	Fireproof Structure	Non-Combustible Materials	Fireproof Structure
Grade 3	Non-Combustible Materials	Non-Combustible Materials	Non-Combustible Materials
Grade 4	Other than above		

Sources Target and application of fire insurance factory items [19]

3 Data Analysis

3.1 Research Methodology

Machine learning develops predictive and decision-making models by identifying patterns in large datasets, enhancing accuracy through supervised, unsupervised, and ensemble methods. Used across fields like computer vision, NLP, biology, and social sciences, it is essential for industrial forecasting and data mining [20–22]. Accuracy improves as data volume grows; models are categorized as supervised or unsupervised by data traits [1]. This study used R-Studio and Python, popular in data mining and machine learning.

$$E(Pure\,premium) = E\left(\begin{array}{c} RP : \frac{Number\ of\ incidents}{Number\ of\ contracts} \times \\ \frac{Incurred\ loss}{Number\ of\ incidents} \end{array}\right) + K \cdot Var \tag{1}$$

$$\begin{aligned} E = E\,(RP &: The\,probability\ of\ an\,incidents\,occurring \\ &\times Incurred\ lossper\,Incidents) \\ &\pm Discount\ or\ extrapremium \end{aligned} \tag{2}$$

$$Clames\,paid = Incurred\ loss \times \frac{Sum\,insured}{Insurable\ value \times 80\%} \tag{3}$$

The C5.0 algorithm, based on entropy reduction, is efficient in speed and memory for large datasets, simplifying models and handling missing data, useful for predicting industrial fire risks (Quinlan, 1998). The CART (Gini) algorithm measures data purity to boost prediction accuracy, suitable for classification and regression across data types, effectively analyzing fire risks in industrial settings [22, 23].

CHAID, using chi-square tests, groups data by relationships with categorical or continuous variables, enabling multi-level splits, widely used in marketing and surveys, suited for analyzing fire patterns and risk zones [24].

Random Forest uses multiple decision trees to boost accuracy and stability through ensemble learning, reducing prediction inter-correlation and overfitting, assessing variable importance, and commonly applied in fire and industrial forecasting [17].

This study uses machine learning to predict fire risks in industrial facilities and design customized fire insurance products. By employing data mining, it predicts fire occurrence likelihood, identifies risk factors through classification, regression, and clustering, supporting fire prevention and insurance design, enhancing industrial safety [25]. To evaluate machine learning model accuracy for fire prediction, mean absolute error (MAE) is commonly used [26].

MAE is the average absolute difference between predicted and actual values, with lower MAE values indicating higher accuracy. Higher classification accuracy also means a more reliable prediction model [27].

3.2 Data Collection

The study is based on "Annual Fire Statistics (2019–2022)" provided by the National Fire Agency, with a focus on industrial facility fire incidents. Out of a total of 235,367 fire cases, 23,127 incidents were categorized for analysis, excluding unidentified and miscellaneous cases. This study specifically examines general fire insurance, with a particular focus on fire occurrences within factory properties [28]. Data from the Korea Statistical Information Service (KOSIS) on fire insurance status was utilized to assess fire incidents by location, month, property damage, and human life impact, based on ignition factors. Additionally, the analysis included building structure data for fire incidents, enabling an investigation of how structural characteristics affect both the likelihood and severity of fire damage. 1%.

The analysis aimed to predict fire occurrences using ten variables: day and night, reason, factors, case, human life damage, deaths, injuries, property damage, place, and type. Data was split into a 70:30 ratio of training and testing sets for model training. Additionally, to compare and analyze contracts and loss conditions by insurance type, data on fire and marine insurance status from KOSIS was collected. This organized information allowed for systematic assessment of risk factors for fire insurance products tailored to industrial facility fires. The study aims to use this data comprehensively to support the development of industrial facility fire insurance products (Table 4).

3.3 Empirical Analysis

The data analysis was conducted using R-Studio, subdividing the nine variables into categorical and dummy variables. Frequency analysis results showed Sparks and Ember were the most frequent in Reason, at 20.4%; Electrical was the main cause in

Table 4 Fire occurrence factor variables

Variable	Data value
Day & night (Time) (T)	Night: 0, Day: 1
Reason (R)	Cigarette fire, Lighter fire, Explosive materials, Fireworks = 1, Friction, Conduction, Radiation = 2, Sparks, Ember = 3, Natural spontaneous ignition = 4, Operating equipment = 5, Chemical fire = 6
Factors (F)	Gas leak (explosion) = 1, Mechanical factor, Product defect = 2, Arson, Suspected arson = 3, Negligence = 4, Natural = 5, Electrical = 6, Chemical = 7
Case (C)	Combustible gas, Hazardous materials, etc. = 1, Food, Trash = 2, Electrical/Electronic devices = 3, Paper/Wood, Hay, etc. = 4, Furniture, Bedding, Signs, Awnings, etc. = 5, Synthetic resin = 6, Automobiles, Railroad cars, Ships, Aircraft = 7(X)
Human influencing premium calculations aclife damage (HD)	None: 0, Yes: 1
Death (D)	None: 0, Yes: 1
Injury (I)	None: 0, Yes: 1
Property damage (PD)	0~10,000 = 1, 10,001~50,000 = 2, 50,001~200,000 = 3,
(1,000 KRW)	200,001~1,000,000 = 4, More than 1,000,001 = 5
Place (P)	Factory, Underground facilities = 1, Animal/Plant facilities, Sanitary facilities = 2, Power plant = 3, Workshop = 4, Warehouse = 5
Building structure grade	Grade1, Grade2, Grade3, Grade4

Factors, at 39.9%; Electricity and Electronics were most frequent in Case, at 36.9%; Factory and Underground facilities were most frequent in Place, at 42.1%.

For property damage, the 0~10,000 range was most common at 77.9%; for injury, none was most frequent at 96.7%; and for time of occurrence, Night was most frequent at 64.1%. For human life damage and death, none was most frequent at 96.6% and 99.8%, respectively (Table 5).

An examination of the property damage status by location, specifically for ignition factors, reveals that major property damage occurred primarily in factory facilities, warehouse facilities, and power plants in 2021. Significant increases in property damage can be attributed to several major incidents, including large fires at Coupang (the leading e-commerce platform in South Korea) Logistics Warehouse, fires at petrochemical plants, and fires at thermal and wind power plants (Table 6).

Grade 1 shows Reason 5 (operating equipment 64.6%), Factors 6 (electrical, 39.0%), and Case 3 (electrical/electronic devices 37.6%) as the main causes of fire.

Table 5 Frequency analysis

Var.	Val.	Fre.	%	Var.	Val.	Fre.	%
R	1	2307	10	T	0	14,823	64.1
	2	1311	5.7		1	8304	35.9
	3	4725	20.4	HD	0	22,332	96.6
	4	131	0.6		1	795	3.4
	5	13,867	60	D	0	23,085	99.8
	6	786	3.4		1	42	0.2
F	1	83	0.4	C	1	1268	5.5
	2	3820	16.5		2	3200	13.8
	3	73	0.3		3	8540	36.9
	4	8711	37.7		4	4305	18.6
	5	201	0.9		5	823	3.6
	6	9237	39.9		6	4931	21.3
	7	1002	4.3		7	60	0.3
P	1	9747	42.1	PD	1	18,020	77.9
	2	5055	21.9		2	2865	12.4
	3	154	0.7		3	1463	6.3
	4	1726	7.5		4	621	2.7
	5	6445	27.9		5	158	0.7
I	0	22,360	96.7				
	1	767	3.3				

Although it has high resistance to fire spread due to its fireproof structure, the fire risk from electrical factors related to operating equipment remains significant.

Grade 2 shows Reason 5 (operating equipment 58.2%), Factors 4 (negligence 40.1%), and Case 3 (electrical/electronic devices 33.3%) as main fire causes. While columns and exterior walls are fireproof, the roof is non-combustible materials, slightly reducing fire resistance, with negligence posing a significant risk.

Grade 3 shows Reason 5 (operating equipment 55.4%), Factors 4 (negligence 39.9%), and Case 3 (electrical/electronic devices 34.0%) as main fire causes. With non-combustible columns, roof, and walls, structural deformation is likely in fires, with high fire risk from user negligence and electronic devices (Fig. 1 and Table 7).

In this study, correlation analysis and multiple regression analysis were conducted using 9 variables (time, reason, factor, case, human life damage, deaths, injuries, property damage, and place) to identify variables useful for fire occurrence prediction.

The analysis revealed a very strong positive correlation between human life damage and injury, with a correlation coefficient of 0.98. This high correlation indicates that instances of human life damage are frequently associated with injuries. Additionally, a moderate positive correlation was observed between ignition factors and causes, with a correlation coefficient of 0.37. This suggests that certain ignition

Table 6 Frequency analysis (An examination of the property damage status by location)

Place	Factors	2019	2020	2021	2022
Factory	Electrical	38.5	18.1	1.9	13.4
	Mechanical	−2.8	25.1	13.2	−21.6
	Chemical	279.2	−70.9	92.4	−31
	Negligence	−25.7	34	−2.1	68.1
	Natural	−64	−34.3	316.5	0.8
	Arson	−75.4	9.2	−67.7	−88
Warehouse	Electrical	16.6	92.5	2858.3	−98.1
	Mechanical	−31.8	220.6	−66.7	−63.4
	Chemical	−26.7	−56	105.2	303.4
	Negligence	−32.4	747.2	−67.3	16.5
	Natural	−99.7	−35	886.3	−75.3
	Arson	14,663.8	3110.7	−94.3	5822.1
Workshop	Electrical	−52.8	62	−29.2	6.2
	Mechanical	248.8	−74.9	−42.9	197.1
	Chemical	111.1	183.6	−75.8	−60.3
	Negligence	−8.2	−57.9	85	−62
	Natural	−99.4	4852.9	−61.4	−82.5
	Arson	2047.1	−100		–
Power plant	Electrical	−85.8	−86.5	1534.6	−91.4
	Mechanical	31.4	−99.2	25,091.5	−8.8
	Chemical	−19.5	−88.8	−10.1	–
	Negligence	−79.1	213.9	−17.8	−90.3
	Natural		40,726	−87.1	–
Animal/Plant facilities	Electrical	−20.2	17.7	28.8	34.7
	Mechanical	−18	−30.7	−32.7	163.2
	Chemical	55.5	−32.7	−49.9	−19.7
	Negligence	40.2	120	−63.2	77.3
	Natural	90	1746.1	−95.2	1364.6
Sanitary facilities	Electrical	−57.4	434.9	−56.3	317.1
	Mechanical	−86.9	2083.8	−71.5	−29.3
	Chemical	−56	103.7	−83.9	573.1
	Negligence	−96.7	5.4	−40.8	−59.3
	Natural	704.4	−97.5	−98.7	781.6

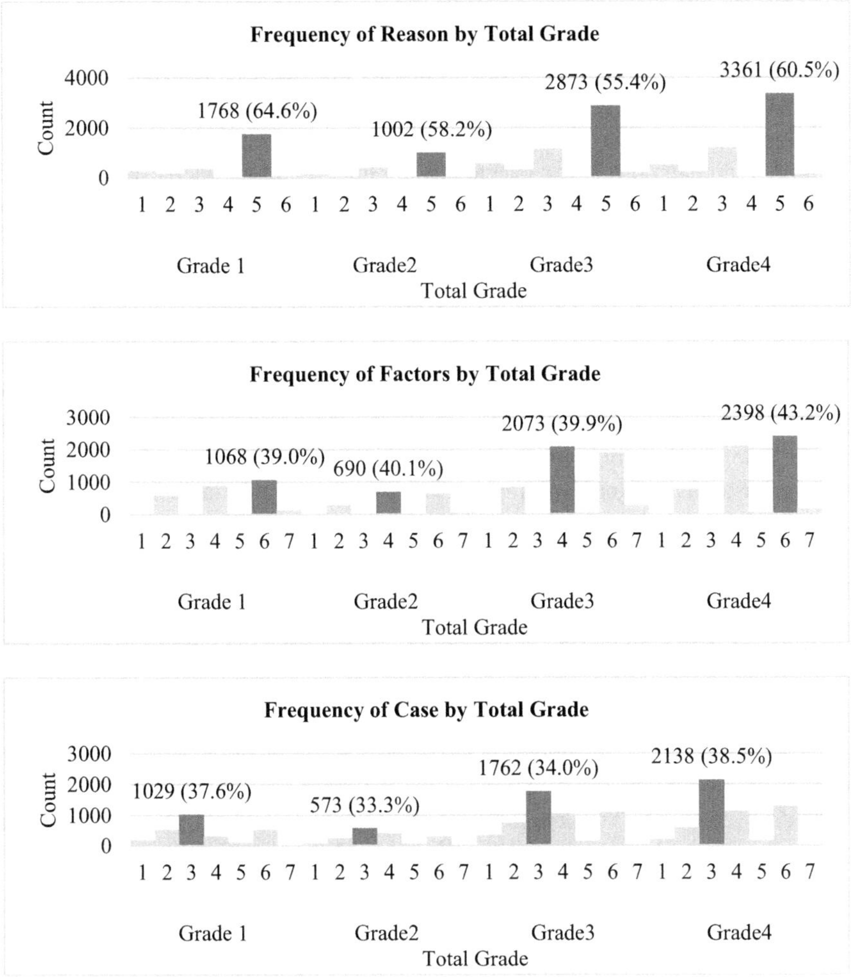

Fig. 1 Frequency and percentage of major fire causes by building grade

Table 7 Frequency and percentage of major fire causes by building grade

Grade	R	Fre	%	F	Fre	%	C	Fre	%
1	5	1768	64.6	6	1068	39.0	3	1029	37.6
2	5	1002	58.2	4	690	40.1	3	573	33.3
3	5	2873	55.4	4	2073	39.9	3	1762	34.0
4	5	3361	60.5	6	2398	43.2	3	2138	38.5

factors are associated with specific ignition causes. As a result of multiple regression analysis, all variables were found to be statistically significant (Table 8).

This study conducted an analysis to predict fire risk factors using C5.0, CART (Gini), CHAID, and RF models. The accuracy of each prediction model was compared and analyzed based on classification accuracy and MAE. The model with the highest predictive power was selected as the final model. Property damage, which directly influences fire insurance premiums, was set as the dependent variable, and the analysis results using C5.0 (Entropy Package) are as follows (Table 9).

The C5.0, CART (Gini), and CHAID models all predicted Factors and Human Damage as key variables. The C5.0 model recorded an accuracy of 0.782534 and an MAE of 0.357410, while the CART (Gini) model recorded an accuracy of 0.780372 and an MAE of 0.366191, and the CHAID model showed an accuracy of 0.779123 and an MAE of 0.358419. The fact that these models commonly predicted Factors as the first priority and Human Damage as the second priority suggests that the main cause of property damage is greatly influenced by Factors and that human damage also has a significant impact. The Factors variable includes key elements related to fire occurrence, such as electrical faults and equipment malfunctions. These factors provide essential information for evaluating and predicting fire risks, thereby enhancing the model's performance.

The RF model utilized Factors and Case as key variables, achieving the highest accuracy of 0.784479 and the lowest MAE of 0.352789. The RF model predicted

Table 8 Multiple regression analysis

Var.	Est.	Std.Error	t val.	p_val.	Sig.
(Intercept)	1.039677	0.025912	40.123	<2e-16	***
T	0.14987	0.010509	14.261	<2e-16	***
R	0.019326	0.003811	5.071	3.99E-07	***
F	0.052312	0.003554	14.72	<2e-16	***
C	0.007245	0.003377	2.145	0.0319	*
HD	−1.371456	0.248786	−5.513	3.57E-08	***
D	2.1158	0.20371	10.386	<2e-16	***
I	1.82457	0.247236	7.38	1.64E-13	***
P	−0.037189	0.002974	−12.505	<2e-16	***

Table 9 Machine learning model performance for predicting property damage

Model	Influential variable			Classification accuracy	MAE
	1st	2nd	3rd		
C 5.0	F	HD	C	0.782534	0.357410
CART (Gini)	F	HD	T	0.780372	0.366191
CHAID	F	HD	T	0.779123	0.358419
RF	F	C	R	0.784479	0.352789

Factors as the primary variable and Case as the secondary variable. The Case variable refers to the initial ignition material, which includes a variety of combustible materials such as electrical and electronic products, and plays a key role in describing the specific ignition path of a fire. This helps in accurately understanding the causes of fire and reinforcing preventive measures.

The high influence of electrical factors across both the Factors and Case variables indicates that electrical issues are major causes of fires. This emphasizes the importance of proper management and prevention of electrical risks. Additionally, the Human Damage variable is an important factor in determining insurance payouts in case of fires, and it was consistently used as a major variable in all the models.

In this study, the RF model demonstrated the best performance, making it the most suitable model for predicting property damage in fire incidents. The key variables, Factors and Cases, significantly contributed to the model's high prediction accuracy, leading to its selection as the optimal model.

4 Result and Discussion

In the analysis of fire occurrences with property damage as the dependent variable, the "Reason" variable indicated "Sparks and Ember" as the cause in 20.4% of cases, while the "Factors" variable identified "Electrical" in 39.9% of cases. In the "Case" variable, "Electrical/Electronic devices" accounted for 36.9%, and "Factory and Underground Facilities" were the most frequent in the "Place" variable, with 42.1%. Property damage was most common in the 0~10,000 range, accounting for 77.9% of cases, while 96.7% of incidents involved no injuries. Analysis by time of occurrence revealed that 64.1% of fires occurred at "Night," and cases with no human injury and no fatalities were observed in 96.6% and 99.8% of incidents, respectively.

An analysis of fire causes by building grade showed that for Grade 1 buildings, with high fireproof structures, the main fire cause was "Operating equipment" (64.6%) in the "Reason" variable, followed by "Electrical factors" (39.0%) in the "Factors" variable, and "Electrical/Electronic devices" (37.6%) in the "Case" variable. In Grade 2 buildings, "Operating equipment" appeared as the main cause in the "Reason" variable at 58.2%, with "Negligence" (40.1%) in the "Factors" variable and "Electrical/Electronic devices" (33.3%) in the "Case" variable showing significant proportions. For Grade 3 buildings, "Operating equipment" accounted for 55.4% in the "Reason" variable, "Negligence" made up 39.9% in the "Factors" variable, and "Electrical/Electronic devices" represented 34.0% in the "Case" variable.

In this study, various predictive models were compared, and the Random Forest (RF) model was selected as the optimal prediction model due to its highest classification accuracy (0.784479) and relatively low Mean Absolute Error (MAE 0.352789). The RF model demonstrated excellent performance by accurately predicting fire risk using key variables such as Case and Factors.

5 Conclusion and Implications

The study highlights fire causes and risks in industrial facilities, considering building structure and specific risk factors, to support the development of customized fire insurance products. Findings show that fires are primarily caused by electrical issues and equipment operation, especially in factories and underground facilities, with factors like deteriorating insulation, short circuits, overloads, and poor contact heightening [29]. It is also indicated that fire causes and damage patterns vary by fireproof construction and non-combustible materials, emphasizing the need for insurance policies tailored to building structure and risk factors.

This study contributes to the literature in two ways. Firstly, while previous studies have largely focused on external factors like population density, building use, and climatic conditions, this research highlights the critical role of structural elements such as fireproof structures and non-combustible materials in impacting fire risk. Examining the interaction between these structural elements and fire causes offers a new perspective on fire insurance design, suggesting that tailored insurance products can better reflect individual facility risks and provide fundamental insights for future fire prevention strategies. Secondly, this study analyzes fire risk factors within industrial facilities, revealing a clear correlation between building grade and fire risk. The high predictive accuracy of the Random Forest model used in this research also supports the effective assessment of fire risk factors. Using loss-based prediction as a guide for premium and coverage design contributes to fire insurance research, while realistic insurance payout estimates underline the relevance of this research for managing fire risks in the insurance sector.

In terms of practical contributions, this study suggests the need for and options for designing fire insurance tailored to industrial facilities. Highly fire-resistant buildings and buildings constructed with non-combustible materials may have lower base premiums, but the additional fire risk caused by electrical factors needs to be reflected. It is important to reduce the likelihood of fire by regularly inspecting facilities and take this into account when designing insurance.

Limitations of this study include its focus on specific industrial facilities and building structures, limiting its applicability across all industrial sectors. Additionally, seasonal and environmental factors were not fully addressed, suggesting the need for future studies on broader influences on fire risk. Further research into premium uncertainty and loss prediction from an insurer's perspective would also provide comprehensive insights for the field.

In sum, this study investigated the main fire risk factors and building characteristics that affect the fire vulnerability and insurance design of industrial facilities. Findings underscore the importance of structural features, such as fireproofing and non-combustible materials, in calculating premiums and assessing risks. This study suggests incorporating additional risk factors like electricity, electronics devices and operating equipment into insurance policy designs, providing foundational data for developing effective fire risk mitigation and tailored insurance strategies. Through this, the study makes academic and practical contributions to fire prevention and risk management in industrial environments.

References

1. Ina Lee., Hyung-Rok Oh., Zoonky Lee, "Risk Prediction and Analysis of Building Fires -Based on Property Damage and Occurrence of Fires-," *The Korean Journal of BigData*, vol. 6, no. 1, pp. 133–144, June 2021.
2. National Statistical Office, 2024, "Contracts and damages by type (fire/maritime) (Monthly April. 2001~December. 2022)," distributed by Korean Statistical Information Service, https://kosis.kr/statHtml/statHtml.do?orgId=382&tblId=TX_38202_A161&vw_cd=MT_ZTITLE&list_id=382_38202_002_021&seqNo=&lang_mode=ko&language=kor&obj_var_id=&itm_id=&conn_path=MT_ZTITLE
3. Min Song Seo., Castillo Osorio, Ever Enrique., Hee Yoo Hwan, "Predictive Analysis of Fire Risk Factors in Gyeonggi-do Using Machine Learning," *Korean Society of Surveying*, vol. 39, no. 6, pp. 351–361, July 2021.
4. Hastie, Chris., Searle, Rosalind, "Socio-economic and Demographic Predictors of Accidental Dwelling Fire Rates," *Fire Safety Journal*, vol. 84, pp. 50–56, August 2016.
5. Shai, Donna, "Income, Housing, and Fire Injuries, "Income, Housing, and Fire Injuries: A Census Tract Analysis," *Public health reports*, vol. 121, no. 2, pp. 149–154, March 2006.
6. Hee-yun Hwang., Kiyoung Baek., Byung-ho Park., Man-Hyung Lee., Jea-hoon Hwang., Eul-Ryul Ryu., TAE HWAN KIM, "Empirical Application for the Urban Disaster Risk Assessment (Fire and Facility Cases in Chongju)," *Chungbuk Research Institute*, vol. 11, no. 1, pp. 1–21, September 2000.
7. Yang-Suk Kang, "The Current State of the Anti-Fire Zone and the Guidelines to Improve It," *Korea Planners' Association*, vol. 38, no. 2, pp. 65–76, April 2003.
8. Jin-Taek Kim., Jung-Sup Um, "The Urban Fire Prediction Mapping Technique based on GIS Spatial Statistics," *International Journal of Fire Science and Engineering*, vol. 21, no. 2, pp. 14–23, June 2007.
9. Jeong Ki Min.,· Kyu Min Lee, Hyeon Seok··Lim, Young Je Woo, Jae Woo·Cho, Sae Hong Min, "A Study on the Relations Analysis between the Current Situation of Fire Accident and the Cause of Damage in Seoul Using SPSS," *Korea Conformity Laboratories*, pp. 117–118, April 2018.
10. Mourão, Paulo Reis., Martinho, Vítor Domingues, "The choices of the fire — Debating socioeconomic determinants of the fires observed at Portuguese municipalities," *In Forest Policy and Economics*, vol. 43, pp. 29–40, June 2014.
11. Chhetri, Prem., Corcoran, Jonathan., Stimson, Robert J., Inbakaran, Robert, "Modelling Potential Socio-economic Determinants of Building Fires in South East Queensland", *Geographical Research*, vol. 48, no. 1, pp. 75–85, January 2010.
12. Sung gwan Hong, "*Development and comparison of fire prediction model of building using machine learning*." Master's thesis. Kookmin University. 2018.
13. Minjoong Kim, "*A Study on Fire Prediction Model Development Using Data Mining*," Master's thesis. Kangwon National University, 2014.
14. Young jin, Kim, "*Prediction of Fire Risk Using Weather Information*," Doctoral dissertation. Soongsil University. 2013.
15. Tae-Hyeung Kim, "*A Study on the fire Development of Fire Prediction Model Using Big Data*," Doctoral dissertation. Daejeon University. (2021).
16. Ina Lee, "*Risk Prediction and Analysis of Building Fires: Based on Property Damage and Occurrence of fires*", Master's thesis. Yonsei University. 2020.

17. Daehoon Lim, "*Development of city-level fire prediction model through analysis of factors affecting fire damage*," Master's thesis. Kyungpook National University, April 2022.
18. Eun Seok Park, "*A Study on the Development of Fire Prediction Platform by Analyzing Fire Occurrence Characteristics*," Master's thesis. Gachon University. 2018.
19. BMCpro, "[Insurance] Property insurance (18) - Targets and application methods for fire insurance factory items," naver blog, https://blog.naver.com/taxaccbm/223268868722. November 22, 2023 (2022).
20. Duk Hyun Kim., Jin Seong Kim, Kyung Jae Lee, "A Study on the Problem of the Debris Value Deduction in the Calculation of the Payment Insurance Benefit in Fire Insurance Practice," *Law Research Institute, Chungbuk National University*, Vol. 29, no. 2, 46, pp. 333–356, December 2018.
21. Jordan, M. I. Mitchell, T. M, "Machine learning: Trends," *perspectives, and prospects Science*, vol. 349, no. 6245, pp. 255–260, July 2015.
22. Leo Breiman, "Random forests," *Machine Learning*, vol. 45, pp. 5–32, January 2001.
23. Nilima Patil., Rekha Lathi., Vidya Chitre.: Comparison of C5.0 & CART Classification algorithms using pruning technique. International *Journal of Engineering Research & Technology (IJERT)*. Vol. 1, no. 4, June 2012.
24. Heejeong Jin., Su Kyung Lee., Siwoo Lee, "Comparison among Algorithms for Decision Tree based on Sasang Constitutional Clinical Data," *Korea Journal of Oriental Medicine*, vol. 17, no. 2, pp. 121–128, August 2011.
25. H. Wang., C. Ma., L. Zhou, "A Brief Review of Machine Learning and Its Application," *2009 International Conference on Information Engineering and Computer Science Information Engineering and Computer Science, 2009. ICIECS 2009. International Conference on*. pp. 1–4, December 2009
26. Min Song, Seo, "*Prediction of Fire Occurrence Factors and Damage Scale by Machine Learning*," Doctoral dissertation. Gyeongsang National University, 2023.
27. Hyunsoo Ahn, "*Development of Occupational Safety and Health Management Cost Calculation Model for Multi-Family Housing Project by Machine Learning Techniques*," Doctoral dissertation. Kyung Hee University. 2021.
28. The Fire Department, 2024, "National Fire Agency_Annual Fire Statistics," distributed by Public Data Portal, https://www.data.go.kr/data/15060386/fileData.do#/layer_data_information
29. Yo-Han Kim, "*Consideration of Electrical Fire Prevention Measures Combing Electrical Fire Statistics and Cases*," Master's thesis. Hanyang University. 2017.

Enhancing Management Information Systems with Large Language Models: A Case Study on Tackling Vietnamese High School Mathematical Problems

Thao Vi Nguyen, Doan Dong Nguyen, and Cong Doan Truong

Abstract This research focuses on the challenges of using large language models (LLMs) to solve high school math problems in Vietnam. Although LLMs have advanced natural language processing, they struggle with math problem-solving. The proposed approach involves using topic classification to identify the relevant math topic, searching for similar problems in a dataset, extracting answers, and using in-context learning for further improvement. Code generation is also used to help with computational problem-solving and provide detailed explanations. By addressing the limitations of LLMs in understanding numbers, computations, and reasoning, this research aims to enhance the accuracy and effectiveness of LLM-based approaches in supporting students in their studies. These findings have the potential to advance educational technology and assist students in confidently navigating high school math.

Keywords Large language models · Natural language processing · Mathematical problem-solving · Educational Information System

1 Introduction

Recent years have witnessed a surge in the application of artificial intelligence to enhance teaching and learning practices, with advances in computer vision and natural language processing enabling the development of innovative educational technologies. For example, a study employed convolutional neural networks to

T. V. Nguyen · D. D. Nguyen · C. D. Truong (✉)
International School, Vietnam National University, Hanoi, Vietnam
e-mail: tcdoan@vnu.edu.vn

T. V. Nguyen
e-mail: vinguyen7202@gmail.com

D. D. Nguyen
e-mail: dongnd@vnu.edu.vn

E. Tsui et al. (eds.), *Management Information Systems in a Digitalized AI World*, Springer Proceedings in Business and Economics,
https://doi.org/10.1007/978-981-96-6526-6_7

monitor and quantify learner attention in real-time, providing actionable insights for educators and administrators to enhance virtual learning and aid in analytical problem-solving strategies [1]. Building upon this foundation of AI-powered educational applications, this work investigates the potential of large language models (LLMs) to provide personalized support and guidance to students working through complex mathematical problems, with the aim of enhancing learning outcomes and fostering deeper understanding.

LLMs have shown promise in solving mathematical problems; however, their performance in complex high school math tasks remains limited. Vietnamese high school math presents challenges due to diverse topics and intricate problem-solving steps. In this context, existing LLM approaches struggle with accuracy and explainability. This research endeavors to enhance LLMs' computational and reasoning abilities specifically for Vietnamese high school math.

To achieve this objective, the proposed approach entails leveraging topic classification techniques to accurately identify the mathematical domain of a given question, retrieving the most relevant problem from a corpus, extracting the corresponding answer, and employing in-context learning to refine the model performance. Additionally, the research seeks to incorporate code-generation techniques to facilitate accurate and efficient computational problem-solving, while also providing comprehensive explanations for the obtained outcomes. By overcoming these challenges, LLMs can effectively support personalized learning and automate the generation of comprehensive solutions. The study focuses on grades 10–12 and utilizes a carefully curated dataset specifically tailored to the requirements of Vietnamese high school math.

One significant contribution of this research lies in the integration of reasoning enhancement and code-based computational power enhancement. By integrating these approaches, LLMs can improve their problem-solving capabilities and provide more accurate and efficient solutions. Moreover, this research provides a tailored solution specifically designed to meet the needs of Vietnamese high school math and establishes a benchmark for evaluating LLM performance in this domain.

2 Literature Review

2.1 Overview of Large Language Models

LLMs are groundbreaking advancements in artificial intelligence, revolutionizing language processing and generation. These models mimic human language patterns by utilizing neural networks. With billions of parameters, LLMs can handle vast amounts of information [2]. The transformative Transformer architecture is central to their success, allowing LLMs to capture contextual relationships, process language efficiently, and generate coherent responses. The transformative Transformer architecture is central to their success, allowing LLMs to capture contextual relationships, process language efficiently, and generate coherent responses.

In recent years, a wave of highly capable LLMs has captured the attention of researchers and practitioners. Models like GPT-4 [3], GPT-3.5 [4], Bard [5], and LlaMA [6] have demonstrated exceptional capabilities across a diverse set of natural language processing (NLP) tasks such as question answering, text summarization, sentiment analysis, information retrieval, etc. However, transcending the boundaries of natural language alone, these extraordinary models possess the ability to handle diverse forms of structured and symbolic data, expanding their utility to various domains. For instance, in the realm of mathematics, LLMs exhibit an impressive aptitude for solving intricate problems [7]. These models demonstrate remarkable deductive reasoning skills, enabling them to draw logical conclusions based on a set of given premises, thus contributing to the field of automated reasoning. Additionally, LLMs trained on a vast amount of programming code can comprehend and generate code snippets efficiently, thereby proving invaluable in software development and automation [8].

2.2 LLMs Performance Assessment on Math

Mathematics is a challenging domain for LLMs, as it requires not only understanding the natural language text that describes the problem but also performing accurate and logical calculations and reasoning based on mathematical rules and principles. Several studies have evaluated the mathematical abilities of LLMs on various tasks and datasets, such as arithmetic operations [9–11], math word problems [12–14], math question answering [15, 16], and theorem proving [17, 18]. Among the existing LLMs, GPT-4 has exhibited exceptional proficiency in mathematical tasks and benchmarks, surpassing other models like ChatGPT and Minerva on diverse datasets such as GSM8K, MATH, and MMMLU-STEM [19]. Furthermore, GPT-4 has demonstrated its efficiency by outperforming InstructGPT, Galactica, and LlaMA in dealing with the arithmetic dataset MATH 401 [20]. This LLM has also exhibited remarkable capabilities in solving Chinese Elementary School Math Word Problems (CMATH) dataset, outshining Chinese-Alpaca, Moss, Ziya-LLaMA-13B, Baichuan-7B, and RWKV-7B [21]. On top of that, GPT-4 has achieved higher scores than the recently developed LLM, Llama 2 by Meta AI, in various evaluations encompassing MMLU, HellaSwag, ARC-E, and GSM8K [22]. In a study conducted by Jessica et al., GPT-4 also outperformed Bard by Google, obtaining a higher score on the Math dataset [23]. GPT-3.5-turbo is a bridge between GPT-3 and GPT-4, it was designed to increase the speed of the model and reduce the cost of running. According to a study that assessed the performance of GPT-3.5-turbo and GPT-4 on Brazilian University Admission Exams, GPT-3.5-turbo attained comparable results to zero-shot GPT-4 when employing techniques such as the three-shot method with Chain Of Thought

(CoT) prompting [24]. Based on these considerations, the attention in this report is directed towards GPT-4 and GPT-3.5-turbo.

These studies have revealed that LLMs can achieve impressive results on some tasks, especially when provided with appropriate prompts or instructions but also face significant limitations and challenges on others, especially when dealing with complex, multi-step, or abstract problems. Despite its remarkable capabilities, GPT-4 faces specific challenges in certain problem-solving scenarios. In particular, when encountering problems that demand intricate reasoning or involve multiple steps, GPT-4 often encounters difficulties in devising suitable plans or selecting optimal solutions, occasionally resulting in errors during plan execution. These challenges are particularly evident in complex domains like Intermediate Algebra and Precalculus. Additionally, GPT-4 occasionally struggles with problems that incorporate specialized symbols or notations, such as fractions, radicals, exponents, or LaTeX expressions. Recognizing and manipulating these symbols can prove to be a demanding task for the model, requiring careful formatting and parsing to ensure accuracy and minimize errors. Due to its reliance on explicit information provided in the problem statement and supporting context, the model cannot make inferences or assumptions beyond what is explicitly stated. Consequently, if a problem lacks clarity, vital details, or is open to interpretation, GPT-4 may encounter difficulties in providing accurate or meaningful answers [25].

2.3 Challenges of Solving Vietnamese High School Mathematics with LLM

Previous studies have identified several challenges and difficulties that LLMs encounter when solving mathematics problems, which can be categorized into two main aspects: mathematical calculation, and mathematical reasoning. Mathematical calculation refers to the ability to perform basic operations, such as addition, subtraction, multiplication, and division, with different types of numbers. On the other hand, mathematical reasoning refers to the ability to apply logical rules, principles, and strategies to solve complex problems. Some math problems involve intricate structures, such as multiple equations, interdependencies, or nested conditions that LLMs may may struggle to navigate, hindering their ability to identify optimal problem-solving approaches. LLMs often exhibit weaknesses and errors in these aspects such as inconsistent embedding, inaccurate computation, incorrect inference, and lack of explanation [20]. Not to mention, some researches have pointed out that the performance of LLMs varies substantially across different languages [26].

Vietnamese high school math is known for its complexity, emphasizing theoretical concepts and requiring abstract reasoning and problem-solving skills. Rather than prioritizing memorization, the educational emphasis in Vietnamese high school math lies in fostering critical thinking, problem analysis, and the development of innovative solutions through the practical application of mathematical concepts in real-world situations. These factors pose significant challenges for LLMs when handling Vietnamese high school math problems.

2.4 *Previous Research on Computational Problem-Solving and Reasoning in Mathematics*

To address the challenges of computational problem-solving and reasoning in mathematics, previous research has proposed various methods and techniques, such as pre-training, fine-tuning, instruction learning, tool-based methods, and chain-of-thought methods. Pre-training refers to the process of training LLMs on large-scale mathematical corpora, such as MathBERT [27], MathGLM [28], and LLEMMA [29], to enhance their mathematical knowledge and skills. Fine-tuning, on the other hand, focuses on adapting LLMs to specific mathematical tasks or domains, such as MetaMath [30], Goat [31], or GenBERT [32], to improve their task-specific performance. Instruction learning revolves around providing LLMs with natural language instructions or prompts that guide them in generating the desired outputs. Examples of instruction learning methods include MathPrompter [33], and WizardMath [34]. This approach involves the paradigm of In-context Learning (ICL) in conjunction with advanced Samples Retrieval (SR), which leverages LLMs to perform novel tasks by providing a few examples as part of the input, as seen in Meta-CoT [35] and CoT-Influx [36]. Tool-based methods entail integrating LLMs with external tools or programs that assist them in carrying out mathematical operations or reasoning. Examples of such methods include SymbLLM [37], PoT [38], and Codex-math [7]. Lastly, CoT methods enable LLMs to generate intermediate steps or sub-goals that lead to the final solution. This approach enhances their problem-solving and reasoning strategies [39].

In the context of this research, CoT, ICL, and Tool Employing (TE) methods present several advantages over fine-tuning and pre-training, making them a more suitable choice. Although fine-tuning has shown success in improving LLM performance on targeted mathematical tasks, it heavily relies on task-specific data and may suffer from catastrophic forgetting, where the model loses knowledge from previous tasks when trained on new ones [25, 40]. Pre-training methods, on the other hand, require extensive data and computational resources and may not fully capture the intricacies of specific mathematical problem-solving tasks [11]. In contrast, CoT, ICL, and TE exhibit appealing characteristics, such as requiring fewer resources, offering flexibility and adaptability across different tasks and domains, and providing enhanced interpretability and user control [41, 42].

3 Methodology

The proposed methodology involves a multi-step process designed to enhance the problem-solving and computational capabilities of the system. Initially, topic classification is employed to accurately identify the relevant subject of the math problem. Once the subject is determined, the system searches through a corpus of mathematical problems to find the most similar problem to the one provided by the user, enabling the extraction of an answer for in-context learning purposes. To enhance computational capacities, a customized code is generated through the utilization of a CoT prompt. The code is then executed using an external code interpreter that is accessed via an API, obtaining tangible results that can be compared against the desired outcome. Finally, given the context and the obtained outcome, the LLM is prompted once again to provide the final explanation (Fig. 1).

3.1 *Sample Problem Datasets*

To ensure the provision of the most suitable sample demonstrations for guiding the LLM, it is essential to begin by gathering a high-quality dataset. The focus is on gathering data on math questions and their corresponding answers from textbooks provided by Vietnamese Ministry of Education so as to increase reliability. Specifically, three distinct math question and answer datasets were collected corresponding to Grade 10, Grade 11, and Grade 12. Each dataset contains three fields: Topic,

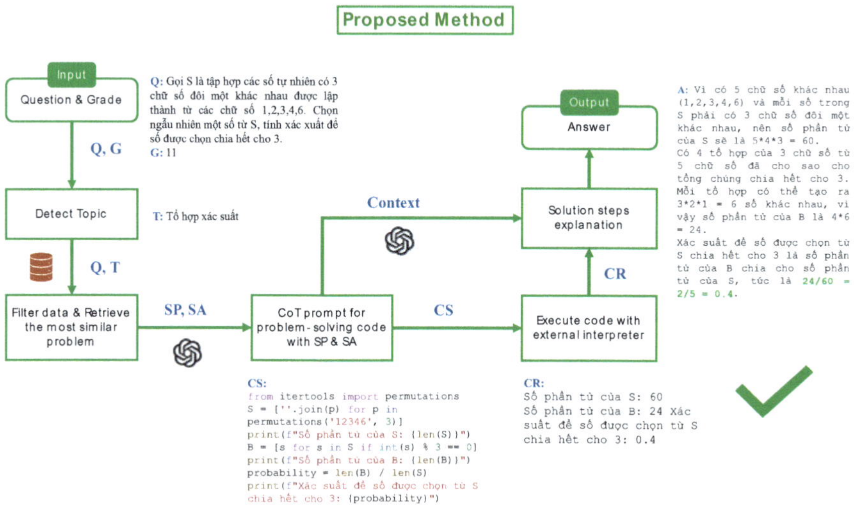

Fig. 1 The interference method to enhance the reasoning and computational capabilities of LLMs

Question, and Answer. The math questions can contain words, math expressions, and formulas in Latex or both.

Tokenizing and vectorizing text before training is necessary as it converts text into numerical form and extracts meaningful features, enabling machine learning models to process and learn from textual data effectively. In this research, the ViTokenizer library from pyvi, a Python library specifically designed for Vietnamese text processing, was utilized for tokenization. In terms of vectorization, the TF-IDF method was utilized to transform the tokenized text into numerical vectors, capturing the importance of each term within the text corpus.

3.2 Topic Classification and Similar Questions Retrieval

A range of machine learning algorithms, including the Linear Support Vector Classifier, Random Forest Classifier, Gradient Boosting Classifier, Multinomial Naive Bayes, K-Nearest Neighbors Classifier, and Multi-layer Perceptron Classifier, were trained and evaluated on the datasets to determine the most suitable approach for topic classification. The finding indicated that the random forest algorithm demonstrated strong suitability for effectively addressing the intricacies presented by Vietnamese mathematical problems and was chosen for the system.

Once the math problem type has been identified, the next step is to search within the questions belonging to that problem type and find the one that most closely matches the input question. To achieve this, cosine similarity was calculated between the question vectors.

3.3 Code Execution and CoT Prompting

The system enhances the computational process by retrieving the most similar question to the user input and incorporating it with the corresponding answer into a CoT prompt. This promotes in-context learning and enables the generation of precise Python code solutions. The code snippet is then executed within a secure Docker environment, facilitated by an Application Programming Interface (API). Docker ensures reliability and isolation, while the API captures the output and provides error messages if necessary. This integrated approach improves code execution, scalability, and error handling for an enhanced user experience. (Fig. 2).

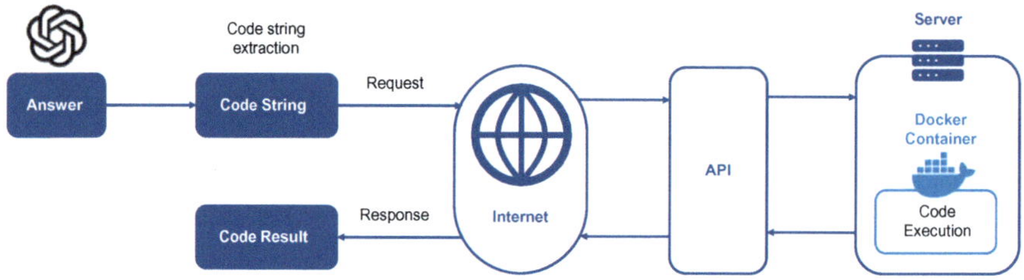

Fig. 2 Code Execution Process via API

4 Result and Discussion

To comprehensively assess the effectiveness and accuracy of the proposed method, three sets of Vietnamese final exam multiple-choice questions for grade 10, grade 11, and grade 12 were collected. Each set contained 50 questions covering a wide range of knowledge. Four scenarios were tested on GPT-4 and GPT-3.5-turbo: zero-shot, computation-focused, reasoning-focused, and combined approaches.

To assess the effectiveness of the proposed method, a designed experiment was conducted. Data was gathered from diverse online sources, consisting of three sets of randomly selected grade 10, 11, and 12 final exam multiple-choice questions. Each set contained 50 questions covering a comprehensive range of knowledge. Four scenarios were tested on two models GPT-4 and GPT-3.5-turbo: zero-shot, computation-focused, reasoning-focused, and combined approaches. In the zero-shot approach, the models processed and responded to questions using their default capabilities, without prior training or fine-tuning. The computation-focused approach relied solely on the code interpreter for accurate calculations. The reasoning-focused approach utilized topic classification and similar problem retrieval techniques to enhance reasoning capabilities. Meanwhile, the combined approach synergistically combined computational and reasoning methods to optimize both accuracy and reasoning quality.

Approaches were graded using a binary system by comparing their responses to a pre-established "ground truth." This objective evaluation method provided insights into the accuracy of the system in generating correct answers.

By adopting the combined approach, which integrated both computational and reasoning improvement methods, the models achieved the highest accuracy rates among all the approaches tested. GPT-3.5-turbo achieved accuracies of 60%, 62%, and 64% for grades 10, 11, and 12, respectively. GPT-4 demonstrated further improvement, with 80%, 88%, and 82% accuracies for the corresponding grades. This reveals that synergistically combining computation-focused and reasoning-focused methods resulted in the most accurate responses, with GPT-4 exhibiting superior performance compared to GPT-3.5-turbo when it comes to solving Vietnamese math problems (Table 1).

Table 1 Experiment Result Summary

	Model	GPT-3.5-turbo			GPT-4		
	Grade	10	11	12	10	11	12
Approach	Zero-shot	44%	52%	48%	52%	78%	64%
	Computation-focused	54%	58%	56%	74%	84%	76%
	Reasoning-focused	48%	54%	50%	66%	82%	68%
	Combined	**60%**	**62%**	**64%**	**80%**	**88%**	**82%**

5 System Implementation

To effectively showcase the outcomes of the proposed method and facilitate its practical implementation, a web application system was developed. The application utilized Flask, HTML, CSS, and JavaScript to create funcional system and intuitive user interface (Fig. 3).

Within the web application, users had the ability to enter their questions, choose grade levels, and selects models (GPT-4 or GPT-3.5-turbo). They could also set similarity thresholds to refine the answers. The application smoothly transitions between models and presented a side-by-side comparison of answers generated through the combined method and the zero-shot approach. In addition, the application provided users with supplementary details including predicted topics, closest matching questions, code snippets, and the outcomes of code execution. In cases of code execution

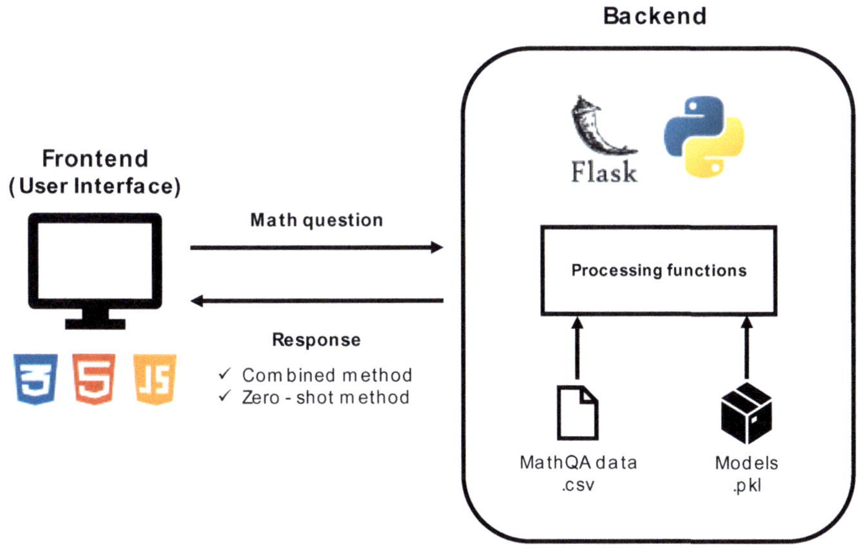

Fig. 3 The architecture of the math solver web app

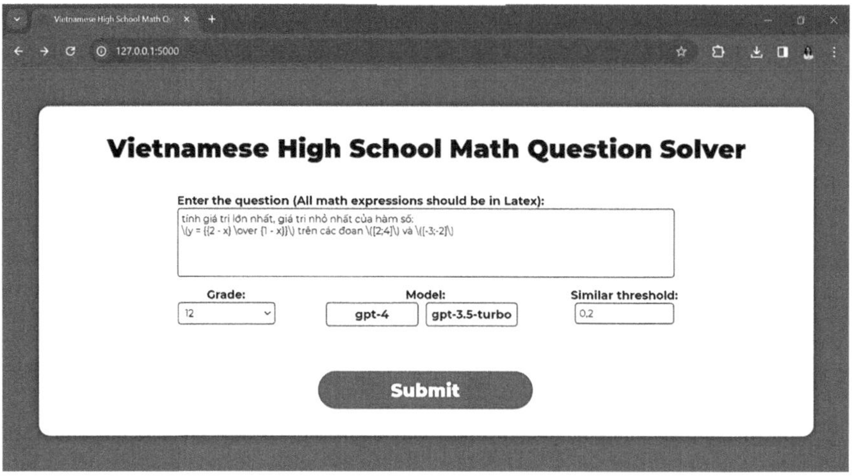

Fig. 4 The web app interface for question input

errors, the web application seamlessly switched to utilizing the GPT-4 model with the CoT prompt (Fig. 4).

6 Limitations and Future Directions

In the pursuit of enhancing Vietnamese highschool math problem-solving abilities for LLMs, it is important to recognize and navigate certain inherent limitations in this research.

Reasoning enhancement data: To improve reasoning abilities through question referencing, it is important to have high-quality questions and sample answers, accurate identification of problem types, and a comprehensive and diverse reference dataset covering various mathematical topics. The current reference corpus may not have a uniform distribution of topics, so efforts should be made to address this imbalance.

Evaluation data and method: The evaluation process consists of a small number of questions and relies on a binary grading system that only focuses on the final answer. To overcome these limitations, the pool of evaluation questions should be significantly expanded to cover a wider range of problem types and ensure a more balanced representation. Additionally, a more nuanced grading system that considers reasoning quality and intermediate steps should be developed.

Math problem retrieval: The tokenization, vectorization, and retrieval process for mathematical formulas face challenges. Existing techniques may not fully capture the unique characteristics and semantic relationships within mathematical formulas.

Advanced techniques such as hybrid tokenization and embedding methods designed for math formulas can be explored to overcome these limitations.

Deployment cost: The cost associated with proprietary models like GPT-4 can be a barrier to entry and hinder widespread adoption. Open-source LLMs like BERT or RoBERTa provide cost-effective alternatives and have robust communities supporting their development. However, thorough evaluation is necessary to ensure their performance meets the research requirements.

7 Conclusion

This comprehensive research proposes and implements a method to enhance the computational and reasoning capabilities of LLMs for solving Vietnamese high school math problems. The method combines techniques such as topic classification, problem retrieval, code generation, and code execution to improve the accuracy and effectiveness of LLM-based approaches. The evaluation on GPT-4 and GPT-3.5-turbo using diverse multiple-choice questions from Vietnamese high school exams demonstrates significant performance improvement compared to the baseline approach. Additionally, an intuitive web application system has been developed to provide direct access to this process. This research contributes to educational technology and has the potential to positively impact the learning experiences of students in Vietnam, though opportunities for optimization remain within the data collection, evaluation, and retrieval methods employed.

References

1. N. T. Son, T. T. Hoang, S. Mishra, N. T. B. Thuy, T. H. Tam, and C.-D. Truong, "Advancing Online Education: An Artificial Intelligence Applied System for Monitoring and Improving Employee Engagement in Enterprise Information Systems," in *Nature of Computation and Communication*, P. Cong Vinh and H. Mahfooz Ul Haque, Eds., Cham: Springer Nature Switzerland, 2024, pp. 3–18. https://doi.org/10.1007/978-3-031-59462-5_1.
2. H. Naveed *et al.*, "A Comprehensive Overview of Large Language Models," arXiv.org. Accessed: Jan. 02, 2024. [Online]. Available: https://arxiv.org/abs/2307.06435v7.
3. OpenAI *et al.*, "GPT-4 Technical Report," arXiv.org. Accessed: Jan. 03, 2024. [Online]. Available: https://arxiv.org/abs/2303.08774v4.
4. J. Ye *et al.*, "A Comprehensive Capability Analysis of GPT-3 and GPT-3.5 Series Models," arXiv.org. Accessed: Jan. 03, 2024. [Online]. Available: https://arxiv.org/abs/2303.10420v2.
5. J. Manyika and S. Hsiao, "An overview of Bard: an early experiment with generative AI".
6. H. Touvron *et al.*, "LLaMA: Open and Efficient Foundation Language Models," arXiv.org. Accessed: Jan. 03, 2024. [Online]. Available: https://arxiv.org/abs/2302.13971v1.
7. I. Drori *et al.*, "A Neural Network Solves, Explains, and Generates University Math Problems by Program Synthesis and Few-Shot Learning at Human Level," Proc. Natl. Acad. Sci. U.S.A., vol. 119, no. 32, p. e2123433119, Aug. 2022, https://doi.org/10.1073/pnas.2123433119.
8. M. Chen *et al.*, "Evaluating Large Language Models Trained on Code." arXiv, Jul. 14, 2021. https://doi.org/10.48550/arXiv.2107.03374.

9. D. Maltoni and M. Ferrara, *Arithmetic with Language Models: from Memorization to Computation*. 2023.
10. M. Muffo, A. Cocco, and E. Bertino, "Evaluating Transformer Language Models on Arithmetic Operations Using Number Decomposition." arXiv, Apr. 21, 2023. https://doi.org/10.48550/arXiv.2304.10977.
11. J. Qian, H. Wang, Z. Li, S. Li, and X. Yan, "Limitations of Language Models in Arithmetic and Symbolic Induction," in *Proceedings of the 61st Annual Meeting of the Association for Computational Linguistics (Volume 1: Long Papers)*, A. Rogers, J. Boyd-Graber, and N. Okazaki, Eds., Toronto, Canada: Association for Computational Linguistics, Jul. 2023, pp. 9285–9298. https://doi.org/10.18653/v1/2023.acl-long.516.
12. K. Niyarepola, D. Athapaththu, S. Ekanayake, and S. Ranathunga, "Math Word Problem Generation with Multilingual Language Models," in *Proceedings of the 15th International Conference on Natural Language Generation*, S. Shaikh, T. Ferreira, and A. Stent, Eds., Waterville, Maine, USA and virtual meeting: Association for Computational Linguistics, Jul. 2022, pp. 144–155. https://doi.org/10.18653/v1/2022.inlg-main.12.
13. "Survey on Mathematical Word Problem Solving Using Natural Language Processing | IEEE Conference Publication | IEEE Xplore." Accessed: Jan. 03, 2024. [Online]. Available: https://ieeexplore.ieee.org/abstract/document/8741437.
14. M. Tan, L. Wang, L. Jiang, and J. Jiang, "Investigating Math Word Problems using Pretrained Multilingual Language Models." arXiv, Nov. 13, 2022. https://doi.org/10.48550/arXiv.2105.08928.
15. D. Saxton, E. Grefenstette, F. Hill, and P. Kohli, "Analysing Mathematical Reasoning Abilities of Neural Models." arXiv, Apr. 02, 2019. https://doi.org/10.48550/arXiv.1904.01557.
16. A. Bhattacharya, "A Survey of Question Answering for Math and Science Problem." arXiv, May 10, 2017. https://doi.org/10.48550/arXiv.1705.04530.
17. M. Johansson, "What Can Large Language Models Do for Theorem Proving and Formal Methods?," 2023, pp. 391–394. https://doi.org/10.1007/978-3-031-46002-9_25.
18. S. Zhang, T. Ringer, and E. First, *Getting More out of Large Language Models for Proofs*. 2023.
19. S. Bubeck *et al.*, "Sparks of Artificial General Intelligence: Early experiments with GPT-4." arXiv, Apr. 13, 2023. https://doi.org/10.48550/arXiv.2303.12712.
20. Z. Yuan, H. Yuan, C. Tan, W. Wang, and S. Huang, "How well do Large Language Models perform in Arithmetic tasks?," arXiv.org. Accessed: Jan. 02, 2024. [Online]. Available: https://arxiv.org/abs/2304.02015v1
21. T. Wei, J. Luan, W. Liu, S. Dong, and B. Wang, "CMATH: Can Your Language Model Pass Chinese Elementary School Math Test?" arXiv, Jun. 28, 2023. https://doi.org/10.48550/arXiv.2306.16636.
22. R. Anil *et al.*, "PaLM 2 Technical Report." arXiv, Sep. 13, 2023. https://doi.org/10.48550/arXiv.2305.10403.
23. J. López Espejel, E. H. Ettifouri, M. S. Yahaya Alassan, E. M. Chouham, and W. Dahhane, "GPT-3.5, GPT-4, or BARD? Evaluating LLMs reasoning ability in zero-shot setting and performance boosting through prompts," *Natural Language Processing Journal*, vol. 5, p. 100032, Dec. 2023, https://doi.org/10.1016/j.nlp.2023.100032.
24. D. Nunes, R. Primi, R. Pires, R. Lotufo, and R. Nogueira, "Evaluating GPT-3.5 and GPT-4 Models on Brazilian University Admission Exams." arXiv, Mar. 29, 2023. https://doi.org/10.48550/arXiv.2303.17003.
25. Y. Luo, Z. Yang, F. Meng, Y. Li, J. Zhou, and Y. Zhang, "An Empirical Study of Catastrophic Forgetting in Large Language Models During Continual Fine-tuning." arXiv, Aug. 21, 2023. https://doi.org/10.48550/arXiv.2308.08747.
26. H. Huang *et al.*, "Not All Languages Are Created Equal in LLMs: Improving Multilingual Capability by Cross-Lingual-Thought Prompting." arXiv, May 11, 2023. Accessed: Jan. 05, 2024. [Online]. Available: http://arxiv.org/abs/2305.07004.
27. S. Peng, K. Yuan, L. Gao, and Z. Tang, "MathBERT: A Pre-Trained Model for Mathematical Formula Understanding," arXiv.org. Accessed: Jan. 04, 2024. [Online]. Available: https://arxiv.org/abs/2105.00377v1.

28. Z. Yang *et al.*, "GPT Can Solve Mathematical Problems Without a Calculator," arXiv.org. Accessed: Jan. 04, 2024. [Online]. Available: https://arxiv.org/abs/2309.03241v2.
29. Z. Azerbayev *et al.*, "Llemma: An Open Language Model For Mathematics," arXiv.org. Accessed: Jan. 04, 2024. [Online]. Available: https://arxiv.org/abs/2310.10631v2.
30. L. Yu *et al.*, "MetaMath: Bootstrap Your Own Mathematical Questions for Large Language Models," arXiv.org. Accessed: Jan. 04, 2024. [Online]. Available: https://arxiv.org/abs/2309.12284v3.
31. T. Liu and B. K. H. Low, "Goat: Fine-tuned LLaMA Outperforms GPT-4 on Arithmetic Tasks." arXiv, May 23, 2023. Accessed: Jan. 04, 2024. [Online]. Available: http://arxiv.org/abs/2305.14201.
32. M. Geva, A. Gupta, and J. Berant, "Injecting Numerical Reasoning Skills into Language Models," in *Proceedings of the 58th Annual Meeting of the Association for Computational Linguistics*, Online: Association for Computational Linguistics, 2020, pp. 946–958. https://doi.org/10.18653/v1/2020.acl-main.89.
33. S. Imani, L. Du, and H. Shrivastava, "MathPrompter: Mathematical Reasoning using Large Language Models," in *Proceedings of the 61st Annual Meeting of the Association for Computational Linguistics (Volume 5: Industry Track)*, S. Sitaram, B. Beigman Klebanov, and J. D. Williams, Eds., Toronto, Canada: Association for Computational Linguistics, Jul. 2023, pp. 37–42. https://doi.org/10.18653/v1/2023.acl-industry.4.
34. H. Luo *et al.*, "WizardMath: Empowering Mathematical Reasoning for Large Language Models via Reinforced Evol-Instruct," arXiv.org. Accessed: Jan. 04, 2024. [Online]. Available: https://arxiv.org/abs/2308.09583v1.
35. A. Zou, Z. Zhang, H. Zhao, and X. Tang, "Meta-CoT: Generalizable Chain-of-Thought Prompting in Mixed-task Scenarios with Large Language Models." arXiv, Oct. 11, 2023. https://doi.org/10.48550/arXiv.2310.06692.
36. X. Huang, L. L. Zhang, K.-T. Cheng, and M. Yang, "Boosting LLM Reasoning: Push the Limits of Few-shot Learning with Reinforced In-Context Pruning." arXiv, Dec. 26, 2023. https://doi.org/10.48550/arXiv.2312.08901.
37. J. He-Yueya, G. Poesia, R. E. Wang, and N. D. Goodman, "Solving Math Word Problems by Combining Language Models With Symbolic Solvers." arXiv, Apr. 16, 2023. https://doi.org/10.48550/arXiv.2304.09102.
38. W. Chen, X. Ma, X. Wang, and W. W. Cohen, "Program of Thoughts Prompting: Disentangling Computation from Reasoning for Numerical Reasoning Tasks," arXiv.org. Accessed: Jan. 04, 2024. [Online]. Available: https://arxiv.org/abs/2211.12588v4.
39. J. Wei *et al.*, "Chain-of-Thought Prompting Elicits Reasoning in Large Language Models," arXiv.org. Accessed: Jan. 04, 2024. [Online]. Available: https://arxiv.org/abs/2201.11903v6.
40. M. Mosbach, T. Pimentel, S. Ravfogel, D. Klakow, and Y. Elazar, "Few-shot Fine-tuning vs. In-context Learning: A Fair Comparison and Evaluation." arXiv, May 30, 2023. https://doi.org/10.48550/arXiv.2305.16938.
41. Q. Dong *et al.*, "A Survey on In-context Learning." arXiv, Jun. 01, 2023. https://doi.org/10.48550/arXiv.2301.00234.
42. T. Schick *et al.*, "Toolformer: Language Models Can Teach Themselves to Use Tools." arXiv, Feb. 09, 2023. https://doi.org/10.48550/arXiv.2302.04761.

Machine Learning Models and Artificial Intelligence in Financial Market Forecasting and Decision Making

A Qualitative Study of the Influence of Artificial Intelligence on Individual Investors in Asian Stock Markets

Ratnakumar Pullagura and Seetharaman Arumugam

Abstract This study assesses how artificial intelligence (AI) affects the behavior of individual investors in Asian stock markets. It aims to provide a research-based understanding of how AI affects investors and stock markets operating in an Asian context. The growing integration of AI in financial markets has impacted the approaches that investors take towards stock price prediction and market-related decision-making, creating a broad range of speculative processes. Based on a literature review, this paper identifies the main trends, benefits, and challenges presented using AI in financial markets. It discusses how AI improves the predictability of market processes and how it boosts investors' trust and confidence, thereby influencing the potential for economic growth. This paper also outlines the main limitations of current research and concludes that a study of the integration of AI technologies and human expertise in this area requires a more comprehensive sector-specific approach.

Keywords Artificial Intelligence (AI) · Stock market dynamics · Behavioral finance · Investor behavior · Market indicators

1 Introduction

Over the last few years, artificial intelligence (AI) technologies have seen rapid advancement, leading to dramatic changes in the financial markets. AI processes big data at scale, and in today's modern data-driven society, it serves as the epitome of efficiency for many financial activities, including stock predictions. AI can improve market efficiency, reduce information asymmetry, and help investors to invest more analytically in Asian stock markets. Despite these benefits, adopting AI technologies

R. Pullagura (✉)
SP Jain School of Global Management, Sydney, Australia
e-mail: ratnakumar.dj24dba004@spjain.org

S. Arumugam
SP Jain School of Global Management, Singapore, Singapore
e-mail: seetha.raman@spjain.org

E. Tsui et al. (eds.), *Management Information Systems in a Digitalized AI World*, Springer Proceedings in Business and Economics,
https://doi.org/10.1007/978-981-96-6526-6_8

in financial markets presents challenges; for example, the complexity of the models developed using AI approaches leads to variability issues related to data quality, while investors' behavioral biases can impact their decision-making.

This paper explores the impact of AI on individual investors in Asian stock markets. Stock price prediction, investment strategies and markets are major in context of the research topic. To better understand the role of AI in investor decisions and market development, we synthesize findings from several research works for this study. Additional, potential limitations have been identified and future work should address extant gaps by identifying emerging challenges in shedding more light on the ethical implications of AI utilization. These findings echo the growing requirement of synergy between AI capabilities and human expertise to create more transparent markets with integrity and enhance investment strategies.

2 Objectives

1. To assess the efficiency of AI-based stock price predictions and their impact on investment decision- making.
2. To investigate the impact of AI on market efficiency and investor behaviour in Asian stock markets.
3. To draw attention to gaps and weaknesses in current research on AI for financial markets.

3 Literature Review

3.1 AI and Stock Price Predictions

An Analysis of Using AI for Stock Price Predictions Various studies have used methods such as neural networks [1], genetic algorithms and machine learning to predict stock prices. Thanks to artificial intelligence, transactions are better predicted, and investors can proceed with more reliable information. In fact, use-cases of AI predicting stock prices have been very successful so far—particularly to exploit non-linear trends and market anomalies that could otherwise remain uncovered from the human eye or traditional statistical methods [2]. Nevertheless, they face data quality variability and high model complexity.

Thanks to AI, it can effectively process massive volumes of data in real-time or close to being real-time which is a huge advantage for the prediction of stock prices. In a fast-paced environment like stock trading, this means that real-time data processing is vastly improved. From the data available, AI algorithms can calculate (among other things) historical price data [3], trading volumes, economic indicators, and even sentiment indicators (which come from news stories or social media opinions).

Table 1 Thematic summary of literature on AI's impact in Asian stock markets

Study Focus	Key themes	Insights	Implications
AI and Stock Predictions	Predictive Accuracy	AI improves stock predictions by analyzing large datasets	Enhanced investment strategies
AI and Market Efficiency	Market Transparency	AI reduces information asymmetry and improves valuation	Increased market stability
Behavioral Insights	Investor Behavior	AI influences investor behavior by providing data-driven recommendations	Reduced impact of behavioral biases

The ability to combine and employ such varied data allows AI models to improve their predictive measures (Table 1).

3.2 *Market Efficiency and Investor Behavior*

AI-driven models offer greater market efficiency in two ways: they reduce information asymmetry and allow better stock market valuations. These improvements lead to healthier investment decisions and fewer dramatic fluctuations in the market. AI and other technologies can be used to identify arbitrage opportunities; because they can do so faster than human traders, this ability helps to maintain market efficiency [4]. However, as behavioral biases such as overconfidence and herding behaviors continue to affect investor decisions, a hybrid approach that combines AI capabilities with human psychology is required.

A concept related to fundamental analysis is the efficient market hypothesis (EMH); according to this theory, stock prices are based on dividend yield. However, the EMH can be called into question by market anomalies to which AI can bring solutions. As noted above, AI models can easily adapt to changing information in stock prices and can do so much faster than a human trader could. In addition, the use of AI lessens the need for expert individual judgement and eliminates (or at least mitigates) behavioral biases by providing data-backed insights that can help curtail emotive or irrational decision-making [5]. Old theory of Efficient market hypothesis is slowly embracing Artificial Intelligence in order to identify efficiency in weak form, semi-strong form and strong form.

Efficient-market hypothesis (EMH) is a theory on investment which states share prices fully reflect all available information hence making so no one can achieve returns above the average market by using stock selection or time to deal. EMH perversely reasoned away any abnormal profits from financial and arbitrage opportunities, as prices quickly converged towards aggregate market information—which promised that dynamic strategies would fare poorly versus static approaches.

However, more recent literature has questioned the universality of EMH by documenting anomalies and inefficiencies that are hard for AI models to resist. For instance, research has indicated that AI may boost predictive accuracy and diminish information asymmetry while revealing select market inefficiencies invisible to more conventional frameworks. This has led to a growing recognition of the need to integrate AI capabilities with human expertise to address behavioral biases and adapt to evolving market conditions [6], suggesting a nuanced approach where AI complements rather than replaces traditional market theories.

3.3 A Comparative Analysis of AI and Human Decision-Making

Comparative studies have shown that AI can outperform human investors, especially in highly volatile market conditions. The results of these studies have suggested that AI-driven funds outperform human-managed ones even when considering relevant risk management factors. For example, if a market suddenly enters an extreme bear phase with high volatility, AI algorithms can adjust to the change in conditions in seconds and modify trading portfolios instantaneously [7]. However, both human and AI methods have their flaws; thus, the best advantages come from combining an AI approach with human expertise [8].

One of AI's strengths is its ability to act without emotion. Human investors can be led by fear or bullish behavior, or they can be swayed by fear and greed. AI algorithms work solely on the data they are provided with, following a tried- and-tested set of rules and thus making consistent and rational investment decisions [9]. However, an in-depth understanding of sometimes intricate market conditions and the ability to plan for future events are requirements that go above and beyond AI's algorithmic capabilities and thus necessitate human expertise (Table 2).

Table 2 Qualitative analysis of AI and investor behavior

Aspect	AI influence	Human factors	Combined impact
Decision Making	Data-driven recommendations enhace decision-making	Behavioral biases can still affect decisions	A hybrid approach is optimal for balanced decision making
Trust and Confidence	AI can increase trust through data transparency	Over-reliance on AI might reduce critical thinking	Combining AI with human expertise can bolster confidence

4 Methodology

The work in this paper is based on a qualitative evaluation of over 30 studies on the use of AI in stock market predictions. The paper synthesizes common themes and gaps in this area through an analysis of the authors' methodologies, results, and conclusions. The selection of studies in this paper was slightly biased as the studies all relate to the use of AI in financial markets with a primary focus on Asian stock markets (Fig. 1).

4.1 Data Collection and Analysis

This paper has considered a range of studies, including academic articles, industry research reports, and conference publications. The main variables studied here are the predictive accuracy of stock prices, market efficiency, and investor behavior [10].

4.2 Research Questions

1. How well do AI models predict stock prices in the most liquid and largest stock exchanges between companies?
2. Does AI affect market efficiency and investor behavior in financial markets?
3. Which type of study does research into the applications of AI in financial markets lack?

5 Findings and Discussion

5.1 Effectiveness of AI in Stock Price Predictions

Increasingly, studies have illustrated that AI technologies are able to predict stock prices that demonstrate non-linear relationships in their metrics and that are anomalies in the financial markets. A neural network can effectively model complex patterns in stock price movements, for example, that a traditional linear model might not capture [11]. Ultimately, however, a neural network will still depend on the quality of the input data selected, while structured parameterization could affect the accuracy of its predictions. A model may make an incorrect prediction either due to poor data quality or inappropriate parameters and, as a result, cause huge financial loss [12].

Even with this limitation, AI models have been outperforming traditional statistical methods. For example, genetic algorithms are used to evolve asset allocations in investment portfolios; these algorithms choose the best combination of assets by

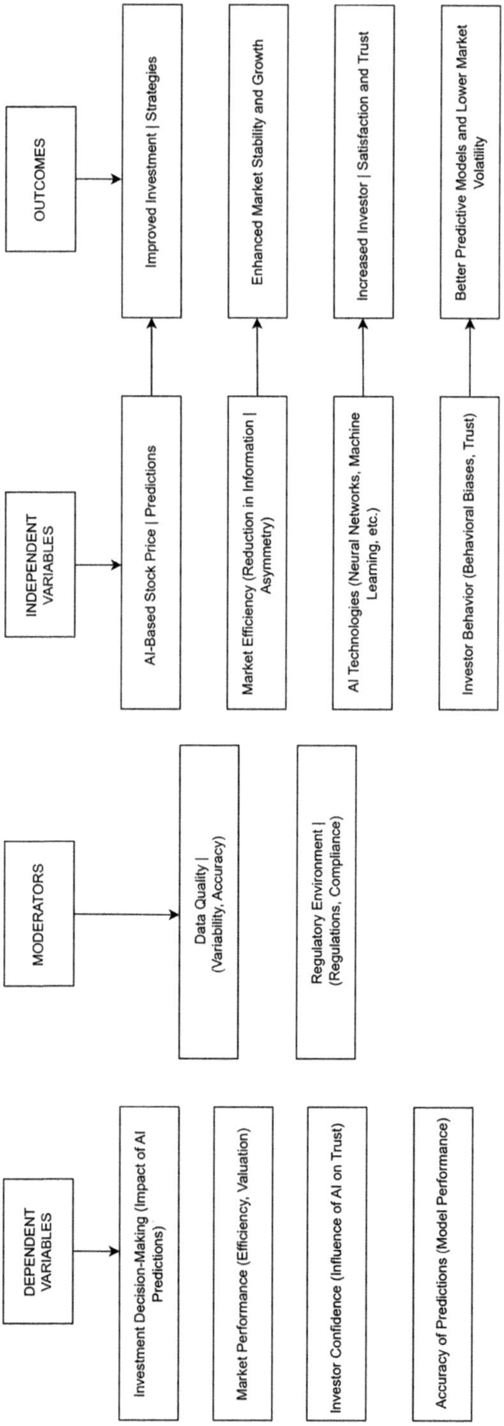

Fig. 1 Conceptual Framework of AI Impact on Asian Stock Markets

observing how the assets have behaved in historical data and extrapolating that information into future returns [13]. This is like the accuracy of machine learning models (namely support vector machines and random forests) which have shown promising results in terms of achieving higher stock price prediction accuracy compared to that possible with traditional methods.

5.2 *Impact on Market Efficiency and Investor Behavior*

AI models also make the market more efficient as they provide greater transparency and reduce information gaps, leading to more accurate stock prices and more logical investment decisions. Confidence in financial markets can be increased using AI to spot fraudulent activities and market manipulation [14]. However, the fact that behavioral biases persist at all suggests that AI is not a magical solution to irrational market behavior. This type of market inefficiency requires a marriage between AI technology and human insight into human behavior to correct issues in the market.

Similarly, AI can affect investor behavior by offering data- driven insights and suggestions. AI trading platforms can even provide personalized investment advice according to a person's risk tolerance and end goals [15]. This approach helps investors to make better decisions, reducing the effect of illusional or cognitive biases. However, a blind belief in AI-driven recommendations also raises concerns about over- reliance on AI and the potential for herding behavior should investors follow AI-generated advice without critically evaluating it.

5.3 *AI and Human Decision-Making: A Comparison of Their Performance*

AI-powered investment strategies have consistently proven that they can outperform their human-powered equivalents, especially in terms of their ability to mitigate risks and create a route through market turbulence [16]. Not only can AI algorithms find and exploit market inefficiencies far more quickly than humans, but they can also generate higher returns. Further improvements can be seen in AI's ability to manage investment portfolios by keeping track of market conditions on a continuous basis and choosing optimal asset allocations in real time.

However, a focus on AI models brings inherent dangers in the form of algorithmic errors and market manipulation. Thus, humans can complement AI's abilities and vice versa; there should be harmony between the two [17]. The addition of human expertise will enable the rapid evaluation of complex market conditions and the identification of strategic decisions; such expertise will work well with AI's data-based insights and suggestions [18].

6 Ethical and Regulatory Concerns

As AI technologies continue to develop and their use cases multiply, ethical questions around the application of artificial intelligence (AI) strategies in financial markets are gaining more attention [19]. The literature also suggests that AI systems are often "black boxes" and, as a result, provide no direct insight into the basis on which decisions have been made; this opacity also makes them difficult to audit (again undermining accountability) while increasing concerns associated with trust. On top of that, AI trading being fast and fully automated can amplify market volatility significantly similar to how books stare us dead in the eye just waiting for a mention about dystopian futures [20]. And someone out there will always find a way (e.g. front-running or collusion) to twist things around per their nefarious wants with this technology-shaped novel toy of discovery! The increased application of AI has made it difficult for regulatory frameworks to keep pace, and this dip in the pool is already sparking calls for meaningful regulations that enable a fair use of technology using transparency. Researchers argue for the implementation of robust guidelines and standards to enhance the interpretability of AI models, safeguard investor interests, and prevent misuse. Additionally, there is a push for integrating ethical considerations into AI development to address potential biases and ensure that AI systems operate within ethical boundaries while protecting market integrity [21].

Researchers have argued that current regulations on the use of AI in stock markets are not strong enough to prevent the kind of ethical challenges highlighted in this study from happening. Transparent, fair, and secure data handling are important to the sustainable acceptance of AI technologies in this area.

7 Limitations and Future Research

While these findings are promising, the current research is not without limitations. The first is around the variability in data quality and availability across different markets (e.g. Asian) which can make it hard to translate AI models developed somewhere else for use here. Second, investor confidence could suffer due to the proprietary nature and complexity of AI algorithms which tend not to explain their decision making well. Finally, merging AI with conventional investment methods recognizes the existing regulatory institutions would be more disruptive and require significant adaptation.

It is important to recognize these limitations when researching in this area. According to Siddhartha Gupta of Mercer Saar [22], this can be particularly challenging for AI models due to the unclear data quality and variability across different Asian markets. Additionally, the complexity of AI algorithms and how they work as black-box decision-making machines make a further few-shots. Addressing these issues is crucial for ensuring the effective and ethical integration of AI technologies in financial markets.

Areas for future research

1. Establish data standards to use the same input variables in a consistent manner across different markets.
2. Providing higher transparency and interpretability for AI models to gain trust from potential investors, and regulatory monitoring.
3. Discovering cornerstone models that integrate AI and human contribution are stronger together, Cross-validation for better investments.
4. Tackling ethical issues in AI on Financial Markets from different angles, Market manipulation is tackled using blockchain properties and data privacy it mitigated by not sending raw contract state to the determiner.

8 Contributions

8.1 Contributions to Theory

Several theoretical areas like behavioral finance or market efficiency have seen significant advances thanks to the integration of artificial intelligence (AI) into financial markets. Theoretical implications are that improved models can be developed which exploit AI's potential to analyse large data sets and identify patterns at scales beyond those perceptible by humans [23]. AI has, for instance, questioned the previously established viewpoints around market efficiency and acted as a technological disruptor by showing that real-time data processing can be utilised to unveil these market anomalies or inefficiencies. In recent years, newer theoretical frameworks combining AI's predictive ability and insights into human behavior provide direction on how AI affects investor behaviors and decision-making processes. For technology, this has resulted in increased appreciation for the role it plays on market dynamics, investor psychology and ultimately how much one can trust our financial predictions [24].

8.2 Contributions to Practice

In practical terms, AI has changed the landscape of investment strategies and market operations by significantly improving predictive power and efficacy. AI-based tools have been picking up in financial industry and with the same purpose i.e. improved decision-making, portfolio management and risk assessment has changed significantly for individual investors this time [25]. In the real world, this resulted in more advanced trading algorithms, personalised financial advice and a higher detection rate for market anomalies or fraud. Additionally, the implementation of AI has inspired and improved regulatory technology (RegTech), assisting with compliance monitoring and fraud detection [26]. Beyond the immediate benefits of an efficiency gain, this real-world example illustrates a valuable competitive advantage in fast-moving financial markets and highlights practical uses of integrating advanced technologies into investment and regulatory applications.

9 Conclusion

Using artificial intelligence in the investment of Asian stock markets would improve predictive power, capital allocation and risk management for decision-making greatly. The use of machine learning in financial markets has made a huge impact on finance, leading to improved stock price forecasts and better trading practices that aim at lower information asymmetry. But even when deploying highly sophisticated AI models, there remain considerable hurdles in extracting value from them, dealing with the noise of datasets and correcting behavioral biases.

A balanced article that focuses on operational productivity and efficiency in the realm of these new promised benefits, rather than terrifying everyone into how AI is going to erase humanity or take over traditional practices. The focus areas of the discussion, however, should be on a) mitigating shortcomings in current research b) regarding issues dealing with data quality c) model interpretability and d) behavioral biases.

Future studies should emphasise the development of guidelines for handling data and enhancing the transparency of AI models. They should also integrate insights from behavioural research to mitigate residual predictions through nudges or policy interventions. In addition, future studies should develop co-methodologies at each step of the processing phases from capturing factsheets to address any ethical and regulatory concerns.

AI has the potential to advance the improvements it has already made to financial decision making and thereby increase market efficiency in Asian stock markets. Further studies and approaches that ensure AI systems are trained to recognize their limitations would make it possible for regulatory authorities or financial institutions to create an appropriate level of transparency within their respective market environments, leaving aside fairness in the financial markets. This holistic mindset will not only benefit retail investors, it will also provide the necessary support and infrastructure to ensure that these markets maintain and improve their stability.

References

1. S. Bahoo, M. Cucculelli, X. Goga, and J. Mondolo, "Artificial intelligence in Finance: a comprehensive review through bibliometric and content analysis," SN Business & Economics, vol. 4, no. 2, Jan. 2024, https://doi.org/10.1007/s43546-023-00618-x.
2. O.-H. Cho, "Analysis of the Impact of Artificial Intelligence Applications on the Development of Accounting Industry," 2024.

3. E. Ghmari, Omar E. Ghmari, Imad T. Sabah, and H. Mohamed, "Análisis de la relación entre el comportamiento financiero y los rendimientos a corto y largo plazo entre los inversores marroquíes: Un enfoque de finanzas conductuales," Ciencia y Tecnología-Serie de Conferencias, vol. 3, p. 1016, 2019, https://doi.org/10.56294/sctconf20241016.
4. R. Chopra and G. Deep Sharma, "Risk and Financial Management Application of Artificial Intelligence in Stock Market Forecasting: A Critique Review and Research Agenda," 2021, https://doi.org/10.3390/jrfm.
5. A. Putri and A. Tanno, "Exploring Market Dynamics: A Qualitative Study on Asset Price Behavior, Market Efficiency, and Information Role in Investment Decisions in the Capital Market," Atestasi: Jurnal Ilmiah Akuntansi, vol. 7, no. 2, pp. 810–827, Jun. 2024, https://doi.org/10.57178/atestasi.v7i2.884.
6. A. Gedikli, G. D. Sharma, S. Erdoğan, and S. Hammoudeh, "Artificial intelligence disruption of financial markets and natural resources economy in the digital era," Resources Policy, vol. 92. Elsevier Ltd, May 01, 2024. https://doi.org/10.1016/j.resourpol.2024.104953.
7. H. A. Abdou, A. A. Elamer, M. Z. Abedin, and B. A. Ibrahim, "The impact of oil and global markets on Saudi stock market predictability: A machine learning approach," Energy Economics, vol. 132, Apr. 2024, https://doi.org/10.1016/j.eneco.2024.107416.
8. S. Nahar, "Modeling the effects of artificial intelligence (AI)-based innovation on sustainable development goals (SDGs): Applying a system dynamics perspective in a cross-country setting," Technological Forecasting and Social Change, vol. 201, Apr. 2024, https://doi.org/10.1016/j.techfore.2023.123203.
9. S. Ahmed, M. M. Alshater, A. El Ammari, and H. Hammami, "Artificial intelligence and machine learning in finance: A bibliometric review," Research in International Business and Finance, vol. 61, Oct. 2022, https://doi.org/10.1016/j.ribaf.2022.101646.
10. E. Kim, M. Kim, and Y. Kyung, "A Case Study of Digital Transformation: Focusing on the Financial Sector in South Korea and Overseas," Asia Pacific Journal of Information Systems, vol. 32, no. 3, pp. 537–563, 2022, https://doi.org/10.14329/APJIS.2022.32.3.537.
11. S. Deng, Y. Zhu, Y. Yu, and X. Huang, "An integrated approach of ensemble learning methods for stock index prediction using investor sentiments," Expert Systems with Applications, vol. 238, Mar. 2024, https://doi.org/10.1016/j.eswa.2023.121710.
12. S. Dawadi, S. Shrestha, and R. A. Giri, "Mixed-Methods Research: A Discussion on its Types, Challenges and Criticisms," Journal of Practical Studies in Education, vol. 2, no. 2, pp. 25–36, Feb. 2021, https://doi.org/10.46809/jpse.v2i2.20.
13. A. Bryman, Social research methods.
14. A. Banerjee and A. Banerjee, "Algorithmic Traders and Volatility Information Trading," 2020.
15. M. Damini and G. Gupta, "Social Media) of Product and Brand Management."
16. S.andCommunicationNetworks,"Retracted:TrendPredictionModel of Asian Stock Market Volatility Dynamic Relationship Based on Machine Learning," Security and Communication Networks, vol. 2024, pp. 1–1, Jan. 2024, https://doi.org/10.1155/2024/9846791.
17. C. Che, Z. Huang, C. Li, H. Zheng, and X. Tian, "Integrating Generative AI into Financial Market Prediction for Improved Decision Making."
18. 19. V.ShunmugasundaramandA.Sinha,"Theimpactofbehavioralbiases on investment decisions: a serial mediation analysis," Journal of Economics, Finance and Administrative Science, 2024, https://doi.org/10.1108/JEFAS-08-2023-0243.
19. N. S. Uzougbo, C. G. Ikegwu, and A. O. Adewusi, "Legal accountability and ethical considerations of AI in Financial Services," GSC Advanced Research and Reviews, https://doi.org/10.30574/gscarr.2024.19.2.0171 (accessed Sep. 7, 2024).
20. Z. Tóth and M. Blut, "Ethical compass: The need for Corporate Digital Responsibility in the use of Artificial Intelligence in financial services," *Organizational Dynamics*, vol. 53, no. 2, Apr. 2024, https://doi.org/10.1016/j.orgdyn.2024.101041.
21. 22. N. L. Rane, S. P. Choudhary, and J. Rane, "Artificial Intelligence-driven corporate finance: enhancing efficiency and decision-making through machine learning, natural language processing, and robotic process automation in corporate governance and sustainability," *Studies in Economics and Business Relations*, vol.5, no.2, pp.1–22, Jun.2024, https://doi.org/10.48185/sebr.v5i2.1050.

22. K. Gupta et al., "International Journal of INTELLIGENT SYSTEMS AND APPLICATIONS IN ENGINEERING Harnessing AI for Strategic Decision-Making and Business Performance Optimization." [Online]. Available: www.ijisae.org.
23. X. Zhan, Z. Ling, Z. Xu, L. Guo, and S. Zhuang, "Driving Efficiency and Risk Management in Finance through AI and RPA," 2024, https://doi.org/10.20944/preprints202407.0083.v1.
24. V. M. Sangala, S. Alamanda, and P. Tirumalareddy, "Smart Finance: Utilizing AI to Predict Stock Prices from News and Market Data," 2024.
25. Wisdom Samuel Udo, Nneka Adaobi Ochuba, Olatunji Akinrinola, and Yinka James Ololade, "Theoretical approaches to data analytics and decision-making in finance: Insights from Africa and the United States," *GSC Advanced Research and Reviews*, vol. 18, no. 3, pp. 343–349, Mar. 2024, https://doi.org/10.30574/gscarr.2024.18.3.0114.
26. Nneka Adaobi Ochuba, Adetumi Adewumi, and David Olanrewaju Olutimehin, "THE ROLE OF AI IN FINANCIAL MARKET DEVELOPMENT: ENHANCING EFFICIENCY AND ACCESSIBILITY IN EMERGING ECONOMIES," *Finance & Accounting Research Journal*, vol. 6, no. 3, pp. 421–436, Mar. 2024, https://doi.org/10.51594/farj.v6i3.969.

Financial Crisis Prediction: A Comprehensive Analysis Using Econometrics and Machine Learning

Ziqian Peng, Mengxi Liu, Jianjie Li, and Rongxin Zhang

Abstract Financial crises have become more frequent in recent years, such as the Great Depression of 1930 and the global financial crisis of 2008–2009. Predicting financial crises is particularly important, so this paper focuses on using econometric models and machine learning to predict the possibility of financial crises. Existing prediction models are limited in variable selection, so this paper uses a wider range of economic indicators. In terms of research methods, this paper preprocessed the data and used techniques such as time series analysis, lagged variable regression, logistic regression, and multicollinearity testing to identify and verify critical variables. The results show that credit, loan growth rate, and loan-to-credit ratio significantly affect the occurrence of financial crises, while real GDP growth can reduce systemic risks. First, this study provides policymakers with a more refined perspective on formulating policies and provides a scientific basis for macroeconomic policy formulation and risk prevention. Second, this study also improves the original model, which helps predict financial crises more accurately.

Keywords Great depression · Financial crisis · Credit boom · Economic growth · Growth rate of bank loans

---

All authors contributed equally to this work and should be considered co-first authors.

Z. Peng (✉)
College of Management,
Nanjing University of Posts and Telecommunications, Nanjing 210003, China
e-mail: Pzi2002@outlook.com

M. Liu
Antai College of Economics & Management,
Shanghai Jiao Tong University, Shanghai 200240, China

J. Li
Mathematics with Statistics, University of Bristol, Bristol, UK

R. Zhang
NYU Arts & Science, New York University, New York, NY, USA

E. Tsui et al. (eds.), *Management Information Systems in a Digitalized AI World*,
Springer Proceedings in Business and Economics,
https://doi.org/10.1007/978-981-96-6526-6_9

1 Introduction

Predicting financial crises is a serious challenge for economists and policymakers, especially given the severe economic and social disruption that such crises can cause. Historical financial crises, such as the Great Depression of 1930 and the Global Financial Crisis of 2008–2009, highlight the importance of developing reliable models that can predict these events and intervene in a timely manner. As the author claimed, the banking panic in the fall of 2008 threw economies around the world into severe recession [1]. The frequency of the Great Depression and financial crises has led to a renewed focus on models for predicting financial crises. However, significant challenges remain, especially in determining the most reliable predictor variables. Researchers have made substantial progress in understanding the factors contributing to financial crises in recent years. Research has identified several economic indicators, such as credit growth rate and leverage rate, as potential predictors of financial instability. As the author proposed, While the importance and significance of the credit growth remains unaffected, this paper's long-run sample data suggest that the risk of financial crises grows with a higher credit-to-GDP level [2]. The motivation for the study stems from the limitations of existing forecasting models, which often rely on a narrow set of variables or focus on specific economic conditions, thereby ignoring the broader factors that contribute to financial instability. In addition, insufficient data processing can skew the results of many studies. For example, insufficient handling of outliers and missing values will ultimately reduce the reliability of the prediction. With the development of the financial system becoming more and more complex, various financial indicators emerge endlessly. So, effective financial indicators are more crucial. As the author put forward, the effects are visible in this paper's long-run data, which show the greater stability of narrow and broad monetary aggregates in financial crises in the postwar era [2]. Especially after World War II and the establishment of the Bretton Woods system, this paper needs long-term data after data processing as a critical indicator to predict the financial crisis. In this work, this paper has done two main things. Firstly, the problems of outliers and missing data are carefully solved. The processing of outliers improves the accuracy of the model. Second, this paper uses statistical methods to identify underlying variables predicting financial crises. These variables cover data from 1870 to 2008 and are all long-term data. This paper runs differences and lags through the data, using economic models and statistics to screen the variables and arrive at a critical model for predicting financial crises.

2 Literature Review

The study by Schularick and Taylor provided the main inspiration for this work [2]. Their work is a milestone in the field of financial crisis prediction. Ultimately, their findings highlight credit growth as a precursor to financial crises. Schularick and Taylor underscore the importance of the idea that credit does not just work to propagate the economy, but also works far beyond [2]. The analyzed data from 14 developed countries between 1870 and 2008 found that rapid credit expansion, especially when economic growth is mismatched, is a reliable predictor of financial crises. The study has profound implications for how economists view the relationship between credit booms and recessions, reinforcing that credit growth can amplify shocks and serve as an independent source of economic instability.

Victoria Ivashina and David Scharfstein 's article also supports that the relevant indicators of the banking industry, especially credit, are closely related to the financial crisis. Ivashina and Scharfstein claimed that the seeds of this panic were sown in the credit boom that peaked in mid-2007 [1].

Gillian Tett proposed that financial crises may not manifest themselves in a way that underlines the unpredictability of such events in the way that the collapse of Lehman Brothers did [3]. So, it is a problem that needs to be solved to consider the predictor variables again and comprehensively. Simply piecing together different pieces of data without more nuanced treatment of the data and models weakens the explanatory power of the models, making their predictions less reliable. Therefore, it is more important to normalize the data to remove noise and selectively not deal with some outliers. Because the choice of data processing will affect the results of model prediction, not processing some outliers and missing values can better reflect the authenticity of the data.

Thus, despite the significance of Schularick and Taylor's findings, their study has partial limitations [2]. A significant problem is the narrow focus on credit and monetary aggregates as the main predictors. This limited choice of variables limits the ability of the model to capture financial crises. Some data issues also need to be addressed, such as handling outliers and filling in missing values.

This study makes improvements in data processing and forecasting methods to build a more powerful financial crisis forecasting model. In terms of data processing, this study preprocessed the data, including eliminating missing data and processing control variables. In terms of forecasting methods, this study attempts to use econometric analysis and advanced machine learning algorithms to comprehensively evaluate various predictors. This study provides a more comprehensive and reliable framework for predicting financial crises.

3 Methodology

3.1 Data Preprocessing Methods

Machine learning regression analysis based on panel data is highly efficient and has good prediction accuracy. However, the analysis of unsteady economic data is prone to time factors affecting the analysis results of this study. To confirm whether these macroeconomic indicator data contain time factors, this study uses the following two methods to test the stability of these data. After the test, the non-stationary data is differentially transformed to reduce the impact of time factors on subsequent data analysis, and the differential data is obtained.

3.1.1 Time Series Graph Observation Method & Unit Root Test Method

The time series graph test determines whether the sequence is stable by observing the trend and volatility of the time series. A stable sequence's mean and variance are constants reflected in the time series graph as the sequence value constantly fluctuates randomly around a constant, with a bounded fluctuation range and no obvious trend or periodicity. The unit root test is a method of statistically testing whether a unit root exists in the sequence. If a time series has a unit root, the series is non-stationary. This test usually uses parametric methods, such as the DF (Dickey-Fuller) test or the ADF (Augmented Dickey-Fuller) test, to evaluate the stationarity of the series.

3.1.2 Lagged Variable in Regression

A lagged variable is a variable that represents the value of another variable at a previous point in time. In economic models, current economic activity is not only affected by other current factors but may also be affected by past economic activity levels. In order to better predict the occurrence of financial crises, this study introduced lagged variables to the independent variables to better explain their temporal dependence. This study uses the following formula to lag variables:

$$Yt = \alpha + \sum_{i=0}^{p} \beta_i X_{t-i} + \varepsilon_t \quad (1)$$

3.2 *Logistic Regression Methods*

Logistic regression is a regression analysis method used for binary classification problems. It models the log odds of the probability of an event occurring. It is basically the same as the model form of linear regression; both have similar $wx + b$, where w is the coefficient of x and b is the constant term coefficient. The difference between them lies in the dependent variable. The dependent variable of linear regression is $wx + b$, that is, $y = wx + b$. In contrast, logistic regression is a hidden state p, which is matched to $wx + b$ by function L, that is, $p = L(wx + b)$, and then calculates the value of the dependent variable through the formula based on the values of p and $1 - p$.

$$logit(P(Y = 1)) = ln\left(\frac{P(Y = 1)}{1 - P(Y = 1)}\right) = \beta_0 + \beta_1 X \tag{2}$$

3.3 *Multicollinearity Test*

Multicollinearity refers to a situation in regression analysis where independent variables are highly correlated, leading to biased regression coefficient estimates and making interpretation difficult. Therefore, when conducting multiple linear regression analysis in this study, it is necessary to test the multicollinearity problem and use appropriate methods to ensure the accuracy and reliability of the analysis results.

3.3.1 Variance Inflation Factor (VIF)

Used to detect the degree of multicollinearity between predictor variables in a regression model. Higher VIF (Variance Inflation Factor) values indicate higher multicollinearity (Usually 10 is the critical point).

3.3.2 Correlation Coefficient Matrix

A matrix of correlation coefficients among the independent variables to identify multicollinearity. The closer the correlation coefficient between two variables is to 1 or -1, the more correlated the two variables are (it can be considered that there is collinearity between the two variables).

4 Exploratory Data Analysis

4.1 *Data Acquisition and Data Preprocessing*

Data analysis is a key part of research in forecasting economic crises. By digging deeper and analyzing historical economic data, it is possible to identify potential crisis signals and provide early warning for macroprudential policies. This section will detail the data acquisition, preprocessing, feature engineering, statistical analysis, and visualization processes. These steps not only help us understand the basic features of the data but also lay a solid foundation for subsequent modelling and forecasting. First, based on a survey of the literature and expertise, it describes the sources of data and selection criteria to ensure that the data used effectively represent the object and problem under study. The next step is discussing the steps of data preprocessing, including cleaning and normalizing the data to remove noise and improve the accuracy of the analysis. Then, the details of the procedure engineering process focus on extracting how to extract key features from the raw data that will aid in prediction.

First, the data acquisition references data taken from Schuianck and Tayla Rcf. This database has economic data for 14 countries from 1870 to 1913. This period included World War I and II, which had particular historical and economic significance. It is also the period covered by more data from 1870 to 1913, which covers the economic data of several countries. This period was essential in global economic history, with a number of economic crises and fluctuations, in particular, the economic cycles of the late nineteenth and early twentieth centuries. This period can provide sufficient sample data for analyzing the causes and characteristics of economic crises. The data types mainly include macroeconomic indicators and financial market indicators like Macroeconomic indicators [4].

Found a lot of missing values in this data, but based on a survey of the literature and expertise so decided to test the stationary of the data first before dealing with the missing values and outliers together. Firstly, it is known through the literature that the stationary of the data needs to be tested before making a stationary on the data. The Augmented Dickey-Fuller test statistic was then used to test whether the data for each country was stationary or not, and the final p-value clearly proved that the data for each country was not stationary. (3) Based on the expertise gained, the data needed to be differenced before it could be stationary. For example, in Fig. 1, you can see the first graph is the state before real GDP diff, an upward trend, it is obviously not stationary. The second picture is the state after the difference, and based on the expertise, the p-value is next calculated again using the unit root test to prove that the post-differential data is stationary [5]

After stationary the data for each country, next started to find the missing values in it, used a box plot to find the outliers in it and intended to treat it as a missing value, but after checking a lot of literature and expertise. Based on a survey of the literature and expertise decided not to do anything with the outliers and missing values. Because every missing value and outlier has some historical significance, these data reflect the changes of each era and the economic direction of the time [5]. As shown in Fig. 2, by using the box plot method in the literature to find outliers, its

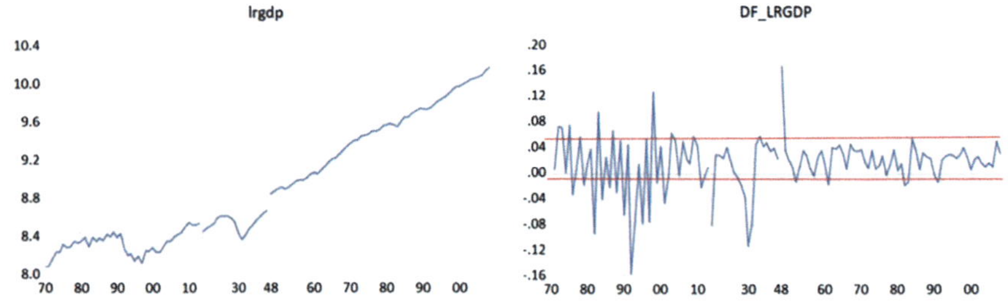

Fig. 1 Comparison of pre-differential and post-differential

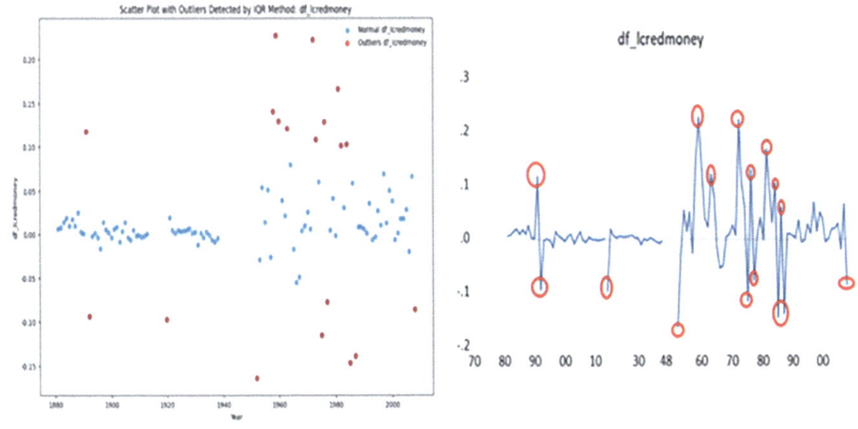

Fig. 2 By using a box plot, find the outlier

graph shows many outliers, but this reflects the economic fluctuations in this period, and these fluctuations have great historical significance and reference value [6].

4.2 Feature Engineering and the Handling of Control Variables

Main variables: The feature engineering section explores in detail how to extract and construct key features from raw data that can best predict economic crises. Feature engineering is a crucial step in the process of data analysis and modelling. Scientific and reasonable feature selection, feature construction, feature dimensionality reduction, and time series feature extraction can effectively improve the model's predictive performance. In the literature and professional knowledge, and find the df_lloansmoney, df_lcredmoney, df_lrgdp, df_lloan_p, df_lcred_p are the five main variables, and according to the out of the data given by the final model, select two of them as main variables of the future model by using the fifth-order lag for each main variable. df_lloan_p, df_lcred_p, these two variables will be the best to be the main variables here [5]. Next is to find the control variables:

The same steps are shown in Fig. 3. First, it has a set of variables. At the outset, the researchers used all 17 variables. These variables may cover a wide range of macroeconomic and financial indicators related to the economic crisis. Elimination of time, region, and unrecorded variables: In this step, the researchers eliminate variables related to time and region, as well as variables that are not logarithms. This step eliminates features that may introduce noise or do not fit the model. In the end, 11 variables were retained and prepared for further analysis.

Dealing with multicollinearity: For the remaining 11 variables, and used the VIF (Variance Inflation Factor) values to demonstrate whether they were multicollinear

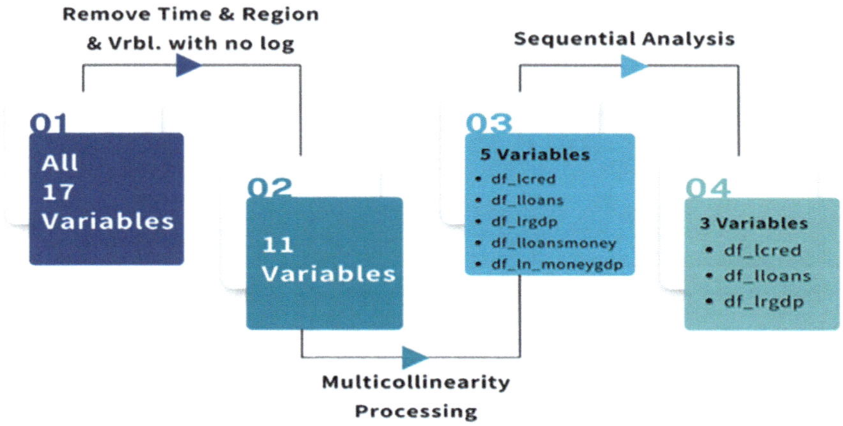

Fig. 3 The process of dealing with control variables

or not, and then plotted them against each variable in a heat map as in Fig. 4. which helped us to more intuitively select the five variables that were less correlated with the main variables. After obtaining the five control variables, and further characterized the five selected variables through serial sum of squares (SS) analysis to determine which variables contributed the most to the model's predictive power. Variables with higher values of sequence sum of squares indicate that they explain more of the variability in the model and are more critical predictors. The following are the results of ranking the importance of the variables: lrgdp: The ordinal sum of squares is 0.6234, which is relatively significant. lcred: The ordinal sum of squares is 0.821630, indicating that this variable has the highest importance in the model and significantly improves the accuracy of economic crisis predictions. lloans: with an ordinal sum of squares of 0.731399, this variable is second only to lcred in terms of importance in forecasting, and is also a key feature: lloansmoney: with an ordinal sum of squares of 0.129809, this variable has a relatively low significance, but still contributes to the model. moneygdp: the sum of squared ordinal values for this variable is 0.068204, indicating that it contributes the least to the model and can, therefore, be considered for exclusion in further analysis. Finally, lcred, lloans and lrgdp were decided as control variables, just like in Fig. 4 [7].

5 Experimental Setting and Results

Baseline Logit Model with perturbations:

$$Y_{financial\ crisis=1} = b_{0i} + b_1(L)M_{it} + b_2(L)C_{it} + e_{it} \tag{3}$$

The lag polynomial $b_2(L)C_{it}$ incorporates five annual lags of the controlled variable.

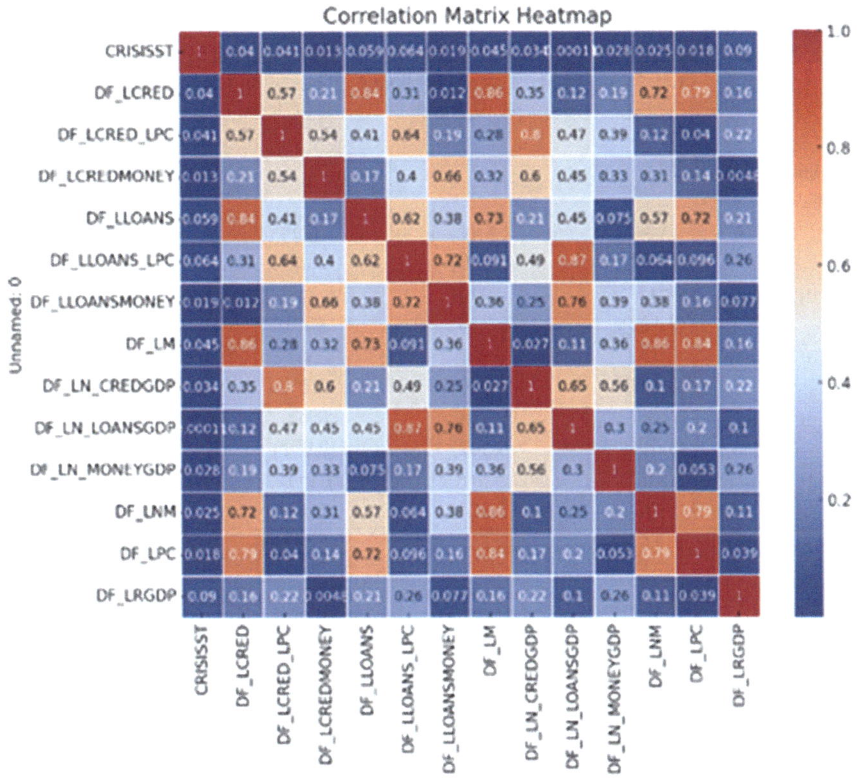

Fig. 4 The heat map of each variable

Specification 5 introduces five lags of credit growth (without deflating). Specification 6 incorporates five lags of loan growth (without deflating) and real GDP growth. Specification 7 integrates five lags of credit growth (without deflating) and real GDP growth. Specification 8 substitutes loans with credit, further augmenting five lags of credit growth (without deflating) and real GDP growth.

Through these settings, this study delves into the impact of nominal loan growth, nominal credit growth, and the growth rate of real GDP, which reflect the underlying monetary policy, market activity, market liquidity, and the level of economic prosperity, among other influencing factors.

Table 1 shows that, although the controlled variables exhibit varying degrees of significance, the primary variables maintain statistical significance across these specifications. All model configurations demonstrate a positive correlation between the growth of loans (or credit) over the preceding five years and the risk of a financial crisis. The quintet of lags is collectively statistically significant, and the overall regression analysis achieves significance at the 1 per cent level.

For the comparative assessment of the models, this work employs AUC [8] & AIC [9] as the evaluative metrics. Additionally, this work utilizes ROC (Experimental

Table 1 Baseline Model with Perturbations

Specification	Baseline Plus 5 Lags of df_lcred	Baseline Plus 5 Lags of df_lloans & df_lrgdp	Baseline Plus 5 Lags of df_lrgdp & df_lcred	Replace loans with credit Plus 5 Lags of df_lrgdp & df_lcred
(Logit country effects)	(5)	(6)	(7)	(8)
L.df_lloan_p	−1.355 (2.952)	3.210 (4.580)	−0.773 (3.084)	−0.418 (5.503)
L2.df_lloan_p	8.718*** (3.122)	−4.391 (5.310)	8.497*** (3.130)	6.133 (6.283)
L3.df_lloan_p	1.766 (3.193)	12.340** (4.956)	3.007 (3.200)	2.895 (6.439)
L4.df_lloan_p	0.109 (3.014)	-3.294 (4.507)	0.996 (2.992)	-1.864 (5.780)
L5.df_lloan_p	7.230*** (2.761)	12.234*** (3.684)	7.327*** (2.816)	9.300** (4.268)
Observations	1174.000	1274.000	1174.000	1244.000
Groups	14	14	14	14
Test for all lags $= 0, \chi^2$	19.04***	21.65***	19.99***	9.70*
p-value	0.0019	0.0006	0.0013	0.0843
Test lags of for added vbl. $= 0, \chi^2$	8.32	38.57***	18.78**	17.46*
p-value	0.1394	0.0000	0.0432	0.0648
Pseudo R^2	0.103	0.148	0.132	0.089
Pseudo likelihood	−148.336	−164.809	−143.475	−161.090
Overall test statistic, χ^2	33.98***	57.157***	43.71***	31.61***
p-value	0.000	0.000	0.000	0.007
AUROC	0.7379	0.7635	0.7602	0.7292
AIC	316.6726	359.618	316.9509	325.1797

Standard errors in parentheses
* $p < 0.1$, ** $p < 0.05$, *** $p < 0.01$

Setting and Result) to scrutinize their predictive capabilities. The ROC (Experimental Setting and Result) curves for the four specifications above are presented as follows (Fig. 5).

In the experimental setting, the nominal loan growth rate positively correlates with the likelihood of a financial crisis. In contrast, the real GDP growth rate demonstrates a negative correlation with the same, aligning with established economic theories and empirical studies [10].

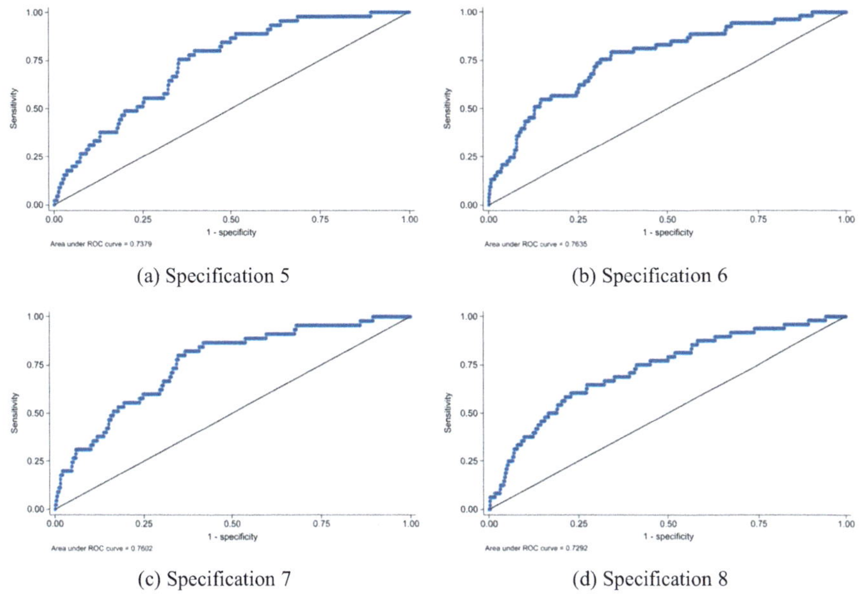

(a) Specification 5 (b) Specification 6

(c) Specification 7 (d) Specification 8

Fig. 5 ROC Curves of 4 Specifications. **a** Specification 5.**b** Specification 6. **c** Specification 7. **d** Specification 8

Notably, the coefficient of the nominal credit growth rate is significantly negative, indicating that it should be integrated with the main variable for its economic implications. Upon a comprehensive evaluation of the four aforementioned specifications, this study has formulated a final model to facilitate a more profound analysis and interpretation.

$$Y(\mathit{financial\ crisis} = 1) = {\beta_1}^2 \nabla lloan\_p + {\beta_1}^5 \nabla lloan\_p - {\beta_2}^5 \nabla lcred - {\beta_3}^3 \nabla lrgdp + ui \tag{4}$$

$$Y(\mathit{financial\ crisis} = 1) = \beta_1^2 \nabla lloan_p + \beta_1^5 \ln \frac{\frac{loan}{p}}{\frac{loan_{(-1)}}{p_{(-1)}}} - \beta_2^5 \ln \frac{cred}{cred(-1)} - \beta_3^3 \nabla lrgdp + u \tag{5}$$

$$Y(\mathit{financial\ crisis} = 1) = \beta_1^2 \nabla lloan\_p + ln(\frac{\frac{loan}{cred}/p}{\frac{loan_{(-1)}}{cred_{(-1)}}/p_{(-1)}})^{\beta_1^5} \cdot (\frac{cred(-1)}{cred})^{\beta_1^5 - \beta_2^5} - \beta_3^3 \nabla lrgdp + ui \tag{6}$$

$$Y(\mathit{financial\ crisis}=1)=\beta_1{}^2\nabla lloan_p+ln(\frac{\frac{loan}{cred}/p}{\frac{loan_{(-1)}}{cred_{(-1)}}/p_{(-1)}})^{\beta_1{}^5}-\beta_3{}^3\nabla lrgdp+ui \quad (7)$$

$$Y(\mathit{financial\ crisis}=1)=\beta_1{}^2\nabla lloan\_p+\beta_1{}^5\Delta ln(\frac{loan}{cred}/p)-\beta_3{}^3\nabla lrgdp+ui \quad (8)$$

"explain: "∇" "means 1st difference".

β_i^j means the the $i-th$ parameter estimator for the $j-th$ lag period $\beta_1\beta_2\beta_3>0$

In this new model, β_1, β_2, β_3 are significantly > 0. Moreover, the result obtains a new variable: the log difference between loan and credit. It reflects how much faster the bank's lending speed is than the growth rate of its assets. And this indicator exhibits a strong positive correlation with the financial crisis [11].

6 Discussion

This study also has its limitations. On one hand, due to the extensive temporal and national scope of the data, the completeness of the data used in this study cannot be guaranteed. Additionally, for reasons yet to be determined, the significance of the newly introduced variable (i.e., the logarithmic difference of loan to credit) disappeared when re-modelled. Furthermore, the predictive power of the model still requires improvement. Future research is anticipated to refine the models for predicting financial crises further. For example, incorporating more reasonable interaction terms.

7 Conclusion

This study examines the key factors that influence the likelihood of financial crises. The results reveal that a significant increase in the growth rate of credit or loans, as well as a rise in the loan-to-credit ratio, signals an elevated level of systemic risk. This increase, in turn, raises the probability of financial crises. Conversely, a higher real GDP growth rate indicates greater economic prosperity, which reduces the risk of financial instability. Unlike previous research, this study focuses on the distinct impact of the loan-to-credit ratio. It provides a deeper analysis of the interaction between credit and loans, rather than assuming these two measures are interchangeable.

From a policy standpoint, several strategies can be adopted to reduce the risk of financial crises. One crucial measure is strengthening regulatory oversight of banks to prevent moral hazards and excessive credit expansion. Policymakers can achieve this by setting limits on the growth of bank lending relative to their assets. Such measures would help control disorderly lending practices. Additionally, regulations should specifically address the risk-taking behavior of banks. Since banks often pursue high- risk activities to boost profits, it is essential to have a regulatory framework that prevents commercial banks from transferring these risks onto depositors. Another effective strategy involves curbing excessive lending during periods of rapid economic growth. When real GDP growth rates are high, restricting bank lending can help manage systemic risk.

To improve the predictive accuracy of the model, further research is needed. Future studies should consider incorporating additional interaction terms to better capture the complexity of economic relationships. Moreover, exploring advanced machine learning techniques, such as ensemble methods or neural networks, could enhance the robustness and precision of crisis predictions. These efforts would refine the model's explanatory capacity and provide a more comprehensive understanding of financial crisis dynamics.

Acknowledgements Ziqian Peng, Mengxi Liu, Jianjie Li, and Rongxin Zhang contributed equally to this work and should be considered co-first authors.

References

1. Ivashina, V. and Scharfstein, D., 2010. Bank lending during the financial crisis of 2008. Journal of Financial Economics, 97(3), pp.319-338.
2. Schularick, M. and Taylor, A.M., 2012. Credit Booms Gone Bust: Monetary Policy, Leverage Cycles, and Financial Crises, 1870-2008. American Economic Review, 102(2), pp.1029-1061.
3. Tett, G., 2018. The next financial crisis may be coming soon—Financial Times, 21 August, p.2.
4. Lin, W. Y., Hu, Y. H., & Tsai, C. F. (2011). Machine learning in financial crisis prediction: a survey. IEEE Transactions on Systems, Man, and Cybernetics, Part C (Applications and Reviews), 42(4), 421–436.
5. Bordo, M. D., & Haubrich, J. G. (2010). Credit crises, money and contractions: An historical view. Journal of Monetary Economics, 57(1), 1-18.
6. Mathur, N., Jain, K., Tiwari, S., & Chebolu, R. M. (2021). Box Plot and Cluster Analysis with Outlier Mining of Indian Listed Firms. IUP Journal of Accounting Research & Audit Practices, 20(1), 15-27.
7. Uthayakumar, J., Metawa, N., Shankar, K., & Lakshmanaprabu, S. K. (2020). Intelligent hybrid model for financial crisis prediction using machine learning techniques. Information Systems and e-Business Management, 18, 617-645.
8. Ling, C.X., Huang, J. and Zhang, H., 2003, August. AUC: a statistically consistent and more discriminating measure than accuracy. In Ijcai (Vol. 3, pp. 519–524).
9. Wagenmakers, E.J. and Farrell, S., 2004. AIC model selection using Akaike weights. Psychonomic Bulletin & Review, 11, pp.192-196.
10. Jickling, M., 2009. Causes of the financial crisis.
11. Demetriades, P.O., Rewilak, J.M. and Rousseau, P.L., 2023. Finance, Growth, and Fragility. Journal of Financial Services Research, pp. 1–21.

How the American Options Early Exercise in the Two-Period Binominal Model

Yuhe Ge, Haoran Wang, and Mingxun Miao

Abstract This paper's purpose is to analyze the early exercise strategy of American options based on the binomial tree model. We use this binomial tree model to analyze the prices of American and European options to determine whether an American option should be exercised early under certain circumstances and to compare the price difference between the two options to calculate the premium. Options are common financial derivatives that have been traded in the financial markets for a long time. As a key tool for hedging, speculation, and enhancing portfolio strategies, options are integral to modern financial markets, which attract a large number of researchers to make research on option pricing. However, in current academic research, there is insufficient investigation into the differences between American put options and European put options, particularly regarding their exercisable time. Therefore, this paper will mainly explore the optimal exercise time for put options using a two-period binomial model, which can help investors make better decisions to seek maximum profit.

Keywords European options · Put options · Call options · The price of options · Optimal exercisable time

Y. Ge (✉)
School of Economics, University of Nottingham, Ningbo, China
e-mail: hmyyg7@nottingham.edu.cn

H. Wang
School of International Exchange, Ningbo University of Technology, Ningbo, China

M. Miao
College of Arts and Sciences, Boston University, Boston, MA, USA

E. Tsui et al. (eds.), *Management Information Systems in a Digitalized AI World*, Springer Proceedings in Business and Economics,
https://doi.org/10.1007/978-981-96-6526-6_10

1 Introduction

An option is a contract and derivative that gives the holder the right to buy or sell the underlying asset at a specified price in the future or at a predetermined time [1]. The binomial tree model is a model that can be used to determine the value of an option because the underlying asset has only two directions at any time—up or down—which move continuously to form a closing tree eventually [2]. Investors can use this model to calculate the value of an option, particularly when valuing US options, which helps them decide whether to exercise the option early and maximize profits.

The value of an option is influenced by six main factors: the strike price, the market price of the underlying asset, the expiration date, the risk-free rate, the volatility of the underlying asset price, and the expected dividend [3, 4]. In an option contract, the option's value is reflected in its price. If the supply and demand dynamics in the market fluctuate, the option price will also fluctuate, affecting the interests of both parties. Thus, the option price is a key issue in options trading, and ensuring reasonable pricing is central to market trading.

Because US options can be exercised at any time, they must be priced correctly. In 2009, Cox, Ross, and Rubinstein published an article called "Options Pricing: A Simplified Approach," in which they proposed a binomial model for pricing options. The principles of this model allow for the correct valuation of European options, but it is not yet applicable to American options [5]. Therefore, in this paper, we examine the difference between the US and European options and the early exercise premium according to the principles of the binomial option pricing model.

2 Variables

Table 1 shows all the variables used in our essay.

3 Methodology: The Two-Period Binomial Model

Binomial model is commonly used to price options and other financial assets. By using binomial model helps investors and financial professionals better assess and manage market risks.

With the binomial model, each iteration results in one of two possible outcomes: an upward move or a downward move, which form a binomial tree. When used in option pricing, the model employs "u" and "d" and repeated application of these up and down process generate the binomial tree, illustrating the potential paths the stock price could follow until the option's expiration.

Table 1 Variables

Variable label	Variable name	Conditions
T	Maturity time	T = 0, 1, 2
u	Upward factor	Constant and positive
d	Downward factor	Constant and positive, assume $d = 1/u$
r	Risk-free Interest rate	Constant and positive
q	Risk-Neutral Probability Measure	Constant, $0 < q < 1$
S_T	Stock price of the option at T	Constant and positive, $S_j = \begin{cases} S_{j-1}u \\ S_{j-1}d \end{cases}, forj = 1, 2$
K	Strike price of the option	Positive
F	The payoff when exercise at T	$F = \begin{cases} (S_T - K)^+, forputoption \\ (K - S_T)^+, forcalloption \end{cases}$
X_T	The value of the option at T	Positive
P^E	The price of European option	Positive
P^A	The price of American option	Positive

* The constant d, u and r satisfy $d < 1 + r < u$

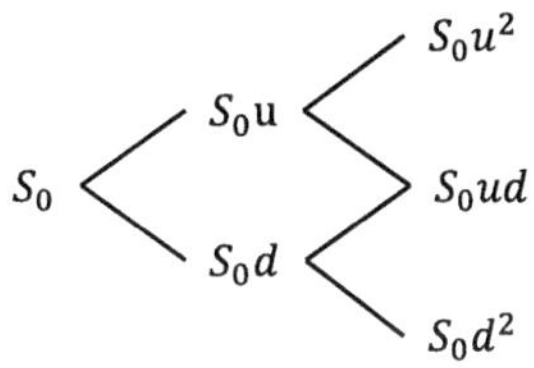

Fig. 1 The binominal tree model

Therefore, the two-period binomial model implies that the model undergoes two up and down processes, resulting in three columns in the binomial tree. Figure 1 shows a two-period binomial model that starts at S_0 with two following periods [6].

3.1 *For European Options*

3.1.1 European Call Options

A European call option grants the holder the right, but not the obligation, to buy one share of stock from the option seller at the strike price K, which is predetermined that allows to make transactions, exercisable only at time T [7].

At maturity time T, if the stock price S_T is less than or equal to the strike price K, the option holder will opt not to exercise the option, as purchasing the stock directly from the market would be more cost-effective. In this case, the option holder receives no payoff [8].

However, if the S_T exceeds the K, the holder can exercise the option, buying the stock at K and selling it in the market at S_T, resulting in a payoff of $S_T - K$ [9].

Then, the option's holder faces a payoff H_T given by

$$H_T = (S_T - K)^+ \equiv \max\{S_T - K, 0\} \tag{1}$$

3.1.2 European Put Options

A European put option grants the holder the right, but not the obligation, to sell one share of stock to the option seller at the strike price K, which is predetermined that allow to make transaction, exercisable only at time T [7].

At maturity T, if the stock price S_T is greater than or equal to the strike price K, the holder will choose not to exercise the option, as selling the stock in the market would be more advantageous. In this case, the option holder receives no payoff [8].

However, if the S_T is less than the K, the holder can exercise the option, selling the stock at K and buying it in the market for S_T, resulting in a payoff of $K - S_T$ [9].

Then, the option's holder faces a payoff H_T given by

$$H_T = (K - S_T)^+ \equiv \max\{K - S_T, 0\} \tag{2}$$

3.1.3 Option Pricing Model

Finally, a pricing formula is employed to determine the current value of an option by discounting the expected payoff under the risk-neutral probability measure q. This method allows for valuing options based on potential future movements of the underlying asset and the prevailing risk-free interest rate [10].

$$X_T = \frac{1}{1+r}(qF(S_T u) + (1-q)F(S_T d)) \tag{3}$$

where,

$$q = \frac{1+r-d}{u-d} \tag{4}$$

3.2 For American Options

3.2.1 American Call Option

An American call option grants the holder the right, but not the obligation, to buy one share of stock from the option seller at the strike price K, which is predetermined that allow to make transaction, at any time τ up to and including T, at the holder's discretion [7, 8].

Holders will face a payout equal to $(S_T - K)^+$ if they choose to exercise the options at time τ [9].

Then, a comparison can be made between payout,

$$(S_T - K)^+$$

And (3)

$$X_T = \frac{1}{1+r}(qF(S_T u) + (1-q)F(S_T d))$$

to get the maximum payout and find the time that is optimal for exercising from

$$\max\left\{(S_T - K)^+, X_T = \tfrac{1}{1+r}(qF(S_T u) + (1-q)F(S_T d))\right\} \tag{5}$$

3.2.2 American Put Option

An American call option grants the holder the right, but not the obligation, to sell one share of stock to the option seller at the strike price K, which is predetermined that allow to make transaction, at any time τ up to and including T, at the holder's discretion [7, 8].

Holders will face a payout equal to $(K - S_T)^+$ if they choose to exercise the options at time τ [9].

Then, a comparison can be made between payout,

$$(K - S_T)^+$$

And (3)

$$X_T = \frac{1}{1+r}(qF(S_T u) + (1-q)F(S_T d))$$

to get the maximum payout and find the time that is optimal for exercising from

$$\max\left\{(K - S_T)^+, X_T = \tfrac{1}{1+r}(qF(S_T u) + (1-q)F(S_T d))\right\} \tag{6}$$

3.3 Early Exercise Premium

The early exercise premium make reference to the additional amount an investor is willing to pay for an American option compared to a European option with all other same conditions such as underlying asset, strike price of K, and expiration time to exercise T. This premium arises because an American option provides more flexibility to exercise early, allowing the holder to potentially react to favorable price movements [10].

Therefore, in this essay to calculate early exercise premium we use a formula,

$$Premium = Price\ of\ American\ Options - Price\ of\ European\ Options \tag{7}$$

4 Analysis of American Put Options Early Exercise

For the put option, we calculate the payoff by $(K - S_T)^+$.

We assume $d = \frac{1}{u}$, so $q = \frac{u+ur-1}{u^2-1}$ and the binominal tree be like the Fig. 2,

Then we are going to discuss how the American put options early exercise with different K. We can calculate the results by (6) and (7).

4.1 Case I: $K > S_0u^2$

If exercise at T, we will get the payoff,

When T = 2, $F(S_0u^2) = K - S_0u^2$, $F(S_0) = K - S_0$, $F\left(S_0\frac{1}{u^2}\right) = K - S_0\frac{1}{u^2}$.

When T = 1, $F(S_0u) = K - S_0u$, $F\left(S_0\frac{1}{u}\right) = K - S_0\frac{1}{u}$.

When T = 0, $F(S_0) = K - S_0$.

For the European option,

$$X_1^E(S_0u) = \frac{1}{1+r}\left[q\left(K - S_0u^2\right) + (1-q)(K - S_0)\right] = \frac{1}{1+r}K - uS_0$$

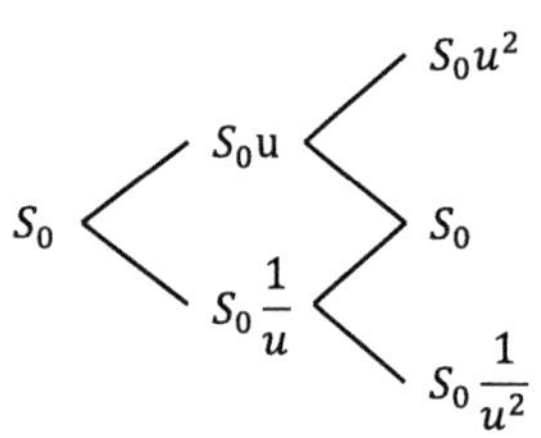

Fig. 2 The binominal tree model

$$X_1^E\left(S_0\frac{1}{u}\right) = \frac{1}{1+r}\left[q(K-S_0) + (1-q)\left(K - S_0\frac{1}{u^2}\right)\right] = \frac{1}{1+r}K - \frac{1}{u}S_0$$

$$P^E = X_0^E = \frac{1}{1+r}\left[q\left(\frac{1}{1+r}K - uS_0\right) + (1-q)\left(\frac{1}{1+r}K - \frac{1}{u}S_0\right)\right]$$
$$= \frac{1}{(1+r)^2}K - S_0$$

For the American option,

$$X_1^A(S_0u) = max\left\{\frac{1}{1+r}K - uS_0, K - S_0u\right\} = K - S_0u$$

$$X_1^A\left(S_0\frac{1}{u}\right) = max\left\{\frac{1}{1+r}K - \frac{1}{u}S_0, K - S_0\frac{1}{u}\right\} = K - S_0\frac{1}{u}$$

$$P^A = X_0^A = max\left\{\frac{1}{1+r}\left[q(K - S_0u) + (1-q)\left(K - S_0\frac{1}{u}\right)\right], K - S_0\right\} = K - S_0$$

Therefore, American option will be early exercised at T = 0 with price $K - S_0$.
The premium can be calculated by (7),
$Premium = P^A - P^E = (K - S_0) - \left[\frac{1}{(1+r)^2}K - S_0\right] = \frac{r^2+2r}{(1+r)^2}K.$

4.2 Case II: $S_0u < K \leq S_0u^2$

If exercise at T, we will get the payoff,
When T = 2, $F(S_0u^2) = 0$, $F(S_0) = K - S_0$, $F\left(S_0\frac{1}{u^2}\right) = K - S_0\frac{1}{u^2}$.
When T = 1, $F(S_0u) = K - S_0u$, $F\left(S_0\frac{1}{u}\right) = K - S_0\frac{1}{u}$.
When T = 0, $F(S_0) = K - S_0$.
For the European option,

$$X_1^E(S_0u) = \frac{1}{1+r}[q \times 0 + (1-q)(K - S_0)] = \frac{1-q}{1+r}K - \frac{1-q}{1+r}S_0$$

$$X_1^E\left(S_0\frac{1}{u}\right) = \frac{1}{1+r}\left[q(K-S_0) + (1-q)\left(K - S_0\frac{1}{u^2}\right)\right] = \frac{1}{1+r}K - \frac{1}{u}S_0$$

$$P^E = X_0^E = \frac{1}{1+r}\left[q\left(\frac{1-q}{1+r}K - \frac{1-q}{1+r}S_0\right) + (1-q)\left(\frac{1}{1+r}K - \frac{1}{u}S_0\right)\right]$$
$$= \frac{1-q^2}{(1+r)^2}K - \frac{(1-q)(u+uq+r+1)}{(1+r)^2u}S_0$$

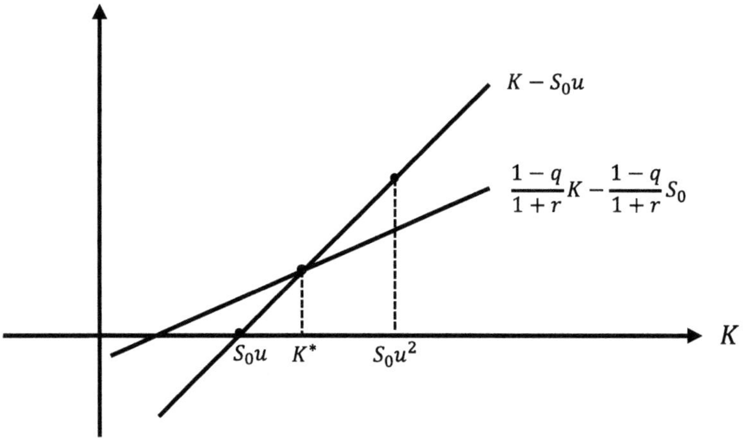

Fig. 3 The two first-order functions

For the American option,

$$X_1^A(S_0u) = max\left\{\frac{1-q}{1+r}K - \frac{1-q}{1+r}S_0, K - S_0u\right\}$$

$$X_1^A\left(S_0\frac{1}{u}\right) = max\left\{\frac{1}{1+r}K - uS_0, K - S_0\frac{1}{u}\right\} = K - S_0\frac{1}{u}$$

for $X_1^A(S_0u)$, we think of these two formulae as two first-order functions with the independent variable K, then set them equal,

$$\frac{1-q}{1+r}K - \frac{1-q}{1+r}S_0 = K - S_0u$$

$K^* = \frac{ur+u+q-1}{q+r}S_0$, where $u < \frac{ur+u+q-1}{q+r} < u^2u < \frac{ur+u+q-1}{q+r} < u^2$.then we can draw the graph (Figure 3),

so, we have two situations, $K^* < K \leq S_0u^2$ and $S_0u < K < K^*$.

4.2.1 When $K^* < K \leq S_0u^2$

$$X_1^A(S_0u) = K - S_0u$$

$$P^A = X_0^A = max\left\{\frac{1}{1+r}\left[q\left(\frac{1-q}{1+r}K - \frac{1-q}{1+r}S_0\right) + (1-q)\left(K - S_0\frac{1}{u}\right)\right], K - S_0\right\}$$
$$= K - S_0$$

In this situation, the American option will be early exercised at T = 0 with price $K - S_0$.

The premium is,

$$Premium = P^A - P^E = (K - S_0) - \left[\frac{1-q^2}{(1+r)^2}K - \frac{(1-q)(u+uq+r+1)}{(1+r)^2 u}S_0\right]$$

$$= \frac{2r + r^2 + q^2}{1 + 2r + r^2}K + \frac{u + r - rq^2 - 2r - r^2}{(1+r)^2 u}S_0$$

4.2.2 When $S_0 u < K < K^*$

$$.X_1^A(S_0 u) = \frac{1-q}{1+r}K - \frac{1-q}{1+r}S_0$$

$$P^A = X_0^A = max\left\{\frac{1}{1+r}\left[q\left(\frac{1-q}{1+r}K - \frac{1-q}{1+r}S_0\right) + (1-q)\left(K - S_0\frac{1}{u}\right)\right], K - S_0\right\}$$

$$= \frac{(1-q)(q+1+r)}{(1+r)^2}K - \frac{(1-q)(qu+r)}{(1+r)^2 u}S_0$$

In this situation, American option will be early exercised at T=1, with price $\frac{(1-q)(q+1+r)}{(1+r)^2}K - \frac{(1-q)(qu+r)}{(1+r)^2 u}S_0$.

The premium is,

$$Premium = P^A - P^E = \frac{rq}{(1+r)^2}K + \frac{(1-q)(-q+u+uq+r+1)}{(1+r)^2 u}S_0$$

4.3 *Case III: $S_0 < K \le S_0 u$*

If exercise at T, we will get the payoff:

When T = 2, $F(S_0 u^2) = 0$, $F(S_0) = K - S_0$, $F\left(S_0\frac{1}{u^2}\right) = K - S_0\frac{1}{u^2}$.

When T = 1, $F(S_0 u) = 0$, $F\left(S_0\frac{1}{u}\right) = K - S_0\frac{1}{u}$.

When T = 0, $F(S_0) = K - S_0$.

For the European option,

$$X_1^E(S_0u) = \frac{1}{1+r}\left[q \times 0 + (1-q)(K - S_0)\right] = \frac{1-q}{1+r}K - \frac{1-q}{1+r}S_0$$

$$X_1^E\left(S_0\frac{1}{u}\right) = \frac{1}{1+r}\left[q(K - S_0) + (1-q)\left(K - S_0\frac{1}{u^2}\right)\right] = \frac{1}{1+r}K - \frac{1}{u}S_0$$

$$P^E = X_0^E = \frac{1}{1+r}\left[q\left(\frac{1-q}{1+r}K - \frac{1-q}{1+r}S_0\right) + (1-q)\left(\frac{1}{1+r}K - \frac{1}{u}S_0\right)\right]$$
$$= \frac{1-q^2}{(1+r)^2}K - \frac{(1-q)(u+uq+r+1)}{(1+r)^2u}S_0$$

For the American option,

$$X_1^A(S_0u) = max\left\{\frac{1-q}{1+r}K - \frac{1-q}{1+r}S_0, 0\right\} = \frac{1-q}{1+r}K - \frac{1-q}{1+r}S_0$$

$$X_1^A\left(S_0\frac{1}{u}\right) = max\left\{\frac{1}{1+r}K - \frac{1}{u}S_0, K - S_0\frac{1}{u}\right\} = K - S_0\frac{1}{u}$$

$$P^A = X_0^A = max\left\{\frac{1}{1+r}\left[q\left(\frac{1-q}{1+r}K - \frac{1-q}{1+r}S_0\right) + (1-q)\left(K - S_0\frac{1}{u}\right)\right], K - S_0\right\}$$
$$= \frac{(1-q)(q+1+r)}{(1+r)^2}K - \frac{(1-q)(qu+r)}{(1+r)^2u}S_0$$

Therefore, American option will be early exercised at T=1, with price $\frac{(1-q)(q+1+r)}{(1+r)^2}K - \frac{(1-q)(qu+r)}{(1+r)^2u}S_0$.
The premium is,
$Premium = P^A - P^E = \frac{rq}{(1+r)^2}K + \frac{(1-q)(-q+u+uq+r+1)}{(1+r)^2u}S_0$,
which is the same result as 4.2.2.

4.4 Case IV: $S_0d < K \leq S_0$

If exercise at T, we will get the payoff:
When T = 2, $F\left(S_0u^2\right) = 0$, $F(S_0) = 0$, $F\left(S_0\frac{1}{u^2}\right) = K - S_0\frac{1}{u^2}$.
When T = 1, $F(S_0u) = 0$, $F\left(S_0\frac{1}{u}\right) = K - S_0\frac{1}{u}$.
When T = 0, $F(S_0) = 0$.
For the European option,

$$X_1^E(S_0u) = 0$$

$$X_1^E\left(S_0\frac{1}{u}\right)=\frac{1}{1+r}\left[q\times 0+(1-q)\left(K-S_0\frac{1}{u^2}\right)\right]=\frac{1-q}{1+r}K-\frac{1-q}{(1+r)u^2}S_0$$

$$P^E=X_0^E=\frac{1}{1+r}\left[q\times 0+(1-q)\left(\frac{1-q}{1+r}K-\frac{1-q}{(1+r)u^2}S_0\right)\right]$$
$$=\frac{(1-q)^2}{(1+r)^2}K-\frac{(1-q)^2}{(1+r)^2u^2}S_0$$

For the American option,

$$X_1^A(S_0u)=0$$

$$X_1^A\left(S_0\frac{1}{u}\right)=max\left\{\frac{1-q}{1+r}K-\frac{1-q}{(1+r)u^2}S_0,\,K-S_0\frac{1}{u}\right\}=K-S_0\frac{1}{u}$$

$$P^A=X_0^A=max\left\{\frac{1}{1+r}\left[q\times 0+(1-q)\left(K-S_0\frac{1}{u}\right)\right],\,K-S_0\right\}$$
$$=\frac{1-q}{1+r}K-\frac{1-q}{(1+r)u}S_0$$

Therefore, American option will be early exercised at T = 1 with price $\frac{1-q}{1+r}K-\frac{1-q}{(1+r)u}S_0$.

The premium is: $Premium=P^A-P^E=\frac{qr+r+q+q^2}{(1+r)^2}K-\frac{(1-q)(u+ur-1+q)}{(1+r)^2u^2}S_0$.

4.5 Case V: $S_0d^2 < K \le S_0d$

If exercise at T, we will get the payoff:

When T = 2, $F\left(S_0u^2\right)=0$, $F(S_0)=0$, $F\left(S_0\frac{1}{u^2}\right)=K-S_0\frac{1}{u^2}$.

When T = 1, $F(S_0u)=0$, $F\left(S_0\frac{1}{u}\right)=0$.

When T = 0, $F(S_0)=0$.

For the European option,

$$X_1^E(S_0u)=0$$

$$X_1^E\left(S_0\frac{1}{u}\right)=\frac{1}{1+r}\left[q\times 0+(1-q)\left(K-S_0\frac{1}{u^2}\right)\right]=\frac{1-q}{1+r}K-\frac{1-q}{(1+r)u^2}S_0$$

$$P^E=X_0^E=\frac{1}{1+r}\left[q\times 0+(1-q)\left(\frac{1-q}{1+r}K-\frac{1-q}{(1+r)u^2}S_0\right)\right]$$

$$= \frac{(1-q)^2}{(1+r)^2}K - \frac{(1-q)^2}{(1+r)^2u^2}S_0$$

For the American option,

$$X_1^A(S_0u) = 0$$

$$X_1^A\left(S_0\frac{1}{u}\right) = max\left\{\frac{1-q}{1+r}K - \frac{1-q}{(1+r)u^2}S_0, 0\right\} = \frac{1-q}{1+r}K - \frac{1-q}{(1+r)u^2}S_0$$

$$P^A = X_0^A = max\left\{\frac{1}{1+r}\left[q \times 0 + (1-q)\left(\frac{1-q}{1+r}K - \frac{1-q}{(1+r)u^2}S_0\right)\right], K - S_0\right\}$$

$$= \frac{(1-q)^2}{(1+r)^2}K - \frac{(1-q)^2}{(1+r)^2u^2}S_0$$

Therefore, the holder will decide no early exercise with price $\frac{(1-q)^2}{(1+r)^2}K - \frac{(1-q)^2}{(1+r)^2u^2}S_0$.
The premium is:
$Premium = P^A - P^E = 0.$

4.6 Case VI: $K \leq S_0d^2$

If exercise at T, we will get the payoff:
When T = 2, $F(S_0u^2) = 0$, $F(S_0) = 0$, $F\left(S_0\frac{1}{u^2}\right) = 0$.
When T = 1, $F(S_0u) = 0$, $F\left(S_0\frac{1}{u}\right) = 0$.
When T = 0, $F(S_0) = 0$.
For the European option,

$$X_1^E(S_0u) = 0$$

$$X_1^E\left(S_0\frac{1}{u}\right) = 0$$

$$P^E = X_0^E = 0$$

For the American option,
$X_1^A(S_0u) = 0$.

$$X_1^A\left(S_0\frac{1}{u}\right) = 0$$

$$P^A = X_0^A = 0$$

Table 2 Results of American put option

No	Range of K	Exercise time	Price of American option	Premium
1	$K > S_0u^2$	T = 0	$K - S_0$	$\frac{r^2+2r}{(1+r)^2}K$
2	$K^* < K \le S_0u^2$	T = 0	$K - S_0$	$\frac{2r+r^2+q^2}{1+2r+r^2}K + \frac{u+r-rq^2-2r-r^2}{(1+r)^2u}S_0$
3	$S_0 < K \le K^*$	T = 1	$\frac{(1-q)(q+1+r)}{(1+r)^2}K - \frac{(1-q)(qu+r)}{(1+r)^2u}S_0$	$\frac{rq}{(1+r)^2}K + \frac{(1-q)(-q+u+uq+r+1)}{(1+r)^2u}S_0$
4	$S_0d < K \le S_0$	T = 1	$\frac{1-q}{1+r}K - \frac{1-q}{(1+r)u}S_0$	$\frac{qr+r+q+q^2}{(1+r)^2}K - \frac{(1-q)(u+ur-1+q)}{(1+r)^2u^2}S_0$
5	$S_0d^2 < K \le S_0d$	T = 2	$\frac{(1-q)^2}{(1+r)^2}K - \frac{(1-q)^2}{(1+r)^2u^2}S_0$	0
6	$K \le S_0d^2$	T = 2	0	0

Therefore, the holder will decide no early exercise with price 0.
The premium is:
$Premium = P^A - P^E = 0.$

4.7 *Results*

We can conclude the results in table 2.

5 Analysis of American Call Options Early Exercise

5.1 *No-Early Exercise*

For the call option, we calculate the payoff by $(S_T - K)^+$. If early exercise at time t, the holder need borrows K to buy the stock at time t. This means he will get a value of $S_T - K(1 + r)^{2-t}$ at the maturity time. If no-early exercise, the holder will get a value of $(S_T - K)^+$ at the maturity time. Therefore, the holder will choose no-early exercise [1].

$$S_T - K(1 + r)^{2-t} < S_T - K < (S_T - K)^+$$

In the binomial tree model, there are many reasons behind the typical decision not to exercise early for the American call options. Mainly because of the time value, it preserves the potential for significant gains in the future when stock prices rise, thus avoiding the loss of prematurely exercising appreciation opportunities. Secondly, capital cost is also an important factor, since holding options postpone the immediate expenditure required to buy the stock, it enables these funds to be invested elsewhere and generate further returns. We should also consider the inherent uncertainty of stock price movements within the model, and since stock prices may trend upward, investors can choose not to exercise their options early to obtain higher future value. Overall, the decision to exercise an American call option early in the binomial tree model depends on the interplay of factors such as market conditions, intrinsic characteristics of the stock, and investor requirements [11].

5.2 *Results*

American call options always have the same value as European call options, which means the holders will never choose early exercise for American call options. The reason is that exercising them before their expiration date means giving up the opportunity to gain higher profits from potential future increases in the price of the underlying asset, so holders typically choose to wait until the option expires to capture the maximum potential profit.

Based on all the research that have been conducted in academia, most have only focused on pricing of either American options or European options, without a comparison between the two. Though our research and literature review, our essay introduces a novel perspective by investigating the relationship between American option and European options, especially examining the special case of call option, where concluded that there is no significant difference in early exercising. By doing so, this study provides investor with insights into their decision making that allows them to maximize their profit. It helps with the current gap in academia and leads the field to development through the analyzing of early exercising strategy and timing for American options and European options from using mathematical models.

6 Conclusion

The use of two binomial model provides a clearer visualization of the potential future price movements of the stock and allows us to better calculate the payoff at different times, which enable us to evaluate and compare the benefits of early exercise versus exercising at expiration more effectively.

As a result, in the context of put options, the value of early exercise increases with a higher strike price K. This results in a higher early exercise premium, indicating that the option holder may gain additional value or benefit from exercising the option before expiration.

Conversely, for call options, early exercise is generally less advantageous compared to waiting until expiration, as the potential benefits of holding the option outweigh the immediate exercise value. Therefore, it is better to wait until the expiration to exercise a call option.

Acknowledgements Yuhe Ge, Mingxun Miao, and Haoran Wang contributed equally to this work and should be considered co-first authors.

References

1. Cox, J. C., Ross, S. A., & Rubinstein, M. (1979). Option pricing: A simplified approach. Journal of Financial Economics, 7(3), 229–263. https://doi.org/10.1016/0304-405x(79)90015-1
2. Albrecher, H., Binder, A., Lautscham, V., & Mayer, P. (2013). The binomial option pricing model. In Compact textbooks in mathematics (pp. 47–54). https://doi.org/10.1007/978-3-0348-0519-3_5
3. Black, F., & Scholes, M. (1973). The pricing of options and corporate liabilities. Journal of Political Economy, 81(3), 637–654. https://doi.org/10.1086/260062
4. Hull, J., & White, A. (1987). The Pricing of Options on Assets with Stochastic Volatilities. The Journal of Finance, 42(2), 281–300. https://doi.org/10.1111/j.1540-6261.1987.tb02568.x
5. Broadie, M., & Detemple, J. (1996). American Option Valuation: new bounds, approximations, and a comparison of existing methods. Review of Financial Studies, 9(4), 1211–1250. https://doi.org/10.1093/rfs/9.4.1211
6. Bayram, K., & Ganikhodjaev, N. (2013, April). On pricing futures options on random binomial tree. In Journal of Physics: Conference Series (Vol. 435, No. 1, p. 012043). IOP Publishing. https://doi.org/10.1088/1742-6596/435/1/012043
7. Musa, M., & Massalesse, J. (2019, October). The Binomial Model for N-Period European Call Option Price. In Journal of Physics: Conference Series (Vol. 1341, No. 6, p. 062037). IOP Publishing. https://doi.org/10.1088/1742-6596/1341/6/062037
8. Vestman, J. (2021). Option pricing in the binomial model.
9. Odegbile, O. O., & Ndogmo, J. C. (2005). Binomial option pricing Model. African institute of Mathematical Sciences.
10. Mou, Y., Li, M., Li, H., & Shi, B. (2022, July). Investigation on the Mechanism of American Put Option Pricing under Binomial Consideration. In 2022 2nd International Conference on Enterprise Management and Economic Development (ICEMED 2022) (pp. 255–261). Atlantis Press. https://doi.org/10.2991/aebmr.k.220603.044
11. Jensen, Mads Vestergaard, and Lasse Heje Pedersen. “Early Option Exercise: Never Say Never.Journal ofFinancial Economics, vol. 121, no. 2, Aug. 2016, pp. 278–299, https://doi.org/10.1016/jjfineco.2016.05.008.

Predicting BTCUSDT Based on the CNN-LSTM Model

Hao Zhang, Zihao Qiu, and Yilan Sheng

Abstract This study explores the modelling, use, and analysis of various machine learning and deep learning models for financial data. It focuses on testing the accuracy of cryptocurrency price prediction and analysing and demonstrating various interpretable features of machine learning models. This paper explains the features and limitations of traditional LSTM and CNN models in detail, combines both advantages and uses the CNN-LSTM model as the research model. In order to verify its superiority, the paper chooses the most common BTCUSDT in the market as the research object, and the data of the basic indicators of BTCUSDT from January 2019 to 31 December 2023 are compared by finding the optimal parameters of the model and establishing the CNN model and LSTM model. The experimental results show that the CNN-LSTM model is more advantageous than the traditional model in predicting the price of BTCUSDT and conclude that the proposed CNN-LSTM model has good feasibility and universality in predicting the effect.

Keywords Deep learning · LSTM-CNN · Bitcoin index · Parametric analysis · Entropy weighting method

1 Introduction

Bitcoin, a decentralised digital currency proposed by the mysterious Satoshi Nakamoto in 2008 and implemented in 2009, is the first application of blockchain technology. This distributed ledger allows multiple nodes to maintain and verify

H. Zhang (✉)
School of Economics, Guangdong University of Technology, Guangzhou, China
e-mail: 3083442385@qq.com

Z. Qiu
School of Economics, Sichuan University, Chengdu, China

Y. Sheng
School of Mathematics and Statistics, Hainan University, Haikou, China

E. Tsui et al. (eds.), *Management Information Systems in a Digitalized AI World*,
Springer Proceedings in Business and Economics,
https://doi.org/10.1007/978-981-96-6526-6_11

transactions without a central authority. Key features of Bitcoin include decentralisation, openness, limited supply, security, and a balance between anonymity and transparency. Bitcoin also offers privacy, as accounts can be created without centralised vetting or personal information. This system is seen as flexible, private, and resistant to regulatory control. Beyond being a decentralised payment method, Bitcoin is viewed as a volatile investment asset, attracting investors and challenging traditional financial systems while influencing markets.

However, the high volatility and complexity of the cryptocurrency market make price prediction a challenging task. Traditional financial market analysis methods often need help accurately capture cryptocurrency price dynamics. As Bitcoin lacks seasonality, machine-learning models are applicable and valuable [1]. Convolutional neural networks have been successfully applied in image data and time classification tasks on image and time-series data with powerful feature extraction and recognition capabilities [2]. Due to steadily growing computational power and increasing data availability, forecasting economic time series via machine learning techniques describes a novel string of techniques and research [3]. Although so far, several deep learning methods have been studied and compared for the Bitcoin price prediction, most previous work has considered only a few deep learning methods, mostly based on a deep neural network (DNN) or a recurrent neural network (RNN) [4]. This study aims to explore a more accurate and efficient cryptocurrency price prediction model by combining the advantages of Long Short-Term Memory Networks (LSTM) and Convolutional Neural Networks (CNN).

Combining LSTM with CNN for Bitcoin price prediction is indeed a clever approach, as it seamlessly integrates the strengths of both models. CNNs excel at extracting local patterns from raw data, akin to swiftly capturing the market's micro-fluctuations and short-term trends. On the other hand, LSTMs are masters at capturing long-term dependencies in time series and adept at modelling Bitcoin's long-term price movements and cycles.

By fusing these two, it is like equipping the prediction model with a pair of eyes that can see both the path ahead (short-term trends) and the horizon beyond (long-term price dynamics). This hybrid approach offers a potent tool for Bitcoin price forecasting and can be readily adapted to other financial time series forecasting tasks, making it incredibly versatile and practical.

The structure of this paper is as follows: Section 2 is a literature review and the work this paper contributes. Section 3 introduces the basic principles of RNN, LSTM, and CNN models and comprehensively summarises the prediction indexes and evaluation criteria. Section 4 describes the sources of data, data selection and the values of statistics. Section 5 brings the data as a training set and validation set into the LSTM, CNN and LSTM-CNN coupled models, respectively, compares the fit of the predictions, and at the same time, adjusts the parameters of the coupled models (seq-length, learning rate, epochs and filters), and analyses the most powerful model and model parameters for Bitcoin prediction parameters. Section 6 analyses the problems of this experiment and possible future improvements.

2 Literature

Svetlana Borovkova et al. developed an ensemble model based on LSTM networks for categorical forecasting of high-frequency stock markets, using a rolling window approach for training and dynamically adjusting weights for each model [5]. Hongrui Zhao et al. proposed a hybrid LSTM-CNN model with an attention mechanism for financial time series forecasting [6]. Ahmad El Majzoub et al. explored deep learning algorithms for cryptocurrency market forecasting, finding LSTM and CNN to perform well [7]. Yi-Qiu Fang et al. proposed a new stock prediction model using LSTM and CNN, addressing the limitations of earlier linear models [8]. Theo Berger et al. compared machine learning techniques, including RNN and LSTM, with the ARMA-GARCH model for predicting Bitcoin returns, finding machine learning techniques to outperform the econometric model in terms of prediction accuracy [9].

The main contributions of this article are (1) constructing a joint CNN- LSTM model to predict the price movement of Bitcoin and (2) adjusting the model parameters to seek better prediction results.

3 Methodology

3.1 Model Analysis

With the increase of neural networks, deep learning has attracted increasing attention [10–12]. Table 1 shows detailed information on the model used in this paper.

3.2 Evaluation Functions

Table 2 shows detailed information on the evaluation functions used in this paper.

4 Data

The data analysed, spanning from January 2019 to December 31, 2023, were sourced from the Coin Exchange. This five-year period captures several significant phases in the cryptocurrency market, including bull and bear markets, sharp market volatility, and shifts in regulatory policies. This diverse dataset offers valuable insights into how the market behaves under different conditions, serving as a useful reference for future market predictions and the development of investment strategies.

Table 1 Model analysis

model	theory	characteristic	formula
RNN	Recurrent Neural Networks (RNNs) process sequences by retaining a "memory" of previous inputs through loops	This allows them to handle tasks like language modelling and time series prediction. RNNs combine the current input with the previous hidden state at each step to generate an output and update the hidden state for the next step	$h_t = \sigma(W_{xt}x_t + W_{hh}h_{t-1} + b_h)$
LSTM	The Long-Short-Term Memory (LSTM) network is a particular class of RNNs, which solves the issue caused by RNN by connecting the cell states in a linear way, thus ensuring strong and stable gradients [5]	It uses a cell state and three gates (input, forget, and output) to control the flow of information, allowing it to remember or forget information over time. This helps LSTMs maintain information across long sequences more effectively than standard RNNs	$f_t = \sigma(W_f \cdot [h_{t-1}, x_t] + b_f)$ $i_t = \sigma(W_i \cdot [h_{t-1}, x_t] + b_i)$ $\tilde{C} = \tanh(W_i \cdot [h_{t-1}, x_t] + b_i)$ $C_t = f_t \cdot C_{t-1} + i_t \cdot \tilde{C}$ $o_t = \sigma(W_o \cdot [h_{t-1}, x_t] + b_o)$ $h_t = o_t \cdot \tanh(C_t)$

(continued)

Table 1 (continued)

model	theory	characteristic	formula
CNN	Convolutional Neural Networks (CNNs) specialise in processing grid-like data like images	CNNs use filters to detect features like edges and textures and reduce spatial dimensions while preserving key information. This makes CNNs effective for tasks like image classification and object detection	$(f*g)(u,v) = \sum_{m=-\infty}^{+\infty} \sum_{n=-\infty}^{+\infty} f(m,n) \cdot g(u-m, v-n)$ $\text{Pooling}(u,v) =$ $\max(\text{or average})\{f(u,v), f(u+1,v), \ldots, f(u+k-1,v), f(u,v+1), \ldots\}$
LSTM-CNN	LSTM-CNN combines LSTM and CNN architectures to handle both sequential and spatial data	The CNN extracts spatial features from inputs like images, while the LSTM processes the sequence of these features to capture temporal dependencies. This hybrid model is adequate for tasks like video analysis, where both spatial and temporal information are essential	

Table 2 Evaluation functions

parameter	definition	formula	use
MSE	MSE (Mean Squared Error) measures the average squared difference between actual and predicted values in a dataset	$MSE = \frac{1}{n}\sum_{i=1}^{n}(y_i - \hat{y}_i)^2$ standardizied MSE = $\frac{MSE}{\bar{y}^2}$	It's commonly used in regression to assess model accuracy, with lower MSE indicating a better fit
RMSE	RMSE (Root Mean Squared Error) is the square root of the Mean Squared Error (MSE)	$RMSE = \sqrt{MSE}$ standardizied RMSE = $\frac{RMSE}{\bar{y}}$	It measures the average error magnitude in the same units as the data, with lower values indicating better model performance
RMAE	RMAE (Relative Mean Absolute Error) normalises MAE by the mean of the observed values	$RMAE = \frac{MAE}{\bar{y}}$	It provides a relative measure of prediction accuracy, with lower values indicating better performance
MAPE	MAPE (Mean Absolute Percentage Error) measures the average absolute percentage difference between actual and predicted values	$MAPE = \frac{1}{n}\sum_{i=1}^{n}\left\|\frac{y_i - \hat{y}_i}{y_i}\right\|$	Lower MAPE values indicate better accuracy

5 Result

5.1 Comparison of LSTM-CNN Joint Model Parameters

See Figs. 1 and 2.

5.1.1 Filters

Through the Fig. 1, With the increasing of Filters, the values of MSE, RMSE, RMAE, and MAPE decrease, which signifies an improvement in prediction accuracy. This is because more filters enhance the model's ability to identify intricate and complex patterns in the data, which in turn leads to better overall prediction performance. However, it is not the case that more filters are always better; using an excessively high number of filters increases computational load and shortens training time. Through experimentation, 64 filters achieved a good balance between performance and efficiency.

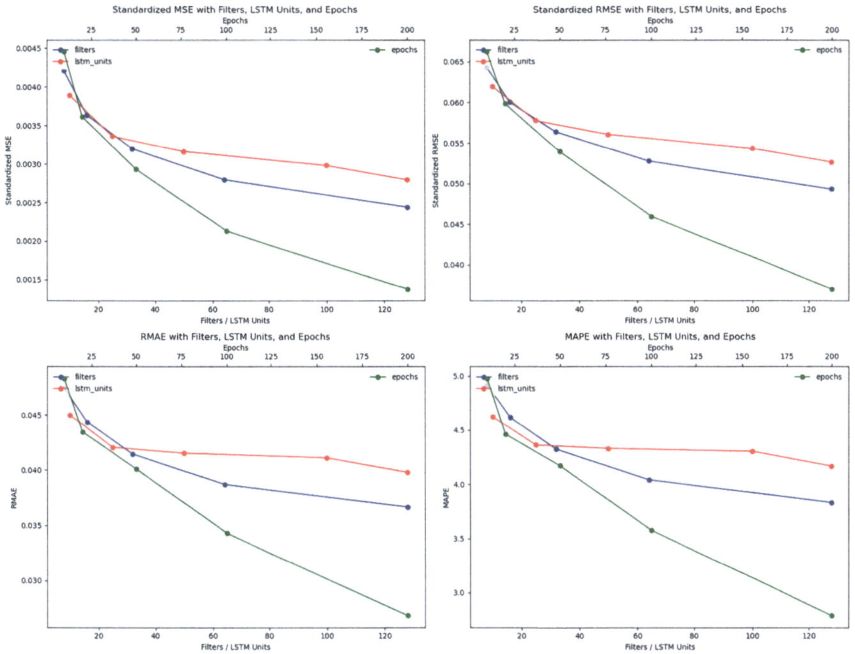

Fig. 1 The coefficient of error versus the parameters of Filters, LSTM Units and Epochs

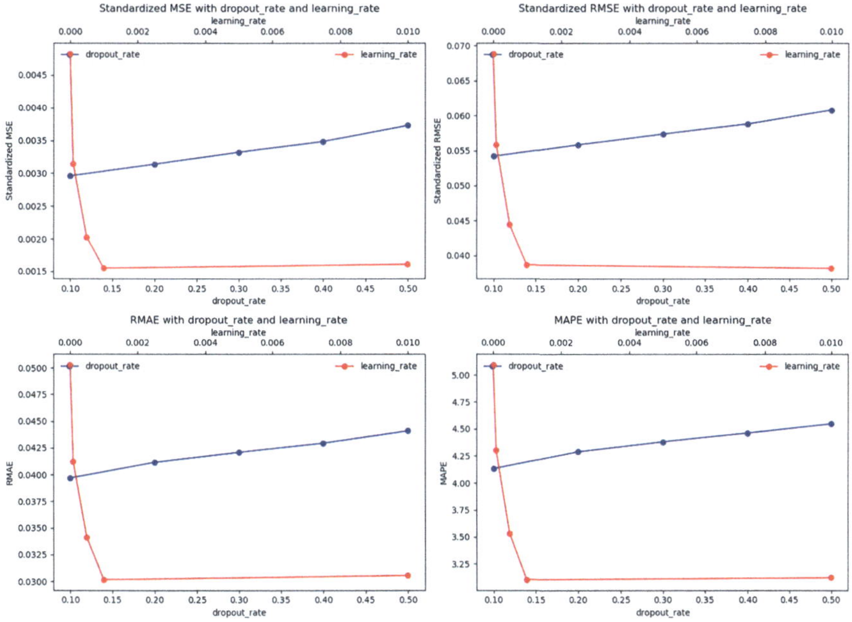

Fig. 2 The coefficient of error versus the parameters of Dropout_rate and Learning_rate

5.1.2 LSTM_units

Figure 1 shows that with the increase in LSTM units, the MSE, RMSE, RMAE, and MAPE values decrease, indicating an improvement in prediction accuracy. This enhancement can be attributed to the fact that boosting the number of LSTM units enhances the model's capacity to capture intricate patterns and long-term dependencies within time series data. However, it is essential to note that using excessive units can elevate the risk of overfitting and escalate computational costs. After comparison, 100 LSTM units achieved a good balance between performance and efficiency.

5.1.3 Epochs

Figure 1 illustrates that as the number of training epochs increases, the MSE, RMSE, RMAE, and MAPE values decrease, improving prediction accuracy. This is because more epochs give the LSTM-CNN model more opportunities to learn from the data, allowing it to adjust its weights and reduce prediction errors. However, the error reduction rate begins to slow as the number of epochs increases. Over-training also increases computational time and the risk of overfitting. Since the improvements in error reduction slow down after 100 epochs, 100 epochs were chosen as the optimal number for training.

5.1.4 Dropout_rate

Figure 2 shows that an increase in the dropout rate is correlated with a rise in MSE, RMSE, RMAE, and MAPE values, indicating an increase in prediction errors. This is because a higher Dropout rate means more neurons are dropped during training, limiting the model's ability to learn complex patterns and decreasing performance. After comparison, the Dropout rate of 0.1 was chosen to prevent overfitting while maintaining sufficient model complexity for accurate predictions.

5.1.5 Learning_rate

Figure 2 shows that the MSE, RMSE, RMAE, and MAPE values first decrease and then increase with the increase in learning rate. In the first half of the curve, the increase in the learning rate helps the model jump out of the local optimal solution and explore a larger parameter space to find a better global optimal solution. In the second half of the curve, the learning rate is too large for the model to converge steadily in these flat regions. Instead, it may oscillate repeatedly within these areas.

5.2 *Comparison of LSTM, CNN and LSTM-CNN Associative Models*

Using the above three models to predict the value of Bitcoin/USD, respectively, the true value and the predicted value are shown in Fig. 3. The problems that the LSTM model and CNN model have with each other when predicting through image analysis were found. The LSTM is mainly for the time series data. However, LSTM focuses on time series data and performs poorly in carving out the corners of the image, and the predicted line segments are smoother. CNN is unsuitable for dealing with long-time series data because it lacks the mechanism to capture the long-time dependency, leading to bias between the true value and the predicted value. The LSTM-CNN model combines the advantages of both models, and it is better in both time series and local performance. The true value is similar to the predicted value, proving that the constructed concatenated model is more predictive than the LSTM and CNN from the perspective of the degree of fit.

Figure 4 shows the prediction error performance of the CNN, CNN-LSTM and LSTM models for different months in 2023 for four metrics: normalised MSE, normalised RMSE, RMAE and MAPE.

In order to measure the comprehensive performance of each model more objectively, the entropy weight method was used to construct an evaluation system to measure the fitting effect of each model.

Figure 5 shows that the CNN-LSTM model, by and large, has the highest combined score in the entropy weighting method as the best-performing model for prediction.

6 Conclusion

This paper evaluates the ability of the Convolutional Neural Network—Long-Short-Term Memory (CNN-LSTM) to predict the variation of BTCUSDT values. The sensitivity of different parameters to the model prediction results was explored by adjusting the parameters and selecting the better solution to compare it with the standard Convolutional Neural Network (CNN) model and Long-Short-Term Memory (LSTM) model.

The results show that CNN-LSTM is an effective prediction method for the value of BTCUSDT. It combines the advantages of the CNN model and LSTM to better predict the future trend of BTCUSDT, and its composite scores are higher than the other two models in almost all monthly results.

By repeatedly adjusting parameters such as the number of filters, LSTM units, dropout rate, and learning rate, the model finally shows better performance. Overall, the CNN-LSTM model is highly feasible for price prediction in the cryptocurrency market and provides effective technical support for predicting future price fluctuations.

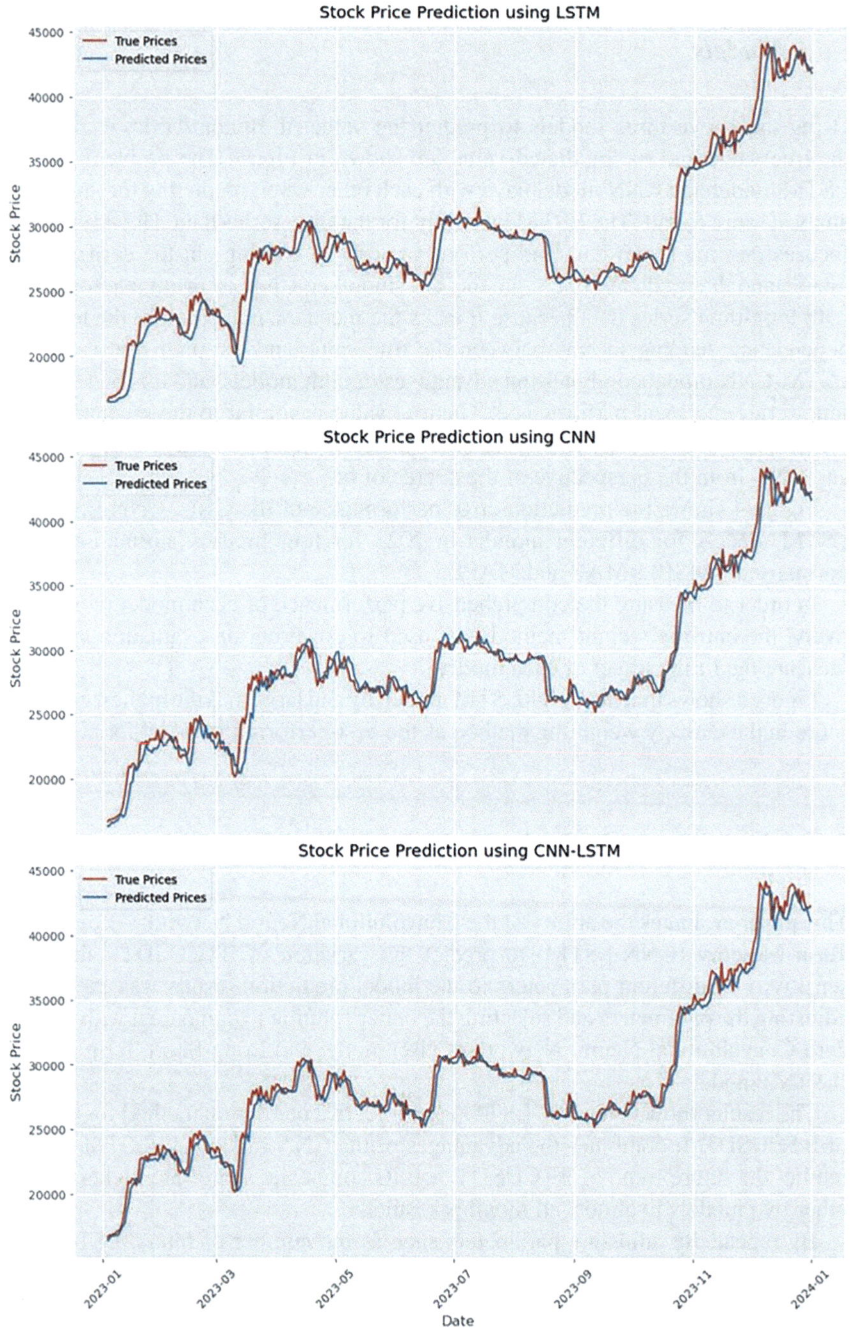

Fig. 3 Comparison of the forecast value with the actual value by using LSTM, CNN and LSTM-CNN

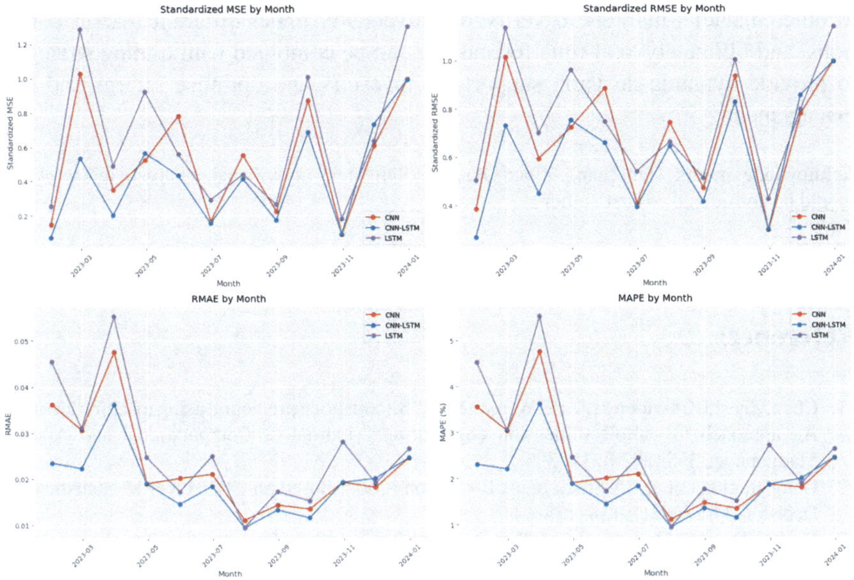

Fig. 4 The prediction error performance of the CNN, CNN-LSTM and LSTM models for different months

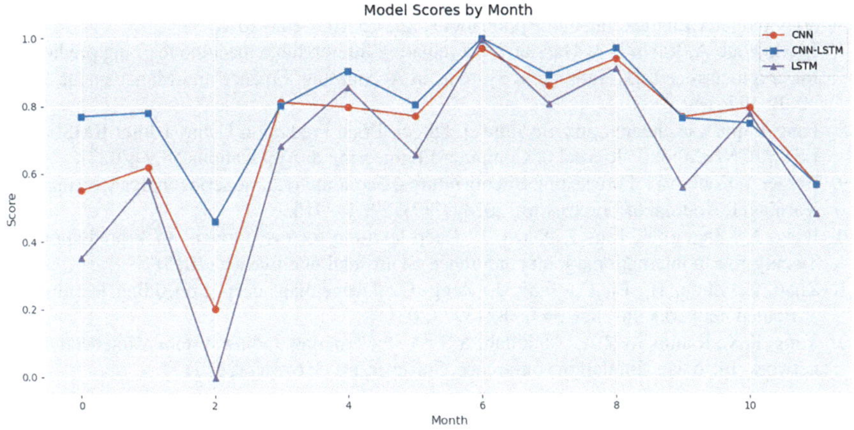

Fig. 5 Model scores by month

Future research can further improve the model's prediction accuracy by introducing more variables that affect market movements, such as trading volume and market sentiment data; at the same time, it can optimise the model's ability to capture long-time dependencies with the help of advanced techniques such as the Attention Mechanism or the Transformer Structure. In addition, the model can be extended to other financial markets to verify its universality under different market conditions, and ultimately, real-time forecasting can be combined with trading strategies to provide dynamic decision support for investors and optimise returns and risk management.

Acknowledgements Hao Zhang, Zihao Qiu and Yilan Sheng contributed equally to this work and should be considered co-first authors.

References

1. Chen, Zheshi, Chunhong Li, and Wenjun Sun. "Bitcoin price prediction using machine learning: An approach to sample dimension engineering." Journal of Computational and Applied Mathematics 365 (2020): 112395.
2. Geng Jingjing, et al. "A Stock Index Prediction Model Based on CNN-LSTM." Statistics and Decision 37.5 (2021): 134–138.
3. Berger, Theo, and Jana Koubová. "Forecasting Bitcoin returns: Econometric time series analysis vs. machine learning." Journal of Forecasting.
4. Rumelhart, D.E.; Hinton, G.E.; Williams, R.J. Learning representations by back-propagating errors. Nature1986, 323, 533–536.
5. Borovkova, Svetlana, and Ioannis Tsiamas. "An ensemble of LSTM neural networks for high-frequency stock market classification." Journal of Forecasting 38.6 (2019): 600–619.
6. Zhao Hongrui, Xue Lei. Research on stock prediction based on LSTM-CNN-CBAM model [J]. Computer Engineering and Applications, 2021,57(03):203–207.
7. El Majzoub A, Rabhi F A, Hussain W. Evaluating interpretable machine learning predictions for cryptocurrencies[J]. Intelligent Systems in Accounting, Finance and Management, 2023, 30(3): 137–149.
8. Fang Yiqiu, Lu Zhuang, and Ge Junwei. "Stock Price Prediction Using a Joint RMSE Loss LSTM-CNN Model." Journal of Computer Engineering & Applications 58.9 (2022).
9. Berger T, Koubová J. Forecasting Bitcoin returns: Econometric time series analysis vs. machine learning[J]. Journal of Forecasting, 2024, 43(7): 2904–2916.
10. Ding, X., Zhang, Y., Liu, T., Duan, J.: Deep learning for eventdriven stock prediction. In: Twenty-fourth international joint conference on artifcial intelligence (2015)
11. Zhao, Z., Zhou, H., Li, C., Tang, J., Zeng, Q.: Deepemlan: deep embedding learning for attributed networks. Inf. Sci. 543, 382–397 (2021)
12. Yong, B.X., Rahim, M.R.A., Abdullah, A.S.: A stock market trading system using deep neural network. In: Asian simulation conference, Springer, pp. 356–364 (2017)

Three Basic Machine Learning Models' Suitability for Predicting Bank Churn

Yibin Li, Mingze Gao, Yanfu Zhang, Changbin Feng, Muxi Chen, and Luyun Zhang

Abstract Credit card customer churn is defined as the situation in which a bank's customer stops using the bank's service and it leads to a potential loss of profit for the bank. Therefore, developing a customer churn prediction model for predicting customer likelihood of churning is essential for banks. This study aims to find out the key factor that influences credit card customer churn and to build a well performing model with high predicting accuracy. Finally, we can give some advice for banks to decrease customer churn. To achieve the goal, three models are employed, including neural network, logistic regression and decision tree model. The results indicate that all three models can be employed in different situations. However, the decision tree model has the best performance in both training and testing phases. The study further reveals that the top three factors influencing the likelihood of customer churn are total transaction count, total transaction amount, and changes in total transaction count. Based on the strengths and weaknesses of each model, this paper will also illustrate the different scenarios in which each model is most suitable.

Y. Li (✉)
Rutgers Business School, Rutgers University-NB, Piscataway, NJ, USA
e-mail: yl1857@rutgers.edu

M. Gao
College of Art & Science, University of Virginia, Charlottesville, VA, USA
e-mail: mg9aam@virginia.edu

Y. Zhang
School of Economics and Management, Xidian University, Xin, China
e-mail: 22061300036@stu.xidian.edu.cn

C. Feng
Department of Economic Management, North China Electric Power University, Baoding, China

M. Chen
Questrom School of Business, Boston University, Boston, MA, USA
e-mail: chenmuxi@bu.edu

L. Zhang
University of Edinburgh Business School, The University of Edinburgh, Edinburgh, UK
e-mail: s2163495@ed.ac.uk

E. Tsui et al. (eds.), *Management Information Systems in a Digitalized AI World*,
Springer Proceedings in Business and Economics,
https://doi.org/10.1007/978-981-96-6526-6_12

Keywords Machine learning · Customer churn · Predicting model · Bank churn

1 Introduction

The cost of acquiring new customers is generally higher than that of retaining existing ones [1]. Furthermore, long-term customers often yield greater profits, making customer retention a critical factor in enhancing overall profitability [1]. In today's increasingly competitive market, retaining existing customers is crucial for any business. According to Nie's research, a bank can increase its profits by 85% by improving the retention rate of existing customers by just 5% [1]. Therefore, customer churn is a critical issue for the banking industry. Customer churn define as "the loss of a customer to a competitor, which leads to losses in profits" [2]. Identifying customers who are likely to terminate their banking services and understanding the patterns associated with these customers can significantly enhance service quality and increase retention rates. In the modern era, machine learning methods are widely employed by banks to predict customer churn. Using big data, these methods classify customers as either churners or non-churners [3–5]. Numerous studies in the literature have developed various predictive models using statistical and data mining techniques, including random forests, logistic regression, neural networks, Bayesian networks, the C5 tree, the chi-square automatic interaction detection (CHAID) tree, and the classification and regression (CR) tree. Using machine learning and statistical methods to predict customer churn is a well-established field that has been studied by many researchers. A bunch of well-trained models have been developed by researchers in the field. In contrast, this paper will not focus on developing the best model for predicting customer churn. The author will focus on developing models, find each model's strength and match the situation the models fit.

2 Literature Review

Churn management is a part of Customer Relationship Management (CRM), it is important for firms to maintain long-term customer relationships and optimize profitability [6]. The phenomenon of customer churn will affect firms in multiple dimensions. First and foremost, the loss of existing customers is one of the biggest factors that diminished profits. This loss not only results in an immediate decline in product sales but also will increase customer acquisition costs. Furthermore, if the services are under contractual agreements, customer churn represents more than just a reduction in sales - it also means the end of the customer relationship [6]. Under today's intensely competitive market, the competition between banks is particularly fierce [7]. Therefore, the ability to predict customer churn and identify the causes of customer churn is crucial for banks seeking to sustain and enhance their competitive ability.

Accordingly, banks are closely monitoring their customers for warning signals that may indicate potential churn. Machine learning becomes a common tool for banks to predict churn by analyzing the data collected from their customers. These methods can make banks uncover hidden patterns behind datasets to build predictive models for predicting customer churn [8].

The prediction of credit card customer churn is a well-established area of research, with numerous studies contributing to the field. One remarkable researcher is Dana, her studies is focusing on developing credit card customer churn prediction models using a feature selection method running by five machine learning models: the Bayesian network, the C5 tree, the chi-square automatic interaction detection (CHAID) tree, the classification and regression (CR) tree, and a neural network [2]. Above this basic idea, Dana constructed three variations of each prediction model, utilizing different independent variable selection methods, including the use of all independent variables, two-step clustering, k-nearest neighbor, and feature selection [2]. According to her research, the C5 tree machine learning model performs the best. It has a test recall value of 0.861. The output of the model reveals that the top three variables influencing customer churn were the total transaction count, the total revolving balance on the credit card, and the change in transaction count [2].

Although Dana's research indicates that the C5 tree model delivers the best performance, different models offer unique advantages and are suited to different scenarios. Recognizing this, the author of this study identifies two research gaps:

Exploring the use of various models, including decision trees, logistic regression, and neural networks, to develop a best predictive model for credit card customer churn.

Uncover the strengths of each model and describe the situations in which each model is most effectively applied.

Using the model's results, provide recommendations for the bank to reduce customer churn.

3 Exploratory Data Analysis (EDA)

The dataset used for this research was collected from https://www.kaggle.com/datasets/teralasowmya/bankchurner in Karggle websit. The dataset comprises 21 features, including both categorical and numerical variables. It contains records of 10,000 customers. The EDA revealed several insights into the factors influencing customer attrition. The distribution of customer age revealed a higher concentration of customers within the 40–60 age group. Attrition rates varied significantly by gender, with female customers exhibiting a slightly higher attrition rate. The credit limit distribution indicated that customers who churned tended to have lower credit limits. Additionally, the scatter plot of total transaction amount versus customer age showed that younger customers generally had higher transaction amounts, with a noticeable distinction between existing and churned customers.

Correlation analysis identified strong correlations between features such as total transaction count, total transaction amount, and average utilization ratio with the target variable. Furthermore, we observed a significant imbalance in the data between churners and non-churners. As a result, we employed undersampling and oversampling methods to balance the data in subsequent model-building steps.

4 Data Preprocessing

4.1 Data Splitting

In the data splitting section, the common approach is to divide the existing dataset into a training set and a test set. However, in this study, we divided the dataset into three parts: the training set, validation set, and test set. The training set is used to train the model, the test set is used to evaluate the model's performance after training and validation, and the newly added validation set is used for fine-tuning the model's performance and parameters after training. The data in the validation set accounts for only 5% of the total data, which is less than the amount in the test set. This approach has two advantages. First, validating the model after training can improve its accuracy during testing. Second, with a smaller amount of data, the time required to optimize the model is reduced, saving time.

4.2 Handling Missing Values

To handle missing values in the dataset, we employed a strategy of filling in the gaps with the most frequent value for each feature. This approach offers several advantages. First, it helps maintain data consistency, as the most frequent value, having already appeared multiple times in the dataset, reflects the common characteristics of the data. Second, it reduces data bias, particularly when compared to methods such as filling with the mean or median, which can be influenced by outliers or extreme values. This is especially advantageous for categorical data, where the most frequent value often represents the predominant category. Additionally, this method is straightforward and requires no complex calculations, making it an efficient and effective way to address missing data. Finally, by using the most frequent value, the original data distribution is better preserved, ensuring that the filled data remains representative of the dataset's overall characteristics. Overall, this approach enhances data quality and, consequently, improves the performance of machine learning models.

Table 1 Recall value after undersampling

	precision	recall	f1-score	support
0	0.97	0.83	0.89	993
1	0.51	0.87	0.64	203
accuracy			0.84	1196
macro avg	0.74	0.85	0.77	1196
weighted avg	0.89	0.84	0.85	1196

5 Model Building

5.1 Model 1: Logistic Regression

Logistic regression is an important method used for classification tasks. It finally obtains the probability of each class in the data set or event existing. Unlike linear regression which predicts a continuous value, logistic regression predicts the probability of a binary outcome. It's commonly used in various fields such as healthcare, finance, and marketing.

5.1.1 Data Processing

Before doing logistic regression, we can find that the imbalance problem in the data set. Undersampling and oversampling are two methods to address this issue. However, among these two resampling strategies, undersampling has been shown to be a better choice than oversampling [9]. Undersampling is an effective data processing method, particularly suitable in two scenarios. First, when the number of majority class samples is very large, undersampling can reduce these samples, thereby alleviating data imbalance. Additionally, for large datasets, undersampling can decrease the computational load. The dataset in this problem contains over 10,000 entries, making it necessary to preprocess the data using undersampling. After applying undersampling and feeding the processed data back into the logistic regression model, there was a significant improvement in the recall value, as shown in Table 1.

The improved recall value indicates that the model is highly fitted to the existing data and performs well in predictions, making the results both feasible and highly reliable.

5.1.2 Model Results

The final results of the logistic regression model are generated by using the SHAP package. The SHAP values method is a feature attribution technique that assigns a value to each feature for a specific prediction, which is useful for interpreting the prediction results [10]. SHAP can generate feature importance plots and other global interpretation charts which can help us to understand the overall behavior of the model and the impact of each feature on customer churn. Additionally, SHAP provides explanations for individual predictions, showing the contribution of each feature in specific cases. This is significant for understanding the model's decision-making process at the individual level. The model analyzed the impact of various user features on the possibility of customer churn, and the results displayed in Fig. 1.

This figure illustrates the impact of each feature on the model's output using SHAP (SHapley Additive exPlanations) values, which highlight how features contribute to prediction results. The color gradient, ranging from blue (lower values) to red (higher values), indicates the magnitude of feature values in each sample. The X-axis represents SHAP values, where positive values indicate a feature's positive impact on the prediction, and negative values indicate a negative impact. The spread of dots along the X-axis reflects the variation in each feature's impact, while the vertical density of dots shows how frequently similar SHAP values occur across

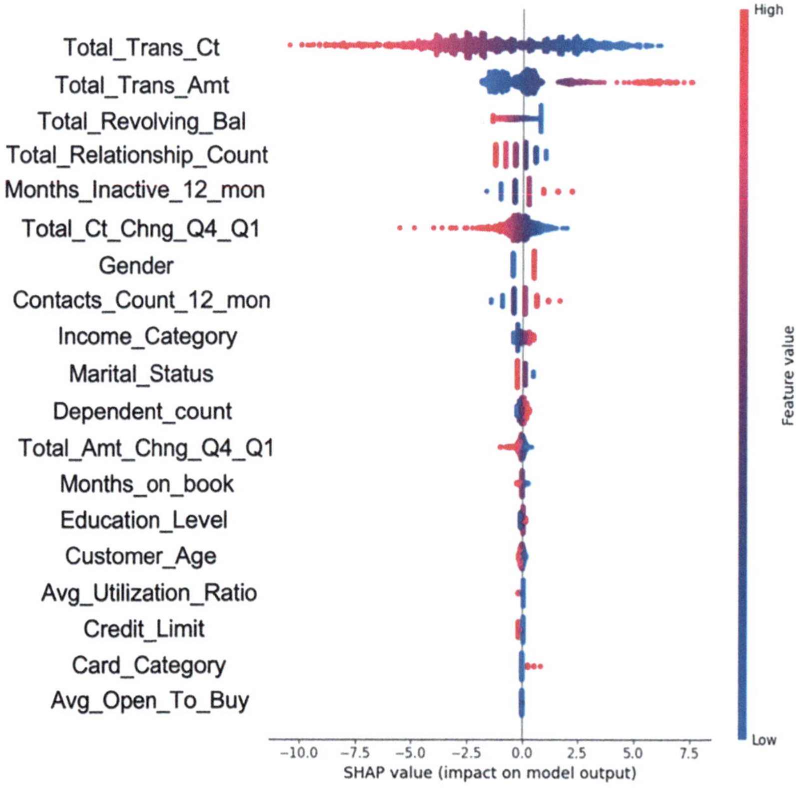

Fig. 1 SHAP result

samples. Analyzing these relationships helps identify the most influential features in predicting customer churn and whether they increase or decrease the likelihood of churn, providing valuable insights for effectively addressing customer retention.

From the above figure, we can easily find that Total transaction count in the last 12 months and Total transaction amount in the last 12 months are two main reasons which infect the churning of the customers. They can also be considered as two key parameters which can predict the future churning of the customers in the neural network.

5.2 *Model 2: Neural Network*

Ref. [11] provide a thorough examination of various machine learning techniques for churn prediction in the banking industry, highlighting the significance of feature importance and model performance. [11] This has some inspiration for us to build models. [12] explore the application of machine learning, including neural networks, for customer churn prediction in banking, emphasizing the relevance of this approach to our study. [12] In this case, the model is designed to predict whether customers will remain with the bank or stop using its services. It does this by analyzing input data that includes 20 features, such as CLIENTNUM, Customer_Age, Gender, and others, to produce an output indicating true or false.

5.2.1 Step One: Determine and Define the Number of Layers and Nodes

Model 1 (Fig. 2).

Model 2 (Fig. 3).

Model 3 (Fig. 4).

The three neural network models increase in complexity and depth, while sharing core features. Each model has an input layer, multiple hidden layers, and a single-output neuron with a sigmoid function for binary classification.

```
# We will be adding the layers sequentially
model_1 = Sequential()

# First hidden layer with 256 neurons and relu activation function, the input shape tuple denotes number of independent variables
model_1.add(Dense(256, activation='relu', input_shape=(X_train_normalized.shape[1],)))

# We will be switching 20% of neurons off randomly at each iteration to avoid overfitting
model_1.add(Dropout(0.2))

# Second hidden layer with 128 neurons and relu activation function
model_1.add(Dense(128, activation='relu'))

# We will be switching 10% of neurons off randomly at each iteration to avoid overfitting
model_1.add(Dropout(0.1))

# The output layer has only one neuron and sigmoid as the activation function will give the probability of losing the user
model_1.add(Dense(1, activation='sigmoid'))
```

Fig. 2 Layers and nodes

```
# Input Layer dan hidden Layer 1
model.add(Dense(units = 12, kernel_initializer = 'uniform', activation = 'relu', input_dim = 10))

# hidden Layer kedua
model.add(Dense(units = 12, kernel_initializer = 'uniform', activation = 'relu'))
model.add(Dense(units = 12, kernel_initializer = 'uniform', activation = 'relu'))

# Output Layer
model.add(Dense(units = 1, kernel_initializer = 'uniform', activation = 'sigmoid'))

# Compile ANN
model.compile(optimizer = adam, loss = 'mse', metrics = ['accuracy'])
```

Fig. 3 Layers and nodes

```
# Input Layer dan hidden Layer 1
model.add(Dense(units = 24, kernel_initializer = 'uniform', activation = 'relu', input_dim = 10))

# hidden Layer kedua
model.add(Dense(units = 24, kernel_initializer = 'uniform', activation = 'relu'))
model.add(Dense(units = 24, kernel_initializer = 'uniform', activation = 'relu'))
model.add(Dense(units = 24, kernel_initializer = 'uniform', activation = 'relu'))

# Output Layer
model.add(Dense(units = 1, kernel_initializer = 'uniform', activation = 'sigmoid'))

# Compile ANN
model.compile(optimizer = adam, loss = 'mse', metrics = ['accuracy'])
```

Fig. 4 Layers and nodes

Model 1 has two hidden layers (256 and 128 neurons) with ReLU activation and dropout layers. Model 2 adds a third hidden layer (64 neurons) and uses tanh activation in all hidden layers, with dropout after the first two. Model 3 includes a fourth hidden layer (32 neurons), maintaining tanh activations and dropout after the first three layers.

All models use weight variables initialized with a uniform function, adjusted during training based on the Mean Squared Error loss function. The Adam optimizer fine-tunes weights to minimize loss and maximize accuracy, using a 0.01 learning rate. Activation functions transform inputs into outputs for each layer, driving the network's predictions through sequential matrix calculations.

5.2.2 Step Two: Training Model

Creating three different models allows the system to study the correlation between feature data and labels through mathematical calculations. This approach ensures that the models can be effectively applied to new data in the future (Fig. 5).

By writing the model_1.fit function and providing certain arguments, the model is trained using normalized feature data (X_train_normalized) and corresponding labels (y_train). The validation_split = 0.1 argument is used to allocate 10% of the training data for validation purposes, helping to monitor the model's performance during training. The epochs = 150 argument sets the number of times the model will

```
history_1 = model_1.fit(X_train_normalized,
                        y_train,
                        validation_split=0.1,
                        epochs=150,
                        verbose=1)
```

Fig. 5 Train the model

```
Epoch 1/150
74/74 ━━━━━━━━━━━━━━━━━━━━ 2s 5ms/step - accuracy: 0.8272 - loss: 0.4946 - val_accuracy: 0.8769 - val_loss: 0.3812
Epoch 2/150
74/74 ━━━━━━━━━━━━━━━━━━━━ 0s 4ms/step - accuracy: 0.8333 - loss: 0.4511 - val_accuracy: 0.8769 - val_loss: 0.3832
Epoch 3/150
74/74 ━━━━━━━━━━━━━━━━━━━━ 0s 3ms/step - accuracy: 0.8333 - loss: 0.4502 - val_accuracy: 0.8769 - val_loss: 0.3848
Epoch 4/150
74/74 ━━━━━━━━━━━━━━━━━━━━ 0s 3ms/step - accuracy: 0.8333 - loss: 0.4493 - val_accuracy: 0.8769 - val_loss: 0.3857
Epoch 5/150
74/74 ━━━━━━━━━━━━━━━━━━━━ 0s 3ms/step - accuracy: 0.8333 - loss: 0.4455 - val_accuracy: 0.8769 - val_loss: 0.3851
Epoch 6/150
74/74 ━━━━━━━━━━━━━━━━━━━━ 0s 4ms/step - accuracy: 0.8333 - loss: 0.4457 - val_accuracy: 0.8769 - val_loss: 0.3857
Epoch 7/150
74/74 ━━━━━━━━━━━━━━━━━━━━ 0s 3ms/step - accuracy: 0.8333 - loss: 0.4457 - val_accuracy: 0.8769 - val_loss: 0.3852
Epoch 8/150
74/74 ━━━━━━━━━━━━━━━━━━━━ 0s 3ms/step - accuracy: 0.8333 - loss: 0.4449 - val_accuracy: 0.8769 - val_loss: 0.3845
Epoch 9/150
74/74 ━━━━━━━━━━━━━━━━━━━━ 0s 3ms/step - accuracy: 0.8333 - loss: 0.4448 - val_accuracy: 0.8769 - val_loss: 0.3852
Epoch 10/150
74/74 ━━━━━━━━━━━━━━━━━━━━ 0s 3ms/step - accuracy: 0.8333 - loss: 0.4404 - val_accuracy: 0.8769 - val_loss: 0.3855
```

Fig. 6 Model training process

go through the entire training dataset during the training process, allowing it to learn and adjust its parameters through forward and backpropagation. The verbose = 1 argument ensures that detailed information about the training process is displayed, including the loss and accuracy for each epoch (Fig. 6).

Figure 6 shows the model 3 training process (one sample taken from the three model designs) with an epoch of 200, with a loss of 0.0491 and an accuracy of 98%.

5.2.3 Step 3: Testing the Model.

The data used in this stage are X_test and Y_test from the dataset to test whether the model can predict from new data, and not only remember the data from the model training process.

Figure 7 shows that the model achieved a recall of 0.86 in testing, compared to 0.98 in training. This indicates that the model can effectively predict new data, rather than simply memorizing the training data.

Table 2 is the result of designing a model from 3 layer and node models that have been created.

In conclusion, deep learning models based on artificial neural networks (ANN) are used to address classification problems and enhance predictive services in the

```
              precision    recall  f1-score   support

           0       0.95      0.95      0.95      1266
           1       0.76      0.76      0.76       253

    accuracy                           0.92      1519
   macro avg       0.86      0.86      0.86      1519
weighted avg       0.92      0.92      0.92      1519
```

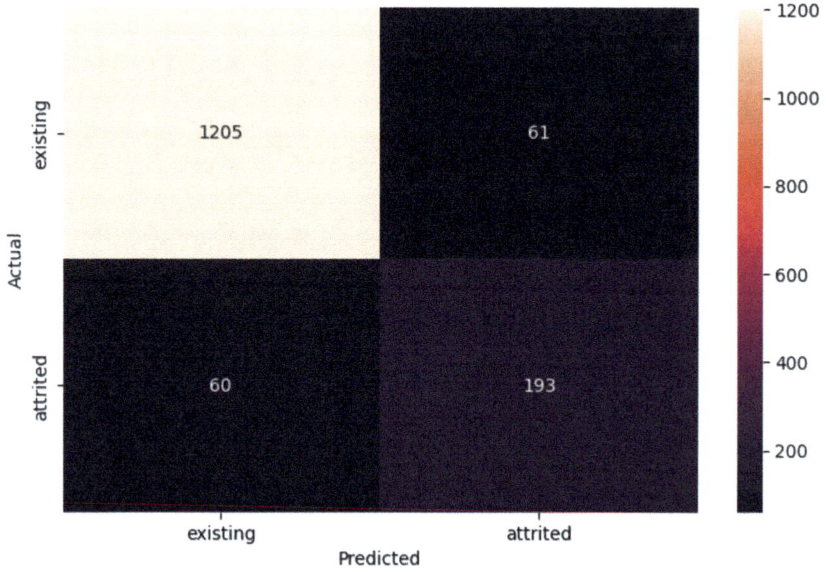

Fig. 7 Accuracy obtained for testing data

Table 2 Recall value

recall value	Recall of Training	Validation Recall
model 1	98%	72%
model 2	98%	80%
model 3	98%	86%

banking industry. With input customer data, the model achieves a recall value of 86%. Designed using supervised machine learning and a dataset of existing bank customer churn data, this model demonstrates the ability to make accurate churn predictions. This accuracy can help the company make informed decisions and mitigate potential losses.

Table 3 Attrition flag class imbalance

Attrition_Flag		Counts	Portion
0	Existing Customer	8500	0.839
1	Attrited Customer	1627	0.161

5.3 Model 3: Decision Tree

5.3.1 Model Construction

Decision tree is one of the predictive modeling approaches used in statistics, data mining and machine learning. [13] The target variable of our decision tree model is Attrition_Flag, indicating whether a customer is an existing or attrited customer. Our primitive tries of decision tree utilized the Decision Tree Classifier with the criterion set to 'gini'. This decision tree classifier was trained on the training data without any constraints on its growth. However, the mismatched accuracy of the training set and test set indicates signs of overfitting, especially with our imbalanced datasets (Table 3).

We further refined our model by pruning which reduces the complexity of the decision tree by removing sections that provide minimal classification power. We constrained the decision tree's depth by setting the maximum depth of 3, and required a minimum sample of 20 to split the internal node and at least 10 samples to be at a leaf node. After pruning, the model showed balanced performance with a high accuracy compared to our initial model, but the recall score still indicates high potential to improve. Even though we further constructed our model using the decision tree classifier with ccp_alpha set to 0.0016994637735378475, there were only slight improvements on the recall score.

By re-examining the zero and ones in our data set referring the attrition flag value, the class imbalance problem is extremely noticeable, therefore we refined our model by employing oversampling and undersampling techniques to address this issue (Table 3).

Oversampling increases the number of minority class instances to balance the dataset using the Synthetic Minority Over-sampling Technique (SMOTE). It is based on sampling data from the minority class by simply generating data points on the line segment connecting a randomly selected data point and one of its K-nearest neighbors. [14] The training data was resampled using SMOTE to balance the class distribution followed by a decision tree classifier trained on this oversampled data.

Our final model is undersampled decision tree model. Under sampling reduces the number of majority class instances to balance the dataset by randomly removing samples from the majority class. The training data was resampled using random under sampling to balance the class distribution. A decision tree classifier was then trained on this under sampled data, achieving the overall best recall score.

Table 4 Performance of accuracy

Model	Training Set Accuracy	Test Set Accuracy
Primitive Decision Tree	1.0	0.9285714285714
Pre-pruning Decision Tree	0.9190123456790	0.9150757077024
Post-pruning Decision Tree	0.9604938271604	0.9391046741277

Table 5 Performance of decision tree model

Model	Training Set Recall	Test Set Recall
Primitive Decision Tree	1.0	0.768687687
Pre-pruning Decision Tree	0.7098765432098766	0.705050505
Post-pruning Decision Tree	0.9629629629629629	0.797979797
Oversampled Decision Tree	1.0	0.785858585
Undersampled Decision Tree	1.0	0.878787878

6 Model Evaluation

Our primitive decision tree model was trained without any constraints on its growth, therefore, there was an asymmetry between a perfect train set accuracy and test set accuracy. By pre-pruning to reduce overfit, the accuracy of training and test sets are 0.919 and 0.915. (Table 4) Similarly, the post-pruning achieved an accuracy score of 0.960 and 0.939, (Table 4) both models solved the overfitting problem, but there was still room for improvement of the recall score.

The recall scores are the key element when we compare the effectiveness of each model. Recall score was chosen as the evaluation metric because it focuses on the model's ability to correctly identify the crucial minority class (attrited customers).

The primitive decision tree achieved a recall score of 0.769, the pre-pruning model 0.705, the post-pruning model 0.798, the oversampled model 0.786, and the undersampled model 0.879 (Table 5). By reducing complexity, pruning significantly improved the model's performance, however, the undersampled decision tree model provided the highest recall score, effectively solving the class imbalance and over fitting issue, obtaining an optimal balance between predictive power and interpretability.

7 Conclusion

Based on the experience of building decision trees, logistic regression, and neural network models, certain characteristics and the suitability of each model for bank churn prediction can be identified. The primary advantage of decision trees is their highly interpretable results, which are presented in an intuitive, tree-like structure that enhances both understanding and the communication of findings [15]. Moreover, the decision tree model has the highest recall value during this study. The weakness of decision tree is prone to overfitting and can be mitigated through pruning and sampling adjustments [16]. Therefore, the decision tree is well-suited for situations where a bank requires highly accurate predictions of churners and a model that can be clearly and effectively presented. Compared to decision trees, logistic regression offers a simpler way to present prediction results. However, its ability to accurately predict churners is generally weaker than that of a decision tree model [17]. Therefore, if a bank seeks to build a straightforward model with reasonable accuracy for predicting churners, a logistic regression model may be appropriate. In contrast to decision trees and logistic regression, neural networks are more complex models. Additionally, the internal workings of a neural network during processing are not visible, making the model less interpretable. The output of a neural network is simply a prediction of whether a customer will churn or not. However, once properly tuned, a neural network can deliver a clear and straightforward prediction. This makes it a valuable tool for banks in identifying potential churners.

By combining the results of the logistic regression and decision tree models (Fig. 1, Fig. 8), we identified the top four features influencing customer churn: total transaction count and amount, total revolving balance, customer age, and total relationship count. Moreover, we identified the suitability of each model for different needs within the banking sector when predicting customer churn.

8 Recommendations for Banks

To improve customer retention and reduce churn, banks should consider implementing several strategic initiatives. First, enhancing customer engagement is crucial. This can be achieved by developing and promoting rewards programs tailored to various customer segments, crafting marketing strategies that appeal to different age demographics, and implementing personalized communication strategies to build stronger relationships with customers. Additionally, banks should focus on improving financial support services by offering financial planning and advisory services, as well as providing balance transfer options and lower interest rates for customers with high revolving balances. Strengthening product cross-selling efforts is also important; banks can encourage customers to use multiple banking products by offering bundled deals and discounts for those who hold multiple accounts. Finally, attention should be given to high-risk segments by closely monitoring transaction activity and engaging low-activity customers with targeted incentives to increase their usage of banking services.

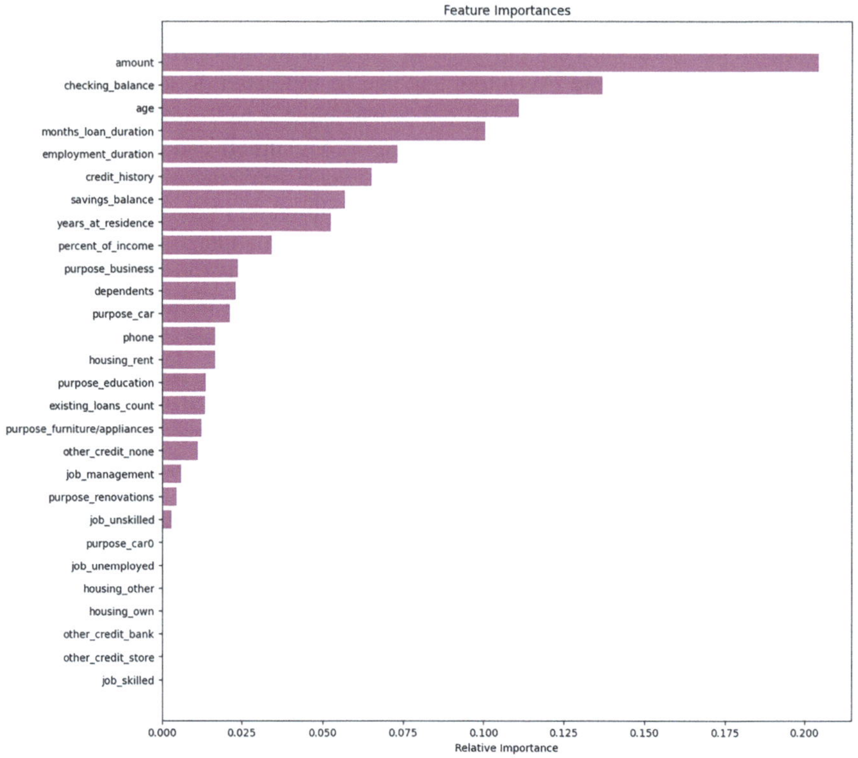

Fig. 8 Feature importances to Customer churning from Decision Tree

Acknowledgements Yibin Li, Mingze Gao, Yanfu Zhang and Changbin Feng contributed equally to this work and should be considered co-first authors.

Muxi Chen, Luyun Zhang contributed equally to this work and should be considered co-second authors.

References

1. Nie, G.; Rowe, W.; Zhang, L.; Tian, Y.; Shi, Y. Credit card churn forecasting by logistic regression and decision tree. Expert Syst.Appl. 2011, 38, 15273–15285. [CrossRef]
2. Al-Najjar, D., Al-Rousan, N., & Al-Najjar, H. (2022). Machine learning to develop credit card customer churn prediction. Journal of Theoretical and applied electronic commerce research, 17(4), 1529–1542.
3. Xia, G.; He, Q. The research of online shopping customer churn prediction based on integrated learning. In Proceedings of the 2018 International Conference on Mechanical, Electronic, Control and Automation Engineering (MECAE 2018), Qingdao, China, 30–31 March 2018; pp. 30–31.
4. Rahman, M.; Kumar, V. Machine learning based customer churn prediction in banking. In Proceedings of the 2020 4th International Conference on Electronics, Communication and

Aerospace Technology (ICECA), Coimbatore, India, 5–7 November 2020; IEEE:Piscataway, NJ, USA; pp. 1196–1201.
5. Khodabandehlou, S.; Rahman, M.Z. Comparison of supervised machine learning techniques for customer churn prediction based on analysis of customer behaviour. J. Syst. Inf. Technol. 2017, 19, 65–93. [CrossRef]
6. Risselada, H., Verhoef, P. C., & Bijmolt, T. H. (2010). Staying power of churn prediction models. Journal of Interactive Marketing, 24(3), 198–208.
7. Kumar, D.A.; Ravi, V. Predicting credit card customer churn in banks using data mining. Int. J. Data Anal. Tech. Strateg. 2008, 1, 4–28. [CrossRef]
8. Anil Kumar, D., & Ravi, V. (2008). Predicting credit card customer churn in banks using data mining. International Journal of Data Analysis Techniques and Strategies, 1(1), 4–28.
9. Lin, W. C., Tsai, C. F., Hu, Y. H., & Jhang, J. S. (2017). Clustering-based undersampling in class-imbalanced data. Information Sciences, 409, 17–26.
10. Meng, Y., Yang, N., Qian, Z., & Zhang, G. (2020). What makes an online review more helpful: an interpretation framework using XGBoost and SHAP values. Journal of Theoretical and Applied Electronic Commerce Research, 16(3), 466–490.
11. Muneer, A., et al. (2022). Predicting customers churning in the banking industry: A machine learning approach. Indian Journal of Electrical Engineering and Computer Science, 26(1), 539–549.
12. Rahman, M., & Kumar, V. (2021). Machine learning-based customer churn prediction in banking. In the 4th International Conference on Electronics, Communication and Aerospace Technology (ICECA) (pp. 1196–1201).
13. Xindong Wu et al. (2007), "Top 10 Algorithms in Data Mining - Knowledge and Information Systems," SpringerLink, December 4, 2007, https://link.springer.com/article/doi.org/10.1007/s10115-007-0114-2.
14. Elreedy, D., & Atiya, A. F. (2019). A Comprehensive Analysis of Synthetic Minority Oversampling Technique (SMOTE) for handling class imbalance. Information Sciences, 505, 32–64.
15. De Ville, B. (2013). Decision trees. Wiley Interdisciplinary Reviews: Computational Statistics, 5(6), 448–455.
16. Esposito, F., Malerba, D., Semeraro, G., & Kay, J. (1997). A comparative analysis of methods for pruning decision trees. IEEE transactions on pattern analysis and machine intelligence, 19(5), 476–491.
17. Long, W. J., Griffith, J. L., Selker, H. P., & D'agostino, R. B. (1993). A comparison of logistic regression to decision-tree induction in a medical domain. Computers and Biomedical Research, 26(1), 74–97.

Econometric Analysis and Financial Mathematics

Real Exchange Rate and GDP Growth: A Regression Analysis Considering Multiple Economic Indicators

Zhewen Meng, Ruichen Tang, Jieya Yang, Jiale Tan, and Liyan Zhang

Abstract This paper examines the relationship between the real exchange rate and GDP growth in both developing and developed countries under the Balassa-Samuelson effect, incorporating various economic indicators. Based on Purchasing Power Parity Theory, the sensitivity of real exchange rate undervaluation to GDP fluctuation is analysed. This study employs panel regression analysis, stepwise regression, and predictive model to assess the impact of the exchange rate on economic growth. The results reveal a positive correlation between the exchange rate and GDP growth, particularly in developing countries, while also highlighting the significance of other factors such as consumption, investment, and trade openness. Additionally, a time series forecasting model is utilized to predict future GDP growth rate and exchange rate trend. The applicability of the model is validated using actual data from China and Britain, revealing that undervaluation can stimulate economic growth, especially during periods of high economic openness. The robustness of the model, including its goodness of fit and multicollinearity, is also discussed. Furthermore, this research suggests that the government should comprehensively regulate exchange rate policy, trade policy, and foreign investment policy to achieve a more flexible and integrated policy mix that promotes economic growth.

Keywords Real exchange rate · GDP growth rate · Regression · Predictive model

Z. Meng (✉)
School of Economics, University of Bristol, Bristol, UK
e-mail: rg22122@bristol.ac.uk

R. Tang
Department of Statistics, University of Toronto, Toronto, Canada

J. Yang
Department of Finance, Jinan University, Guangzhou, China

J. Tan
Department of Economics, Jinan University, Guangzhou, China

L. Zhang
Department of Business Administration, Jincheng College of Sichuan University, Sichuan, China

E. Tsui et al. (eds.), *Management Information Systems in a Digitalized AI World*,
Springer Proceedings in Business and Economics,
https://doi.org/10.1007/978-981-96-6526-6_13

1 Introduction

With the deepening of globalization and the trend of multinational business operations, the real exchange rate has become an increasingly significant topic. On August 5, 2019, after the CNY exchange rate fell below the "7" mark, the U.S. Treasury Department officially labeled China as a currency manipulator, arguing that China had taken deliberate steps to devalue its currency while maintaining large foreign exchange reserves. The U.S. Treasury Department accused China of gaining significant trade advantages through this action, which caused the U.S. dollar to tumble and pushed gold prices higher. This statement drew widespread attention from the international community. In this research, panel regression analysis is employed to examine the relationship between the real exchange rate and economic growth rate in both developed and developing countries, considering multiple economic indicators. Following this, tests for correlation, multicollinearity, and heteroscedasticity will be conducted on the selected variables. The analysis will then proceed with a Hausman test, followed by stepwise regression and interpretation of the results.

Over the past decade, numerous studies have explored the mechanisms through which the exchange rate impacts economic growth. These studies have examined how the exchange rate influences factors such as terms of trade, international balance of payments, and capital flows. However, the Balassa-Samuelson effect remains particularly important. When productivity gains lead to higher per capita income levels and price levels, the estimated undervaluation of the exchange rate may be overstated or understated. This can create the impression that exchange rate undervaluation is driving economic growth, when in fact, the contribution may be due to productivity improvements alone [1, 2]. While this paper will not delve into political discussions, it seeks to clarify the questions: "Can a country improve its growth prospects by controlling its currency? To what extent? And how can this be achieved?".

This paper will focus on several research questions, including whether a changed real exchange rate (relative to purchasing power parity or other benchmarks) has significantly boosted a country's long-term economic growth rate, and how this impact differs across economies (e.g., developed versus developing countries). The study will also explore how and to what extent a changed exchange rate influences economic growth through mechanisms such as boosting exports, attracting foreign investment, and increasing domestic productive activities.

2 Literature Review

2.1 Real Exchange Rate and GDP Growth Rate

Research has long explored the mechanisms and extent of exchange rate impacts on economic growth. The real exchange rate, has been extensively studied in relation to various aspects of economic performance. Although its direct influence on economic growth may not always be significant, it becomes crucial in certain contexts, such as in export-oriented economies. Adjustments in the real exchange rate can affect resource allocation and production efficiency, thereby indirectly impacting economic growth [3]. For instance, the real exchange rate can serve as an incentive to shift resources toward manufacturing, potentially increasing national income if manufacturing productivity exceeds agricultural productivity.

Moreover, the effect of the real exchange rate on economic growth is not simply linear but exhibits a threshold effect [2]. When the real exchange rate deviates from its equilibrium level, it can negatively impact economic growth. To capture this dynamic, a new variable, undervaluation, is introduced and measured. Empirical analysis of cross-country data reveals that excessive appreciation or depreciation can have adverse effects on economic growth, highlighting the importance of maintaining the real exchange rate within a reasonable range. Additionally, when using different classification criteria and empirical strategies, the effect of currency undervaluation on economic growth appears larger and more robust for developing economies. However, the relationship between real exchange rate undervaluation and GDP per capita is non-monotonic, as evident in both the least developed and wealthiest countries [4].

Upon reviewing the extensive literature on the relationship between the real exchange rate and GDP growth, it becomes clear that much of the research ties back to Rodrik and his seminal work, Real Exchange Rate and Economic Growth. In this study, Rodrik argues that an undervalued currency—which corresponds to a high real exchange rate—can promote economic growth. He developed a comprehensive model to clarify the link between the real exchange rate and subsequent economic growth rates. Significantly, many later academic studies have drawn on his core ideas, establishing Rodrik's paper as a pivotal reference in this field of research.

Rodrik's (2008) study, has yielded some influential insights and findings. Nevertheless, like all research endeavors, it possesses certain limitations and scope for improvement. Our group has enumerated some of his shortcomings: 1. Data reliability and source issues: Rodrik relies on data from the Penn World Table to evaluate the real exchange rate. However, these data might not be precise or updated in specific countries, which could potentially impact the general applicability and accuracy of the conclusions. 2. Adjustment for the Balassa-Samuelson effect: Even if the Balassa-Samuelson effect is adjusted in the study, this adjustment might introduce bias if there exists a third variable influencing per capita income and the price level. 3. Relying on a single measure of real exchange rate undervaluation: This study primarily relies on "undervaluation" as a metric of the level of real valuation of the currency, without taking into account other factors that might affect economic growth. 4. Endogenous issues: The research might not fully contemplate the reverse causality between the real exchange rate and economic growth, that is, economic growth might affect the real exchange rate and vice versa.

2.2 Optimization

This paper utilizes the GDP deflator as the macro price level to calculate the exchange rate and further computes the exchange rate and its growth rate. In the empirical analysis phase, the paper conducts regressions on two different forms of the exchange rate and selects one as an independent variable for further regression analysis and the development of prediction models, based on comparative results. Additionally, to enhance the model's accuracy, the concept of undervaluation as discussed by Rodrik was incorporated. The findings indicate that these adjustments have notably improved the model's fit.

2.3 Selection Variable

In examining the relationship between exchange rate and GDP growth rate, consumption, investment rate and trade openness are selected as regression variables.

2.3.1 The Role and Impact of Consumption

Consumption and Economic Growth: According to New Growth Theory, consumption is a primary driver of national economic growth and accounts for the majority of GDP. An increase in consumption can lead to a rise in domestic demand, which may boost imports and influence the exchange rate. If the national currency depreciates relatively, it can enhance the competitiveness of exports and further promote GDP growth. A consumption-driven economy not only directly impacts economic growth but is also closely associated with various factors such as globalization, corruption, economic freedom, the knowledge economy, and FDI [5, 6].

2.3.2 The Role of Investment Rate

Investment, Exchange Rate, and GDP Growth: Movements in the real exchange rate significantly affect GDP growth, with investment playing a crucial role. Investment impacts not only the exchange rate but also the GDP growth rate through its effect on the exchange rate [7]. An increase in investment typically signals anticipated economic growth, potentially causing the currency to appreciate. However, if the investment proves inefficient, the exchange rate may face long-term depreciation pressures, adversely affecting GDP.

2.3.3 The Importance of Trade Openness

Trade and International Markets: The index of trade openness is measured by the total value of imports and exports as a percentage of GDP. A depreciation in a country's currency generally makes its exports more competitive in global markets, thereby increasing exports. Conversely, if the currency appreciates, it may reduce export competitiveness and negatively impact GDP. Similarly, the relative prices of currencies can also influence changes in imports. Several studies affirm the positive effects of trade openness on economic growth and discuss its regional heterogeneity and nonlinearity. Aligning with classical economic growth theory, which posits that trade openness can stimulate economic growth in various ways, trade openness is recognized as one of the principal drivers of economic growth [5]. In general, exchange rates are closely related to trade openness and GDP.

3 Methodology

3.1 Data Description

In establishing and improving the model, this paper mainly used relevant data from Penn World Table version 10.0, IMF, World Bank and China National Bureau of Statistics. The following tables provide a detailed breakdown of the key data.

Table 1 lists the data mainly used to establish the model in the early stage, among which part of the data is the original data obtained and part of the data is the result obtained after recalculation. For the main data real exchange rate in this study, the following calculation methods were mainly adopted in the acquisition process:

$$P_{USA} = \frac{v\_gdp_{USA}}{q\_gdp_{USA}} \tag{1}$$

$$P_{domestic} = \frac{v\_gdp_{domestic}}{q\_gdp_{domestic}} \tag{2}$$

$$RER = xr * \frac{P_{USA}}{P_{domestic}} \tag{3}$$

Equation (1) and (2) are calculated the overall price level of a country based on real GDP(q_gdp). This study takes the GDP deflator as a macro price level and calculates the real interest rate on this basis. The data in this paper are mainly taking the country as a whole and using annual data. To facilitate the research, we did not take all data

Table 1 Main data

Variable	Description	Unit
countrycode	3-letter ISO country code	None
Level	Country's development level	None
Year	None	None
q_c	Household consumption at constant national 2017 prices	Million
q_i	Investment at constant national 2017 prices	Million
q_x	Exports at constant national 2017 prices	Million
q_m	Imports at constant national 2017 prices	Million
q_gdp	GDP at constant national 2017 prices	Million
xr	Exchange rate (market)	National currency/USD
v_gdp	GDP at current national prices	Million
gdp_growth_rate	None	%
nation_deflator	A macro measure of the price level	None
cgdp	Consumption as a percentage of GDP	%
igdp	Investment as a percentage of GDP	%
openness	Total imports and exports as a percentage of GDP	%
RER	Real exchange rate	None

for all countries, but selected eight representative developing countries and eight developed countries based on the contents of the World Economic Outlook released by the IMF and combined with geographical factors. In the process of collecting the forecast data set, the data in Penn World Table is only listed until 2019. To improve the accuracy of the data and maintain consistency with the data in Penn World Table, this paper converts some data found after 2020 into data with 2017 as the base year. To reduce the error of the prediction model and ensure the data authenticity.

3.2 *Statistical Analysis and Visualization*

To more intuitively explore the relationship between key variables and GDP growth rates, this paper visualizes data from selected countries and makes preliminary assessments that will inform further research. Figure 1 displays year-to-year changes in the real exchange rates of countries at different development levels. The line chart suggests a correlation between the real exchange rate and a country's development status. Developed countries generally exhibit lower real exchange rates, whereas developing countries typically show higher rates. However, there are exceptions in the developed world, such as South Korea and Japan, which have unusually high real exchange rates compared to other developed nations. In the developing world,

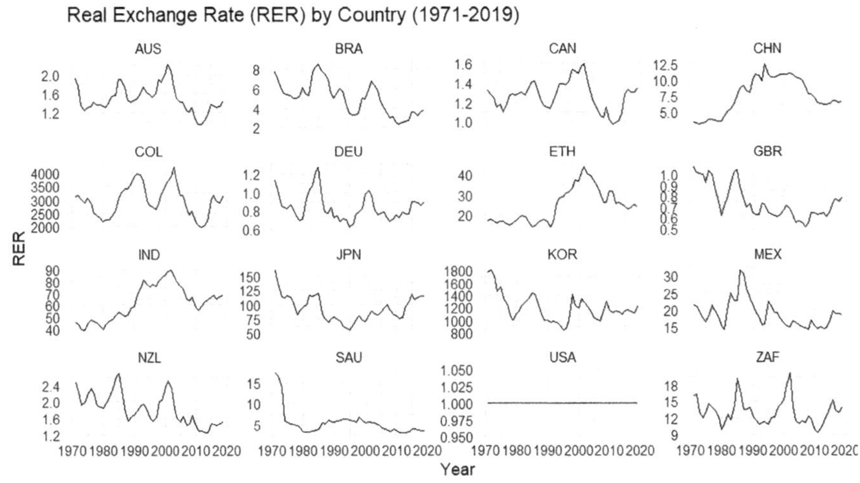

Fig. 1 Real exchange rate

Colombia is an outlier, with its real exchange rate soaring above 2,000. Since calculation errors have been ruled out in this study, the reasons for these anomalies may not be due to data processing issues. This prompts consideration of incorporating different real exchange rate variations into the model.

The study also examines major factors that can impact GDP, such as trade openness, consumption, and investment, and evaluates their contributions to GDP growth. Figure 2 focuses on trade openness (The openness data needs to be multiplied by 100 to fit the scale of the chart). It reveals that in some countries, like Saudi Arabia (SAU) and Ethiopia (ETH), there is a noticeable similarity between the trends of the red curve (GDP growth rate) and the blue curve (openness). This trend is also observable in developed countries like Canada (CAN) and Japan (JPN), though the convergence effect of openness and growth rates is more pronounced in developing countries. Figure 3 addresses consumption and its share of GDP (The consumption data needs to be multiplied by 100 to fit the scale of the chart). It shows that in selected countries, the two curves do not always move in the same direction and sometimes even display opposite trends, an observation incorporated into the model.

As illustrated in Fig. 4, it examines investment, another component of the GDP formula, and its effect on GDP growth rate (The investment data needs to be multiplied by 100 to fit the scale of the chart). It clearly shows a significant synergistic trend between the two curves in countries like Colombia, South Korea, South Africa (ZAF), and New Zealand (NZL). This positive association appears to be unaffected by the level of development.

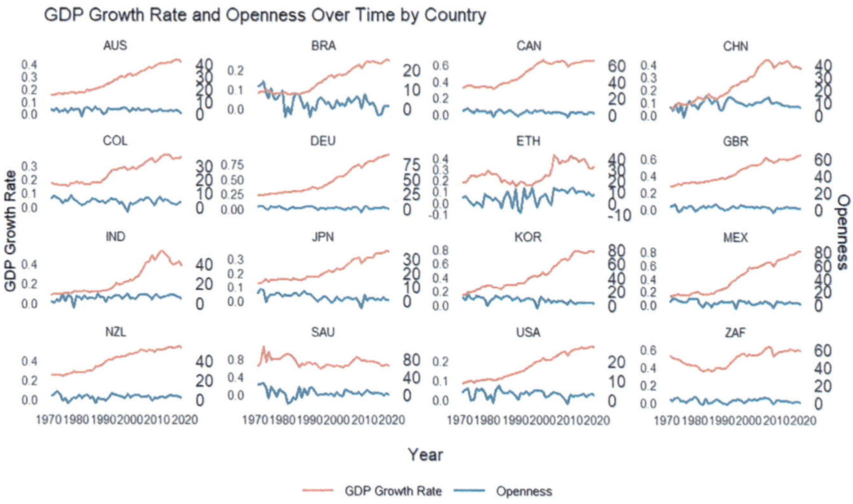

Fig. 2 Openness

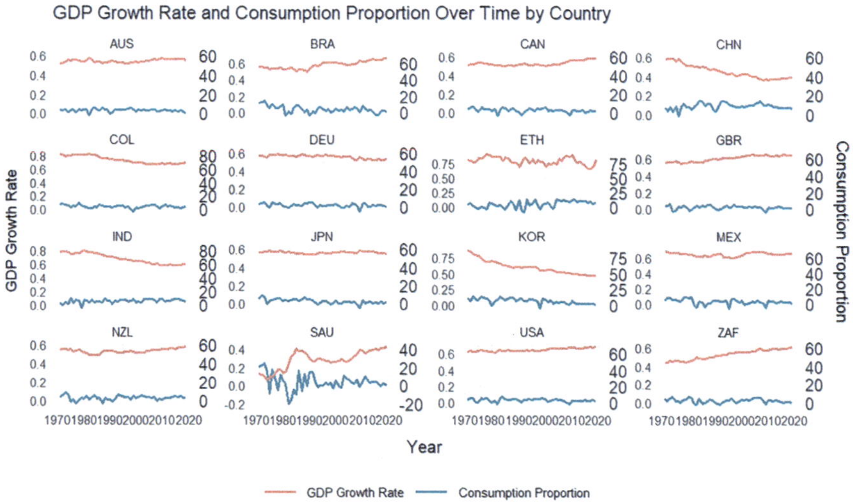

Fig. 3 Consumption proportion

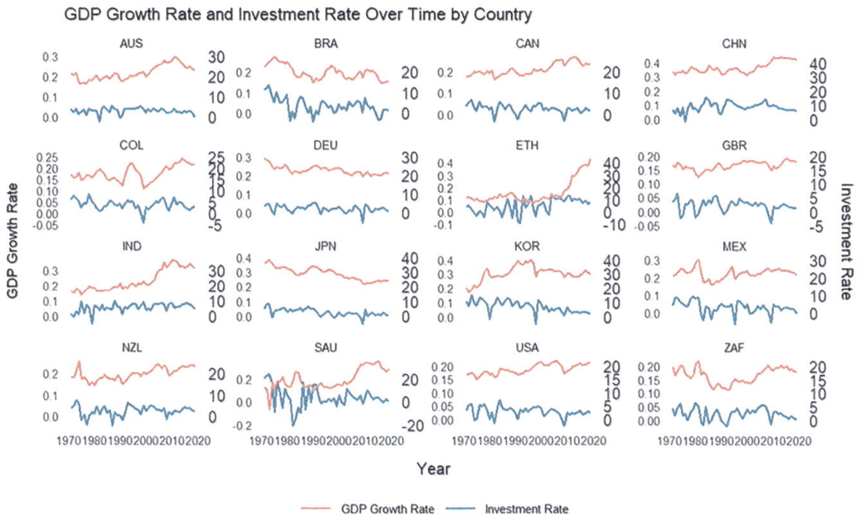

Fig. 4 Investment rate

4 Model Fitting and Experiment Results

4.1 Model Fitting

In this article, data from eight representative developing countries and eight developed countries spanning the years 1971 to 2019 will be utilized as research and analysis samples. Key regression variables selected for this study include the exchange rate, consumption rate, trade openness, and investment rate, to explore the relationship between the exchange rate and GDP growth rate. This examination will consider three aspects of the exchange rate: its overall form, its growth rate, and its degree of undervaluation. To further probe the relationship between these variables, this paper employs empirical analysis techniques including stepwise regression and classification regression. The specific procedures and results of these regressions are detailed below.

4.2 Quantitative Analysis of Variable Selection

In part 2.3, this essay conducts a qualitative analysis of the variable section. Subsequently, it selects variables including the exchange rate, consumption rate, trade openness, investment rate, and real GDP to conduct a correlation test. The results indicate that all values are below 0.05, except for real GDP. Further analysis reveals that the presence of a long-term trend in real GDP means that the growth rate reflects the relative change. This underlying trend results in differing behavioral patterns for these two variables, thereby diminishing the statistical correlation between them, and thus the correlation test results for real GDP do not meet the significance threshold. However, the other variables demonstrate significant correlations, warranting further tests.

4.3 Regression Results and Variable Model Selection

Firstly, this part will test the collinearity and multicollinearity and all the selected variables pass the test as shown in Fig. 5. Then the next step will be running a single regression on each variable.

As depicted in Table 2, the regression coefficient between the exchange rate and GDP growth rate is 0.002, which is statistically significant at the 0.1% level, indicating a positive correlation. Thus, for every 1% increase in the exchange rate, the GDP growth rate increases by 0.002/100, suggesting that faster exchange rate growth correlates with faster GDP growth. The regression coefficient of 0.114 between the investment rate and GDP growth rate is also statistically significant at the 0.1% level, showing a positive correlation; a one-unit increase in investment rate leads to a 0.114 increase in GDP growth rate, indicating that higher investment rates contribute to faster GDP growth. Conversely, the regression coefficients between trade openness and GDP growth rate, as well as between consumption rate and GDP growth rate,

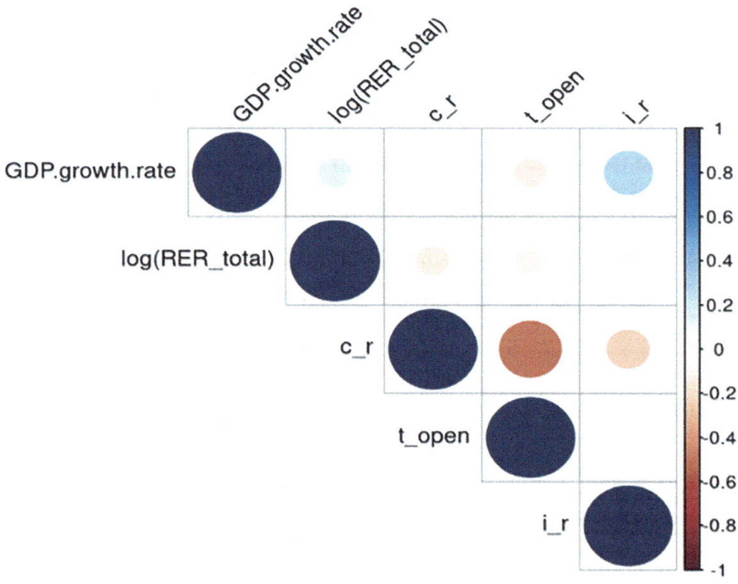

Fig. 5 Correlation

are both statistically significant and negative at the 0.1% level. A one-unit increase in trade openness and consumption rate leads to a decrease in GDP growth rate by 0.025 and 0.069 respectively, suggesting that faster growth in trade openness and consumption may hinder GDP growth.

To further examine the impact of the exchange rate on GDP growth rate, a stepwise regression analysis will be conducted to explore how the regression results for the exchange rate change when controlling for other variables. Table 3 presents the stepwise regression under a fixed effect model and shows that the coefficient of the exchange rate remains highly significant even after the inclusion of the consumption rate, indicating an independent and significant effect on GDP growth rate. However, when trade openness and investment rate are added to the regression, the coefficient gradually decreases and eventually becomes insignificant, suggesting that these two control variables have substantial confounding effects on the exchange rate. After passing the correlation and multicollinearity tests, comparing the R-square values indicates that the inclusion of trade openness and investment rate may have improved the model's fit, enhancing its explanatory power. Consequently, the independent effect of the exchange rate may become less significant because the investment rate accounts for a larger portion of the variance.

The interpretation of the regression results of the random effect model shown in Table 4 would be the same as the fixed effect, but the Hausman test concludes that the fixed effect model is better. The above sections are all analyses of regression results for the exchange rate. In the following, the regression analyses will be performed with the growth rate of the exchange rate, and then the two forms will be compared. Firstly, the test of collinearity and multicollinearity are also passed in Fig. 6. Then in Tables 5 and 6, in the stepwise regression, the outcome indicates that the coefficient of growth rate of exchange rate would gradually increase but stays negative and becomes

Table 2 Single regression

Regression results summary table

	GDP growth rate	GDP growth rate	GDP growth rRate	GDP growth rate
Log (RER)	0.002 *** (0.000)			
Investment rate		0.114 *** (0.026)		
Trade openness			−0.025 *** (0.010)	
Consumption rate				−0.069*** (0.021)
Observations	784	784	784	784
adjusted R^2				

Standard errors in parentheses
$^{*}p < 0.10$, $^{**}p < 0.05$, $^{***}p < 0.01$

Table 3 Fixed effect with exchange rate

	GDP growth rate	GDP growth rate	GDP growth rate	GDP growth rate
Log (RER)	0.00162*** (3.72)	0.00146*** (3.36)	0.00104* (2.29)	0.000853 (1.88)
Consumption rate		−0.0834*** (−3.38)	−0.109*** (−4.19)	−0.105*** (−4.06)
Trade openness			−0.0319*** (−2.94)	−0.0430*** (−3.86)
Investment rate				0.110*** (3.80)
Constant	0.0337*** (19.00)	0.0827*** (5.66)	0.110*** (6.38)	0.0882*** (4.87)
Observations	784	784	784	784

t statistics in parentheses
$*p < 0.05$, $**p < 0.01$, $***p < 0.001$

statistically insignificant. In addition, it still compares fixed effect and random effect and concludes that the fixed effect is better through the Hausman test.

Comparing the R-square, AIC, and BIC outcome, shows that the model with exchange rate is better than the growth rate of the exchange rate model as the R-square is bigger and both AIC and BIC are smaller. Therefore, in the next regression and last prediction parts, the exchange rate will be put into regression.

Table 4 Random effect with exchange rate

	GDP growth rate	GDP growth rate	GDP growth rate	GDP growth rate
Log (RER)	0.00153*** (3.69)	0.00140*** (3.37)	0.00100* (2.30)	0.000826 (1.95)
Consumption rate		−0.0624** (−2.88)	−0.0894*** (−3.85)	−0.0741*** (−3.38)
Trade openness			−0.0327** (−3.12)	−0.0418*** (−4.01)
Investment rate				0.118*** (4.40)
Constant	0.0340*** (6.77)	0.0706*** (5.14)	0.0991*** (6.03)	0.0680*** (4.11)
Observations	784	784	784	784

t statistics in parentheses
$*p < 0.05$, $**p < 0.01$, $***p < 0.001$

Fig. 6 Correlation

Table 5 Fixed effect with the growth rate of exchange rate

	GDP growth rate	GDP growth rate	GDP growth rate	GDP growth rate
RER growth rate	−0.0270** (−2.67)	−0.0230* (−2.27)	−0.0156 (−1.52)	−0.0138 (−1.35)
Consumption rate		−0.0859*** (−3.46)	−0.115*** (−4.40)	−0.109*** (−4.22)
Trade openness			−0.0364*** (−3.45)	−0.0469*** (−4.35)
Investment rate				0.114*** (3.95)
Constant	0.0370*** (26.58)	0.0872*** (5.99)	0.117*** (6.95)	0.0925*** (5.20)
Observations	784	784	784	784

t statistics in parentheses
*$p < 0.05$, **$p < 0.01$, ***$p < 0.001$

4.4 Comparative Analysis by Country

In this section, countries will be classified as either developing or developed countries. The Table 7 indicates that the exchange rate coefficient is significant for both groups in separate regressions, with a greater effect observed in developing countries. However, when the exchange rate is regressed alongside other factors, the results are

Table 6 Random effect with the growth rate of exchange rate

	GDP growth rate	GDP growth rate	GDP growth rate	GDP growth rate
RER growth rate	−0.0260** (−2.60)	−0.0236* (−2.36)	−0.0160 (−1.57)	−0.0149 (−1.49)
Consumption rate		−0.0663** (−3.06)	−0.0949*** (−4.13)	−0.0784*** (−3.62)
Trade openness			−0.0365*** (−3.56)	−0.0447*** (4.38)
Investment rate				0.122*** (4.54)
Constant	0.0371*** (7.52)	0.0757*** (5.55)	0.106*** (6.63)	0.0724*** (4.47)
Observations	784	784	784	784

t statistics in parentheses
*$p < 0.05$, **$p < 0.01$, ***$p < 0.001$

not significant. Therefore, it can be concluded that the exchange rate has a significantly positive effect on economic growth, particularly in developing countries. However, economic growth is influenced by many factors, and the exchange rate is just one of them. The impact of the exchange rate can also be indirectly realized by affecting other variables, such as consumption, investment, and trade openness, as explored in this essay. Thus, while the government can influence the economy by regulating the exchange rate, it is important to also assess and coordinate the effects of other economic variables to achieve broader macroeconomic objectives.

Table 7 Regression of two country categories

	Developing GDP growth rate	Developing GDP growth rate	Developed GDP growth rate	Developed GDP growth rate
Log (RER)	0.00526*** (3.75)	0.00278 (1.66)	0.00125* (2.38)	0.000338 (0.62)
Investment rate		0.166*** (4.80)		0.108** (2.93)
Consumption rate		0.0937*** (3.33)		−0.0944*** (−3.36)
Trade openness		−0.0455*** (−5.37)		−0.0405* (−2.17)
Observations	392	392	392	392
R-squared				

t statistics in parentheses
*$p < 0.05$, **$p < 0.01$, ***$p < 0.001$

4.5 *Prediction Model*

This essay employs a time series prediction model, utilizing data from 1971 to 2019, to forecast both the GDP growth rate and exchange rate for the period from 2020 to 2023. China and the United Kingdom are projected as representatives of developing and developed countries, respectively. The prediction model in Fig. 7 suggests that China's GDP growth rate would gradually increase starting in 2020. However, the rate decreased from 2019 to 2020, surged sharply in 2021, and then declined again between 2021 and 2023. The exchange rate in Fig. 8 was predicted to remain stable over these three years but instead experienced continuous fluctuations.

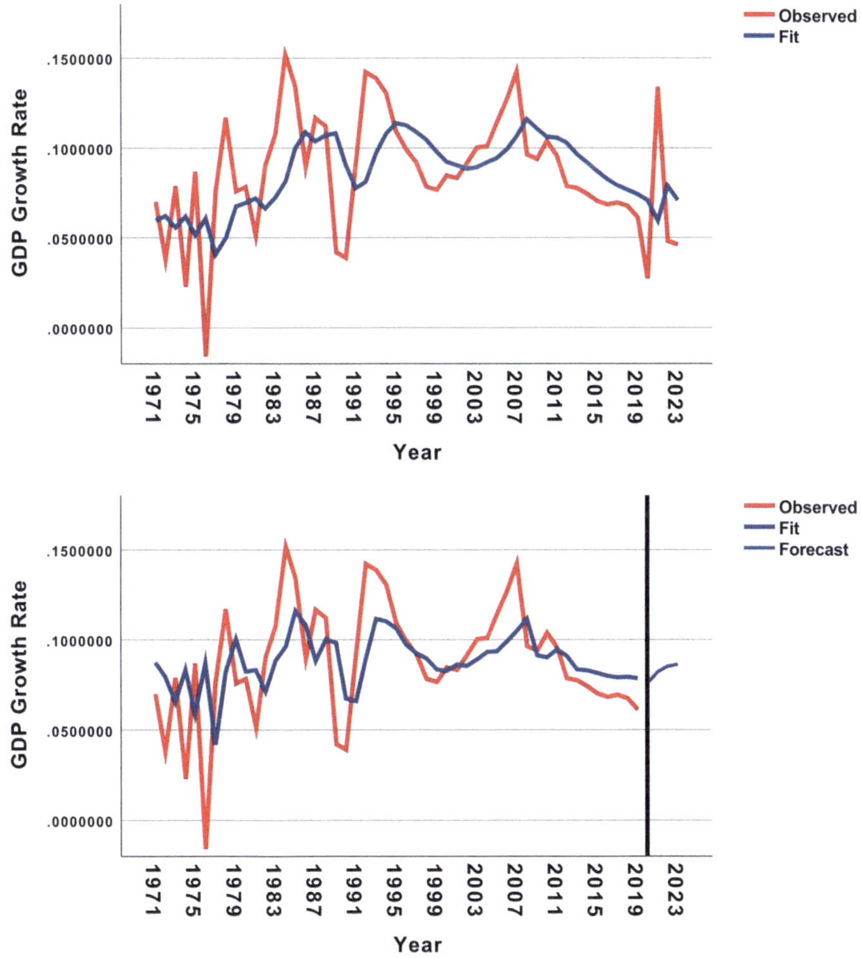

Fig. 7 GDP growth rate prediction (China)

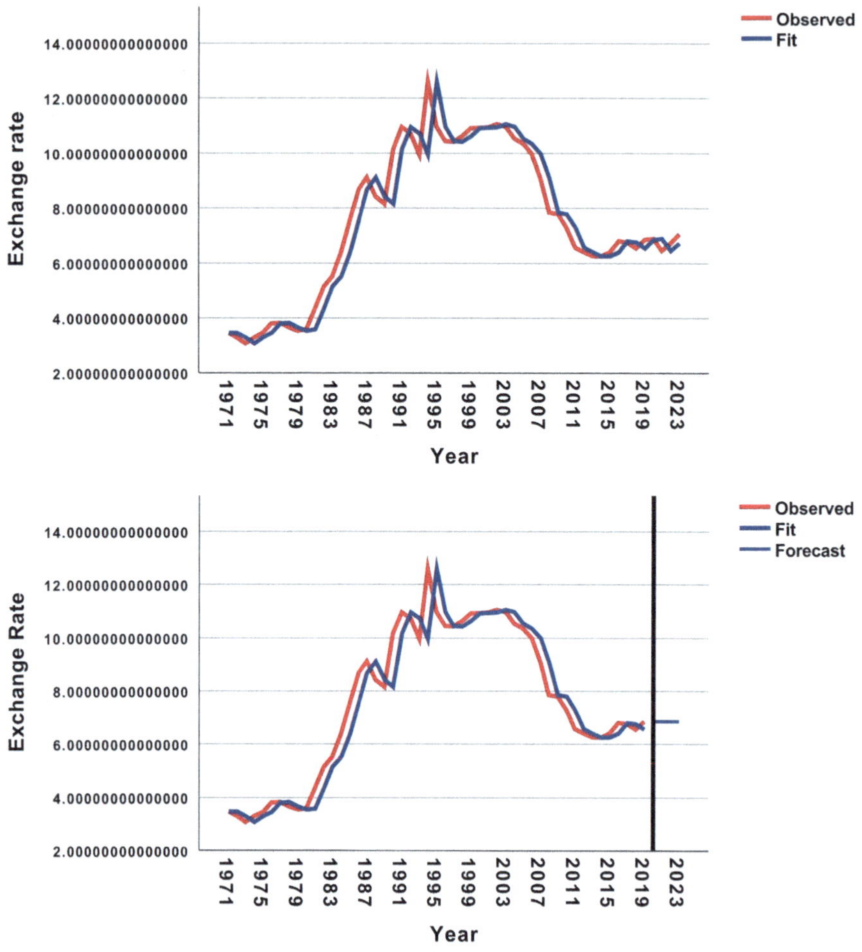

Fig. 8 Exchange rate prediction (China)

For the United Kingdom in Figs. 9 and 10, the forecasted GDP growth rate shows a consistent upward trend, while the observed trend exhibits sharp fluctuations, particularly between 2019 and 2020, where the rate even dropped to -0.104, indicating a negative growth. The predicted and actual exchange rates for the UK show trends like those observed in China.

These discrepancies highlight the significant impact of the epidemic on GDP, leading to substantial fluctuations and even declines. This situation underscores the limitations of the prediction model, which is typically trained on historical data that did not account for global shocks of this magnitude. Additionally, the trend of exchange rate movements does not align consistently with that of GDP growth. While the exchange rate may serve as an important indicator for forecasting GDP growth, relying solely on it may be insufficient, as the relationship between these

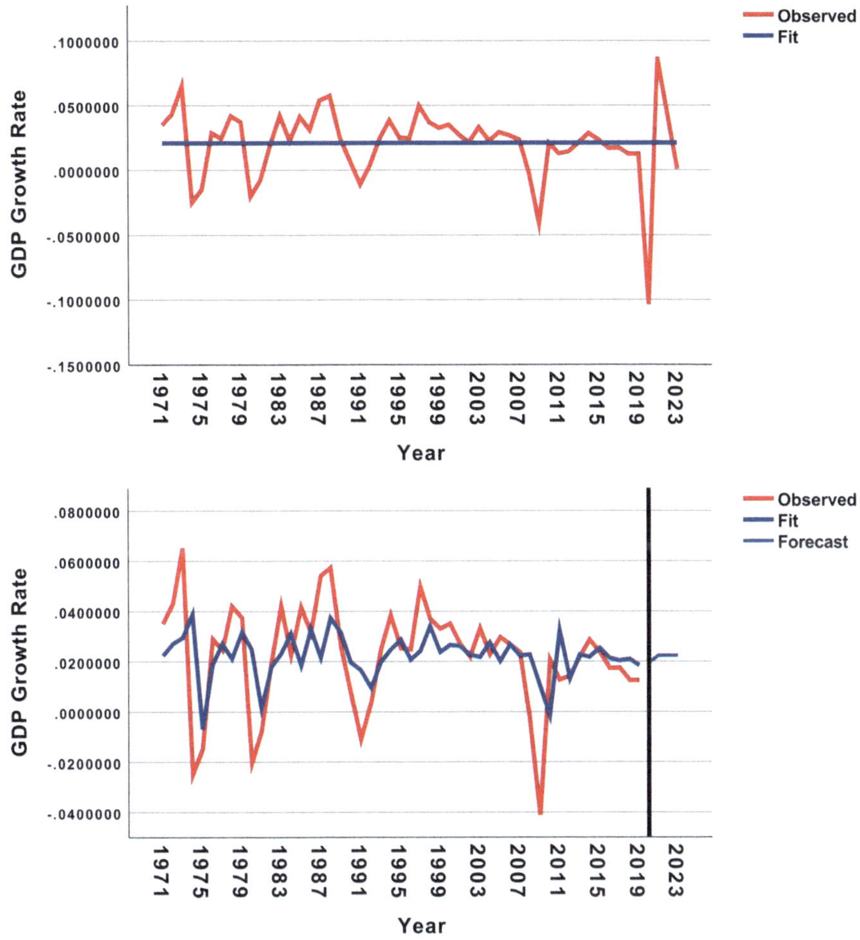

Fig. 9 GDP growth rate prediction (The United Kingdom)

two variables is not linear and may become more complex during global events like the epidemic. However, as the global economy gradually recovers, the GDP growth rate may return to its normal trend in the future.

4.6 Undervaluation and Real Exchange Rate

This study introduces currency undervaluation as a variable to estimate the annual growth rate, proposing that the undervaluation of the real exchange rate (RER) serves as a precise and sensitive indicator of GDP fluctuations. Purchasing Power Parity (PPP) theory generates the concepts of undervaluation and overvaluation:

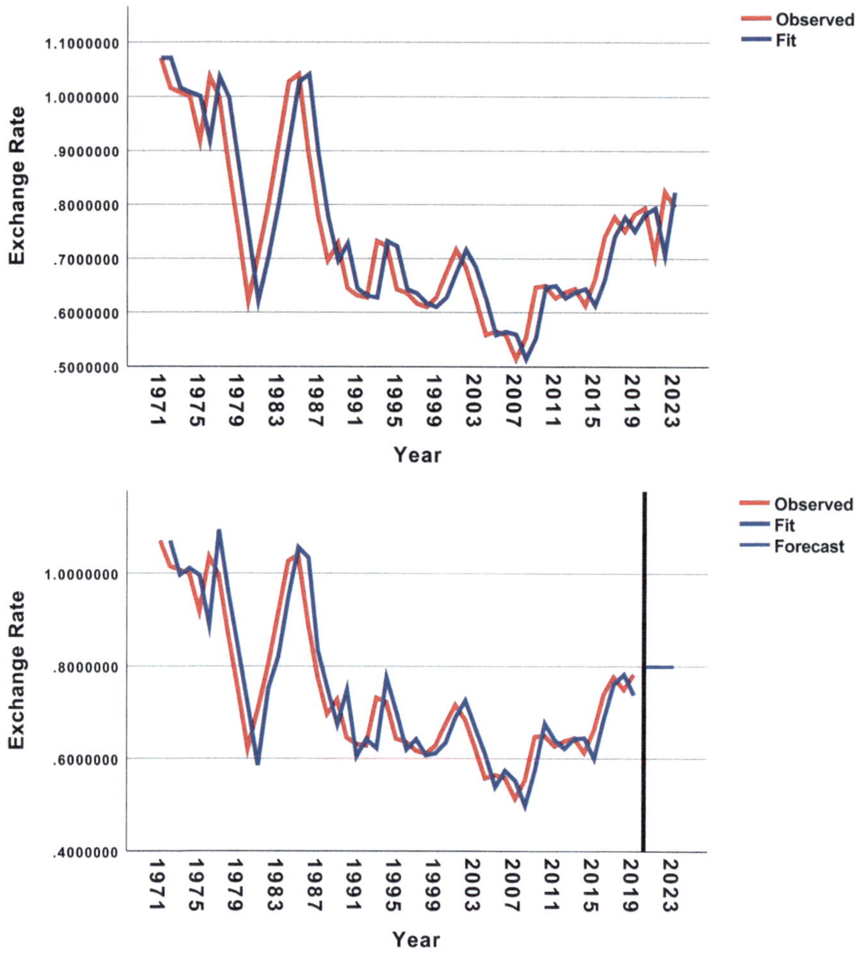

Fig. 10 Exchange rate prediction (The United Kingdom)

$$\frac{exchangerate*USpricelevel}{domesticpricelevel} = 1 \tag{4}$$

which traditionally evaluates whether a currency is mispriced [7]. However, the application of PPP is primarily relevant to tradable goods, ignoring the price variations in non-tradable goods and services, such as housing and local services, can significantly influence the accuracy of PPP calculations. Consequently, adjustments to the real exchange rate (RER) have been incorporated to refine the standard model, acknowledging that fluctuations in RER can notably impact GDP growth rates. Through the Balassa-Samuelson effect (BS effect), this study focusses on the relationship between productivity and real exchange rates [8]. Hence, we reveal this effect by regressing RER on real GDP per capita (reflecting the productivity) and the ratio of the price level of non-tradeable over tradeable sectors for each country:

$$\ln \widehat{RER}_t = \alpha + \beta \ln \ RGDPCH_t + \delta RA_t + f_t + \in \quad (5)$$

where f_t stands for a fixed time effect on the regression. In this model, the estimates of RGDPCH (β_1) and the ratio of price level (β_2) are approximately 0.44 and 1.71, shown in picture.

Table 8 shows that a 1 percent increase in GDP per capita corresponds to a 0.44 percent appreciation of the real exchange rate, assuming the price level ratio remains constant. This result corroborates the Balassa-Samuelson (BS) effect, suggesting that enhanced productivity within the tradable sector, as reflected by an increase in real GDP per capita (RGDPCH), contributes to currency appreciation. Moreover, a higher price level ratio significantly impacts RER, further demonstrating the BS effect. Increased productivity leads to higher wages in tradable sectors, which subsequently spill over into the non-tradable sector (such as services), elevating a country's overall price level. This wage spillover effect encapsulates the relative cost of non-tradables compared to tradables. The coefficient of the relative price level (RA) indicates that a higher ratio intensifies this spillover effect, fostering growth in the real exchange rate [9]. Thus, variations in relative price levels are fundamental to understanding the dynamics of real exchange rates among different countries, in line with the predictions of the Balassa-Samuelson effect [8]. The discrepancy between the real exchange rate from the Penn World Table data and the predicted value from the model serves as the basis for estimating undervaluation:

$$\ln UNDERVAL_t = \ln RER_t - \ln \widehat{RER}_t \quad (6)$$

Table 8 Coefficients of panel regression of RER on GDP per capita and ratio of price level

	Coefficient	Std. Error	*t*-value	*p*-value
log ***RGDPCH***	0.443	0.072	6.167	$< 0.001^{***}$
RA	1.713	0.539	3.177	$< 0.0015^{**}$
Observations	800			
R-squared	0.073			
Adjusted R-squared	0.010			
F statistic	29.356*** (df = 2;748)			

Note $*p<0.1$; $**p<0.05$; $***p<0.01$

4.7 Undervaluation and GDP Growth

To overcome the inaccuracy of RER, we replace original variable RER to UNDERVAL:

$$GDP\ growth\ rate = \alpha + \beta \ln UNDERVAL_{it} + \gamma CR_{it} + \delta TO_{it} + \varepsilon IR_{it} + \pi IR : TO_{it} + f_t + f_i + \in \quad (7)$$

where f_t is the fixed effect of time and f_i is the fixed effect of countries. In this model, we concentrate on the coefficients of UNDERVAL and how it changes the dependent variable GDP growth rate [10]. Table 9 shows that the estimate of UNDERVAL is 0.0011(with a p-value of 0.006), which implies if the undervaluation increases by 100 percent, the GDP growth rate increases by 0.11 percent. This follows our hypothesis that undervaluation will influence GDP in a subtle amount. From the correlation plot, GDP growth rate and UNDERVAL have a weak correlation, revealing that UNDERVAL has a certain impact on Economic growth, but it is not the decisive factor. In Economics, an undervalued exchange rate makes domestic products more competitive in the international market, and an increase in exports leads directly to GDP growth. For example, in the early days of China's reform and opening, by keeping the yuan relatively undervalued, China greatly increased its exports, thus driving high economic growth. Furthermore, it attracts foreign investors because they can access domestic assets and resources at a lower cost, which increases capital inflows and boosts financial growth. This explains the independent variables and IR has the highest correlation in the diagram.

Table 9 Coefficients of panel regression of GDP growth rate on undervaluation of RER

	Estimate	Std. Error	t-value	p-value
log ***UNDERVAL***	0.0012	0.0004	2.7437	0.0062***
c_r	-0.0864	0.0244	-3.5384	0.0004***
i_r	0.4504	0.0480	9.3782	$<2.2\,e^{-16}$
t_open	0.1265	0.0254	4.9718	0.0000
i_r : t_open	-0.8804	0.0966	-9.1096	$<2.2e^{-16}$
Observations	800			
R-squared	0.1621			
Adjusted R-squared	0.0829			
F statistics	28.2435*** ($df = 5; 730$)			

4.8 Robustness of Model

4.8.1 Fitness

To test the fitness of the improved model which consists undervaluation as the coefficient, this paper still uses the data of Britain and China to contrast the predicted GDP growth rate with the actual one. As shown in Fig. 11, the GDP growth rate and projected GDP growth fit very well in many years but have differed significantly, especially during periods of high economic volatility (such as the 1980s and the 2008 financial crisis). The projected growth rate shows a certain leveling off after 2000, but the overall trend is almost consistent with the downward trend of the actual growth rate. As shown in Fig. 12, the real GDP growth rate has been higher than the forecast GDP growth rate for a long time, especially in the early years of reform and opening and in the 1990s when the economy was growing rapidly [11]. Although the projected growth rate has improved in recent years, it is still below the actual growth rate, suggesting that the forecast model may be underestimating the real growth potential of the Chinese economy. Hence, although there were some deviations between the predicted and actual values in some years, the overall trend was consistent, and real exchange rate undervaluation has a significant positive impact on GDP growth, suggesting that competitive exchange rate policies may help boost economic growth.

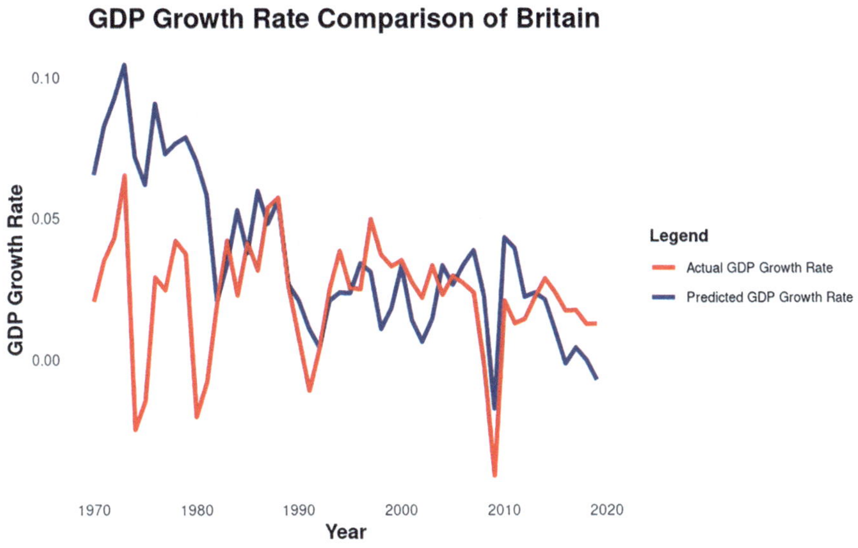

Fig. 11 Comparison of real GDP growth rate and predicted GDP growth rate for Britain

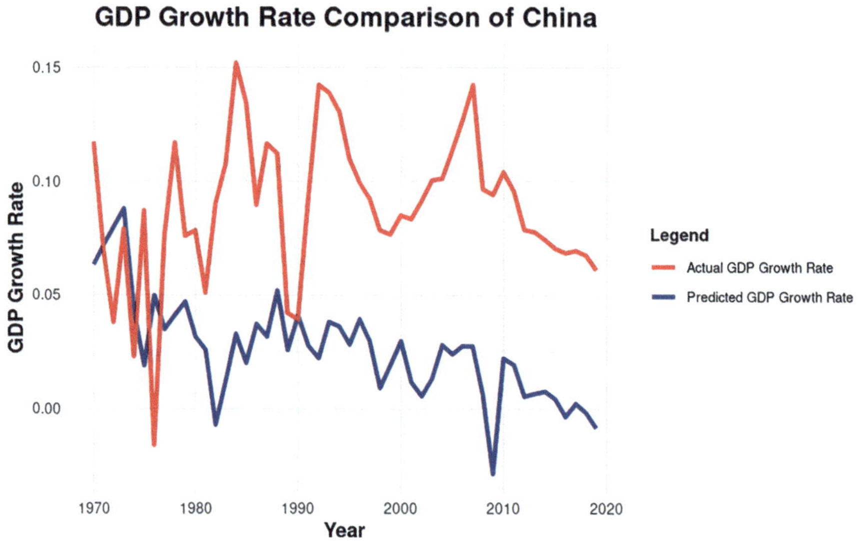

Fig. 12 Comparison of real GDP growth rate and predicted GDP growth rate for China

4.8.2 Multicollinearity

This paper constructs correlation plots to assess multicollinearity among the independent variables. Figure 13 reveals a positive correlation between UNDERVAL and investment, represented by the blue circle in the UNDERVAL and IR variables. This suggests that undervaluation can influence domestic savings and investment behavior. As exports and personal incomes rise, so does the savings rate, which can be converted into investment, thereby increasing the overall investment rate. However, this correlation is minimal and can be overlooked. Overall, the correlation between the independent variables is not significant, though there is a relatively strong negative correlation between the consumption rate and trade openness.

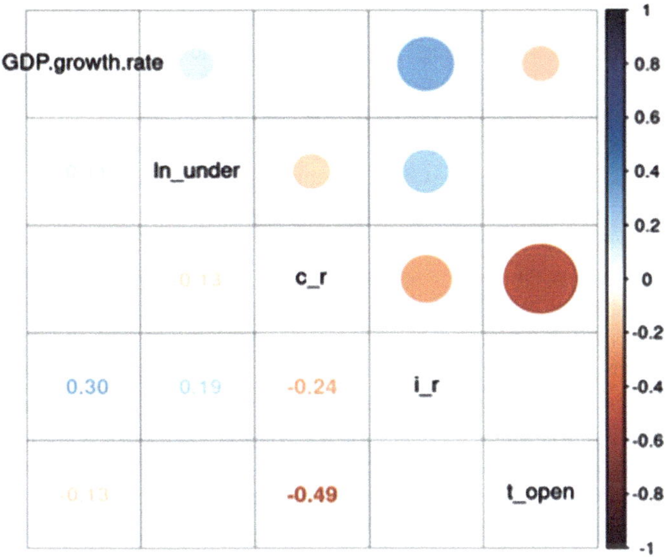

Fig. 13 Correlation plot of the coefficients of panel regression model

5 Innovation Points

This paper uses the GDP deflator as the macro price level to calculate the exchange rate, drawing on both domestic and international studies. It further computes the exchange rate and its growth rate based on extensive data. During the empirical analysis, two forms of the exchange rate are rigorously regressed and compared, after which the exchange rate is selected as the independent variable for subsequent categorized regression analysis and forecasting models. To enhance the model's accuracy and in line with Rodrik's (2008), the paper incorporates exchange rate undervaluation into the regression, resulting in an improved model fit. Additionally, this paper utilizes the latest data to explore the development trends of GDP growth rate and exchange rate, providing explanations for these trends.

6 Conclusion

In conclusion, the primary objective of this research is to examine whether a country can enhance its growth prospects by controlling the exchange rate. The findings indicate a positive relationship between the exchange rate and GDP growth rate, with the effect being most significant for developing countries. However, this effect diminishes when other variables are controlled for. Therefore, governments should consider the indirect effects of the exchange rate on other economic variables, such as by coordinating exchange rate policy with trade and foreign investment policies, to avoid over-reliance on exchange rate adjustments and achieve a more flexible and integrated policy mix that supports economic growth. This research makes significant contributions to both the theoretical and practical understanding of how changes in the exchange rate impact GDP growth. Key contributions include the use of a novel calculation method involving the GDP deflator, the adoption and rigorous comparison of three forms of independent variables, and the use of the latest data along with a time series prediction model to forecast future trends in GDP growth. However, the regression analysis in this study is based on data from only 16 countries, which means that the results may differ if a broader range of countries, particularly poorer nations, are included. Additionally, the complexity of the regression model is somewhat limited; further improvements in fit and accuracy could be achieved by incorporating interaction terms and other refinements. Future research will focus on expanding the dataset to include more countries and further disaggregating country categories. It will also explore additional relevant independent variables and enhance regression models. Furthermore, the use of multivariate time series forecasting models will be pursued to conduct more comprehensive predictive analyses.

References

1. Feenstra, Robert C., Robert Inklaar, Marcel P. Timmer (2015), “The Next Generation of the Penn World Table” American Economic Review, 105(10), 3150–3182, available for download at www.ggdc.net/pwt
2. Rodrik D. (2008) The real exchange rate and economic growth. Brookings Papers on Economic Activity, 365–412.
3. Eichengreen B. (2007) THE REAL EXCHANGE RATE AND ECONOMIC GROWTH. Social and Economic Studies, 7–20.
4. Rapetti M., Skott P., & Razmi A. (2012) The real exchange rate and economic growth: are developing countries different? International Review of Applied Economics, 735–753.
5. Idris J., Yusop Z., Habibullah M.S., (2016). Trade openness and economic growth: a causality test in panel perspective. Int. J. Bus. Soc. 17.
6. Kim H.S., (2021) An Analysis of Patterns of World Economy: Consumption and Economic Growth [J]. Journal of Global Economics, 1–4.
7. Edwards S. (1989) Real Exchange Rates, Devaluation, and Adjustment: Exchange Rate Policy in Developing Countries. MIT Press.
8. Krekó J., Oblath G. (2020) ‘Economic growth and real exchange rate misalignments in the European Union’, Acta Oeconomica, 297–332.
9. Glüzmann P.A., Levy-Yeyati E., Sturzenegger F. (2012) ‘Exchange rate undervaluation and economic growth: Díaz Alejandro (1965) revisited’, Economics Letters, 666–672.
10. Micossi S. (1994) Real exchange rates and the prices of nontradable goods, SSRN Electronic Journal [Preprint].
11. Zhang C. (2020) Inflation dynamics, Inflation in China, 137–157.

Navigating Uncertainty: The Role of Corporate Innovation in Influencing Firms Revenue Amid the COVID-19 Pandemic

Longda Shen, Yulin Yang, and Xinyuan Jiang

Abstract During the period of the pandemic, COVID-19 swept across the globe and deeply affected the production and performance of most enterprises. Notoriously, innovation has a positive impact on firm revenue, but considering the influence of the pandemic, the result is unknown and worth investigating. To figure out the relationship between corporate innovation and firm revenue, this paper concentrates on the data of some Chinese enterprises during the period of the pandemic, uses the scientific skills of econometrics based on the model of the multivariate linear regression function and chooses revenue over scale as the dependent variable, innovation ability, innovation quality, ESG rating as the independent variables. According to the regression result, this paper reaches an astonishing conclusion that the negative impact of the epidemic on enterprises is far more significant than the positive impact of corporate innovation on firms' revenue, which means that the more enterprises invest in innovation, the less return they will get. The last part of this paper offers suggestions that can help enterprises change their strategies when faced with inevitable factors.

Keywords Enterprise innovation · Innovation quality · Innovation Ability · Covid-19 · Regression

L. Shen
School of Foreign Language, Huazhong University of Science and Technology, Wuhan, China

Y. Yang
School of Economics and Management, University of Xidian, Xi'an, China

X. Jiang (✉)
School of Economics and Management, University of North China Electric Power, Beijing, China
e-mail: jiangxinyaun@outlook.com

E. Tsui et al. (eds.), *Management Information Systems in a Digitalized AI World*,
Springer Proceedings in Business and Economics,
https://doi.org/10.1007/978-981-96-6526-6_14

1 Introduction

In early 2020, the COVID-19 pandemic broke out in Wuhan, China, and spread globally. During the pandemic control period, the quarantine policies and related entry restrictions implemented by various countries to prevent the spread of the virus profoundly impacted the global economy. Against this backdrop, the pandemic exerted significant downward pressure on China's economic growth, with enterprises facing numerous "bottlenecks", "breakpoints", and "pain points" [1], including insufficient effective demand, shortages of raw materials, logistical challenges, and shortages of capital and labour. As a result, the growth rate of Gross Domestic Product (GDP) fluctuated significantly, remaining stable at 6–7% from 2015 to 2019 but varying between 2.2% and 8.4% from 2020 to 2023 in Statistical Bulletin of the People's Republic of China on National Economic and Social Development from National Bureau of Statistics of China. In recent years, technological innovation has become a key strategy for Chinese enterprises to achieve innovation-driven development. More and more companies recognize the importance of technological innovation in enhancing their capabilities. In the context of the pandemic, as businesses strive to cope with unprecedented external economic shocks, the role of technological innovation has received close attention. While the pandemic has brought challenges, it has also created opportunities, and companies face relentless pressure to adapt and grow, whether operating on a global scale or within niche markets.

The primary purpose of this study is to explore the impact of innovation ability and innovation quality on the annual revenues of Chinese publicly listed companies during the COVID-19 pandemic. Analyzing companies' performance during this period aims to understand the critical role of innovation in crisis management and long-term corporate development. The results show that COVID-19 significantly reduced the positive effect of firm innovation.

This paper explores the impact of corporate innovation on profitability under the influence of the COVID-19 pandemic. The significance of studying this topic includes the following two points:

First, it helps to better understand the economic dynamics during a crisis for businesses. Innovation has always been crucial in driving recovery and growth after economic downturns. By examining how innovation affects earnings in the context of the pandemic, strategies and practices can be identified for companies to improve financial performance under adverse conditions.

Second, studying how innovation in two dimensions affects revenue can guide companies in effectively innovating and adjusting their strategies to meet new market demands. Furthermore, this research is of great importance for the government in accurately guiding the economic recovery of businesses after a shock.

This paper is organized as follows: in the next section, we review the relevant research on the role of corporate innovation in influencing firms' revenue amid the COVID-19 pandemic. In Sect. 3, we report data collection and variable measurement. Section 4 focuses on the empirical results. Finally, we discuss the main conclusions, suggestions, and research limitations in Sect. 5.

2 Literature Review

2.1 Existing Studies

Fitz-Oliveira and Wasgen explore the relationship between innovation capability and sustainability, highlighting how firms with robust innovation strategies were better equipped to navigate the challenges posed by the pandemic [2]. Their bibliometric analysis suggests that innovation drives sustainability and enhances resilience in uncertain times.

Sahoo investigates the link between quality management, innovation capability, and firm performance within Indian manufacturing SMEs [3]. The study reveals that firms with strong innovation capabilities experienced improved performance metrics, even during economic downturns. This underscores the importance of integrating quality management practices with innovation strategies to sustain competitive advantage.

Le et al. provide empirical evidence from Vietnam, indicating that innovation significantly boosts SME performance [4]. Their research demonstrates that firms investing in innovation saw increased productivity and profitability, which was crucial during the pandemic when traditional business models faced unprecedented disruptions.

Sun and Li focus on the financial performance of Chinese firms during the COVID-19 outbreak, emphasizing the role of corporate culture and social responsibility [5]. Their findings suggest that firms with a strong innovative culture and commitment to social responsibility were better positioned to maintain financial stability, highlighting the broader impact of innovation beyond immediate financial gains.

Li Xiaokai and Wang Peipei examine the influence of innovation capability on stock returns in Chinese firms [6, 7]. Both studies conclude that firms with higher innovation capabilities experienced better stock performance during the pandemic, reinforcing that innovation is a crucial driver of financial success in volatile markets.

2.2 Limitations

2.2.1 Lack of Data Support

Some of the research lacks sufficient empirical data to support their conclusions. This limitation affects the robustness and reliability of their findings, as comprehensive datasets are necessary to assess the impact of innovation capability and quality management accurately.

2.2.2 Insufficient Consideration of Extraordinary Circumstance

Certain studies do not adequately account for the abnormal impacts of the COVID-19 pandemic when exploring the influence of innovation on revenue. The pandemic introduced unique challenges and disruptions that significantly affected market dynamics, which is essential for a complete understanding of innovation's role during such periods.

3 Data and Methodology

3.1 Dependent Variable

This study examines the impact of corporate innovation on business income during the pandemic. Thus, the time frame for the dependent variable is set from 2020 to 2023. Among all the indicators measuring corporate income, total operating revenue can intuitively and effectively reflect the income situation of a company. Additionally, since company size significantly affects income, large companies can leverage economies of scale to reduce unit costs, increase revenue and utilize their more significant market share to gain more sales opportunities and higher income. Therefore, to standardize the income situation of companies of different sizes, corporate income can be divided by company size to reasonably present the true income situation of companies of various sizes, denoted as RS. Company size can be measured by total assets, representing the company's assets and resources, reflecting production capacity and market share information. Furthermore, the impact of corporate innovation on businesses tends to be lagged [8], so the explanatory variable from three years prior will be used to explain the dependent variable three years later, with the dependent variable denoted as RS3. Therefore, this study selects the indicator of total operating revenue divided by total assets from 2020 to 2023 as the dependent variable.

3.2 Explanatory Variables

3.2.1 Innovation Ability

A company's investment in innovation and development is essential to its innovative capability. This paper measures the company's innovation ability by dividing its development investment by its total cash inflows, denoted as IA [9]. This ratio helps assess the extent of the company's investment in development activities and its impact on cash flow, thereby providing insights into the company's investment strategy and financial condition. Generally speaking, the stronger a company's innovation capability, the higher its revenue.

3.2.2 Innovation Quality

The number of patents a company obtains is a significant indicator of its technological innovation. The number of patents can also measure the intensity and quality of a company's innovation [10]. This paper adds one to the number of patents obtained to reduce the influence of extreme values on the statistical results and ensure that the results are more normally distributed. It takes the logarithm, using the result as an indicator of the quality of the company's innovation, denoted as innovation quality. Patents obtained by enterprises are categorized into two types: independent patents and joint patents. Independent patents refer to patents applied for and obtained by an enterprise alone, reflecting the enterprise's independent R&D capability and depth of innovation in technological innovation. Joint patents refer to patents applied for and obtained by enterprises together with other organizations or enterprises, reflecting the ability of enterprises in technological cooperation and joint research and development. By analyzing independent patents and joint patents separately, we can more comprehensively assess the quality of enterprises' innovations at different levels, thus revealing the mechanism of the impact of enterprises' innovations on revenues after the epidemic.

3.2.3 ESG

Additionally, since under contingencies, firms' ESG performance has a significant positive effect on cumulative abnormal stock returns during the event window [11], this paper includes the ESG index to assess the company's contribution to promoting sustainable economic development and fulfilling social responsibilities, denoted as ESG. In response to the fact that some companies have missing ESG data for different years and that ESG performance indices are generally published four times a year, we averaged the ESG indices of companies for each year to obtain the average ESG performance of each company for each year.

3.3 Model Specification

This paper studies how multiple variables influence one variable (the company's revenue indicator). In econometrics, the overall regression function used to describe the linear relationship between an explained variable and multiple explanatory variables is the multiple linear regression function. When researching the impact of innovation during the pandemic on company revenue, there are multiple explanatory variables, thus initially establishing the following multiple linear regression function:

$$Y_{t+\tau} = \alpha + \beta_1 IA_t + \beta_2 IQ_t + \beta_3 ESG_t + \varepsilon_t \quad (1)$$

4 Empirical Results

4.1 Descriptive Statistics

After organizing all the data, descriptive statistics for all explanatory and dependent variables were conducted using STATA (see Table 1). Table 1 displays the sample's number of observations, mean, standard deviation, minimum, median, and maximum. Table 1 shows the statistical characteristics of six variables in this descriptive statistic. RS3 has a low mean but a high standard deviation, indicating a relatively dispersed data distribution. The maximum value is significantly higher than the mean, suggesting the presence of some outliers. The mean and median of RS are relatively close, indicating a more concentrated data distribution. The standard deviation is also large, reflecting a higher degree of dispersion. The mean and median of innovation ability are both low, indicating that most data points cluster around lower values of innovation capability. The standard deviation is relatively small, suggesting a lower degree of dispersion. The mean and median of IIU are close, indicating a concentrated data distribution. The standard deviation is large, showing a higher degree of dispersion. The mean of CIU is significantly higher than the median, indicating a right-skewed distribution (i.e., more low values and fewer high values). The standard deviation is large, reflecting a higher degree of dispersion. The mean and median of the Total are close, and the data distribution is relatively concentrated. The standard deviation is large, indicating a higher degree of dispersion. The mean and median of ESG are relatively close, suggesting a concentrated data distribution. The standard deviation is relatively small, indicating a lower degree of dispersion. The variables in Table 1 exhibit varying degrees of dispersion and concentration trends. Some variables (such as RS3 and RS) have large standard deviations and outliers, indicating a more dispersed distribution, while other variables (such as Innovation_ability and ESG) show a more concentrated data distribution.

4.2 Parameter Estimation

Parameter estimation using the least squares method in STATA software (see Table 2) yields the following results for the model's parameter estimates based on the results in Table 2.

Table 1 Summary statistics

VarName	Obs	Mean	SD	Min	Median	Max
RS3	399	1.29e + 00	2.37e + 00	0.09953399	0.72389193	1.86e + 01
RS	399	1.11e + 00	1.51e + 00	0.07457330	0.68799829	1.50e + 01
Innovation_ ability	399	0.02032255	0.03114717	0.00000376	0.01146371	0.21384722
IIU	399	2.00e + 00	1.55e + 00	0.00e + 00	1.95e + 00	6.17e + 00
CIU	399	0.88002899	1.17e + 00	0.00e + 00	0.00e + 00	5.02e + 00
Innovation_ quality	399	2.24e + 00	1.52e + 00	0.00e + 00	2.20e + 00	6.21e + 00
ESG	399	7.55e + 01	5.56e + 00	6.32e + 01	7.58e + 01	8.99e + 01

Table 2 Parameter estimation

	(1)	(2)	(3)
Variables	RS3	RS3	RS3
Innovation_ability	−12.527***	−13.009***	
	(−3.28)	(−3.38)	
Innovation_quality	−0.206**		−0.219***
	(−2.58)		(−2.71)
ESG	0.043*	0.028	0.047**
	(1.93)	(1.29)	(2.09)
Constant	−0.668	0.038	−1.078
	(−0.40)	(0.02)	(−0.64)
Observations	399	399	399
R-squared	0.076	0.060	0.050
Year	Yes	Yes	Yes

t-statistics in parentheses
***$p < 0.01$, , **$p < 0.05$, * * $p < 0.1$

4.3 Robustness Test

In order to test the robustness of the model results, a robustness test is conducted by replacing the key variable Innovation_quality in the original model with two different substitution variables, IIU (firm independent patents) and CIU (corporate joint patents). The purpose of the test is to ensure that the model results remain consistent under the different variable choices remain consistent, thus verifying that the model is robust.

Table 3 Robustness test (use IIU to replace Innovation_quality)

	(1)	(2)	(3)
Variables	RS3	RS3	RS3
Innovation_ability	−12.819***	−13.009***	
	(−3.35)	(−3.38)	
IIU	−0.160**		−0.166**
	(−2.06)		(−2.11)
ESG	0.037*	0.028	0.041*
	(1.70)	(1.29)	(1.83)
Constant	−0.377	0.038	−0.768
	(−0.23)	(0.02)	(−0.46)
Observations	399	399	399
R-squared	0.070	0.060	0.043
Year	Yes	Yes	Yes

t-statistics in parentheses
***$p < 0.01$, , **$p < 0.05$, * * $p < 0.1$

4.3.1 Selection of Alternative Variables

In this robustness test, we selected two variables, IIU and CIU, as alternatives to Innovation_quality, which were chosen to explore the impact of different innovation inputs on the model results.

4.3.2 Robustness Test Results

According to Table 3, after the robustness test, it was found that the estimation results of the model remained relatively the same whether IIU (as shown in Table 3) or CIU (as shown in Table 4) was used to replace Innovation_quality. This indicates that the introduction of alternative variables did not substantially affect the model's conclusions, which suggests that the model is highly robust. This result further validates the reliability of the model, indicating that the estimation results of the model remain stable by replacing different variables.

Table 4 Robustness test (use CIU to replace Innovation_quality)

Variables	(1) RS3	(2) RS3	(3) RS3
Innovation_ability	−11.554***	−13.009***	
	(−3.00)	(−3.38)	
CIU	−0.281***		−0.327***
	(−2.62)		(−3.05)
ESG	0.046**	0.028	0.052**
	(2.06)	(1.29)	(2.31)
Constant	−1.141	0.038	−1.666
	(−0.67)	(0.02)	(−0.97)
Observations	399	399	399
R-squared	0.076	0.060	0.055
Year	Yes	Yes	Yes

t-statistics in parentheses
*** $p < 0.0\ 1$, ** $p < 0.05$, * * $p < 0.1$

5 Conclusion

This article primarily studies the relationship between innovation and corporate revenue under the impact of the pandemic. Focusing on A-share listed companies in Shanghai and Shenzhen from 2020 to 2023, it conducts an empirical analysis of the effects of innovation capability and innovation quality. Based on the empirical results, the following conclusions are drawn: contrary to popular belief, during the COVID-19 pandemic, the negative impact of the pandemic on businesses far outweighs the positive impact of independent innovation on corporate revenue. This suggests that the more companies invest in innovation, the lesser the returns they receive. Corporate innovation is a high-risk, high-reward activity in the current market economy environment. Only a few companies with strong financial resources and advanced R&D capabilities have the capacity to bear such risks. Therefore, the sampled companies still need to improve in converting capital investments into operating revenue. The total number of patent grants in China has steadily increased, reflecting the achievements made in technological innovation in recent years. Additionally, patents have been relatively affected by the pandemic, with a noticeable decline in the number of patents independently obtained by companies around 2020.

For businesses, the interruption of supply chains during the pandemic significantly reduced production and logistics efficiency, making it easier to obtain raw materials and production equipment in a timely manner. At the same time, market demand plummeted, leading to a decline in consumers' purchasing power and willingness. Additionally, government-imposed lockdowns in some cities restricted normal business operations, causing many companies to face a sharp drop in sales. The economic uncertainty triggered by the pandemic has also increased the risks associated with business investment and expansion. Although current innovation investments have yet to yield positive returns, companies need to maintain confidence in the market, increase R&D spending, and continuously enhance the competitiveness of their products and services through technological innovation. Companies should also keep pace with market changes and technological advancements, adjust their strategies flexibly, seize development opportunities, and turn the situation around.

For the government, it is essential to strengthen tax reductions and fee cuts for businesses, ensuring the implementation of these policies to boost corporate confidence. At the same time, this will also encourage companies' willingness to innovate and enhance their ability to withstand external shocks. Furthermore, government spending encouraging businesses plays a crucial role in innovation activities. First, government innovation subsidies can effectively alleviate cash flow pressures, enabling companies to increase their investment in technological innovation, thereby improving innovation output to some extent. Second, technological innovation activities, such as the invention of COVID-19 vaccines, demonstrate significant positive externalities. Therefore, the government should adopt policy measures to control the impact of these externalities. The government also needs to optimize the operating environment for manufacturing enterprises. China's regulatory environment plays a key role in shaping the innovation landscape. Government policies and regulations can both promote and hinder innovation. In recent years, the Chinese government has implemented a series of policies to promote innovation and entrepreneurship. These measures include financial incentives for R&D, support for high-tech startups, and protections for intellectual property. Such policies create a favourable innovation environment for businesses, allowing them to leverage new technologies and business models to enhance profitability. Alternatively, business decision-makers, in the context of the pandemic, the industry faces unprecedented disruptions and shifts in consumer behaviour, making innovative responses crucial. Companies that innovate effectively can adjust their strategies, adapt to new market demands, and manage risks more adeptly than those that lag behind in innovation.

Like other studies, this research design has certain limitations that can provide direction for future research. First, This study primarily focuses on companies listed on the Shanghai Stock Exchange and the Shenzhen Stock Exchange without an in-depth examination of non-listed companies. Therefore, the conclusions drawn from this study do not apply to all types of companies. The question of whether the COVID-19 pandemic has impacted the innovation of small and medium-sized enterprises is worth investigating. Second, since 210 out of 399 research samples are from the biotechnology industry, This study mainly concentrates on this sector and only comprehensively and evenly covers some industries. Thus, the conclusions are not applicable to companies in other industries. Studying the differences among listed companies in various industries during the pandemic would be meaningful.

Acknowledgements Xinyuan Jiang, Longda Shen, and Yulin Yang contributed equally to this work and should be considered co-first authors.

References

1. Fitz-Oliveira, M., Wasgen, A. M. (2023) Innovation capability and sustainability: A bibliometric analysis. Technological Sustainability, 2: 156–176.
2. Jie Z., Wenping Z. (2018) Is China's Innovation Catch-Up Strategy Stifling Patent Quality? Economic research, 53: 28–41.
3. Le, D. V., Le, H. T. T., Pham, T. T., Vo, L. V. (2023) Innovation and SMEs performance: Evidence from Vietnam. Applied Economic Analysis, 31: 90–108.
4. Naxin L., Sihan L. (2022) A study of the lagged impact of innovation investment on firm performance. Journal of Hunan University of Finance and Economics, 38: 56–65.
5. Peipei W China. (2024) The Impact of GEM Firms' Innovative Capacity on Stock Returns. https://doi.org/10.27047/d.cnki.ggudu.2023.002914.
6. Qi W China. (2022) The Impact of Firms' ESG Performance on Stock Returns under Unforeseen Events. https://doi.org/10.27310/d.cnki.gshsy.2021.000018.
7. Sahoo, S. (2019) Quality management, innovation capability and firm performance: Empirical insights from Indian manufacturing SMEs. The TQM Journal, 31: 1003–1027.
8. Xiaokai L China. (2022) A study of the impact of corporate innovation capacity on stock returns. https://d.wanfangdata.com.cn/thesis/D02703631.
9. Yang, Y., Yingming, Z., Jiazhen, D. (2024) Does digital transformation help mitigate firm innovation dilemma? A quasi-natural experiment based on the COVID-19 pandemic in China. Chinese Management Studies.
10. Yudong L China. (2024) A study on the impact of tax cuts and fee reductions on the high-quality development of the manufacturing industry. https://doi.org/10.27283/d.cnki.gsxcc.2023.000739.
11. Yunpeng, S., Ying, L. (2021) COVID-19 Outbreak and Financial Performance of Chinese Listed Firms: Evidence from Corporate Culture and Corporate Social Responsibility. Frontiers in Public Health, 9.

Pricing American Options Based on the Binomial Tree Model

Zhuohao Cao, Xiaohui Huang, Wentao Xiao, and Qiqian Zeng

Abstract Due to their inherent flexibility to be exercised at any time before expiration, American options present a valuation challenge that is more complex and costly compared to European options, which can only be exercised at expiration. This paper seeks to elucidate the premium of American options through a 2-period binomial tree model under the assumption that the product of downside and upside probabilities equals one. This work explores the price differential between American and European options across a spectrum of interest rates r and strike prices K. Furthermore, this work investigates the implications of dividends on American call option premiums by employing a 1-period binomial tree model. The inclusion of dividends adds a layer of complexity to the valuation process, necessitating the derivation of risk-neutral probabilities that account for dividends while maintaining no-arbitrage conditions. Our analysis reveals how variations in interest rates, strike prices, and the presence of dividends significantly influence American option premiums. By providing a detailed framework, our findings contribute to a deeper understanding of the pricing dynamics of American options, enabling better strategic decision-making for investors and financial practitioners alike. This comprehensive approach sheds light on the intricate relationships that govern option valuation in diverse market conditions.

Keywords Binomial tree model · American option price · European option price · Dividend · Premium

---

All authors contributed equally to this work and should be considered co-first authors.

Z. Cao (✉)
Finance School, Central University of Finance and Economics, Beijing, China
e-mail: 2056352864@qq.com

X. Huang · Q. Zeng
University of Birmingham Joint Institute, Jinan University, Guangzhou, China

W. Xiao
Management School, Lancaster University, Lancaster, UK

E. Tsui et al. (eds.), *Management Information Systems in a Digitalized AI World*,
Springer Proceedings in Business and Economics,
https://doi.org/10.1007/978-981-96-6526-6_15

1 Introduction

American options refer to options that can be exercised at any point before expiration [1]. In contrast, European options must be exercised on the expiration date. Therefore, due to their flexible exercise time, American options are generally more expensive and complex than the same expiration European options.

Since this work observed that the literature on American option premiums has been rarely studied, and there has yet to be a mathematical discussion on premiums between American and European options by adjusting K and r in the past. Therefore, the main content of this article is to discuss the changes in the pricing and premium of American options according to the exercise time node of European options under different K and r conditions. To carry out this research, this work used the binomial tree model to price options [2], choosing this model was inspired by the pioneering work of Cox, and Ross in the paper Option Pricing: A Simplified Approach, where binomial tree model was constructed to simulate the possible price paths of the underlying stock at each time step, thereby calculating the present value of the option [3]. This work uses the 2-period binomial tree model to calculate the American option price, European option price and the difference in price between them, considering different r and K. Furthermore, the researchers briefly studied the premium of American options with dividends added in the 1-period binomial tree model to explore the influence of dividends on the exercise time of American call options [1, 4].

2 Literature Review

The origins of European options can be traced back to the Black–Scholes model by Black and Scholes, which laid the foundation for European options pricing [5]. For American options, Cox, Ross, and Rubinstein introduced the binomial tree model for American option pricing [3], and Hull and White improved on the binary tree model, taking into account stochastic volatility [6]. Later, Benede and Vorster proposed a method for adjusting volatility to improve the accuracy of American option pricing [7]. The fact that American options can be exercised at any point before expiration increases the complexity of pricing. Barone-Adesi and Whaley suggested using finite difference methods, which enhance accuracy but come with high costs [8]. Additionally, Longstaff and Schwartz developed a simulation-based least-squares approach, which simplifies valuation while accommodating early exercise features in American options [9]. Geske and Johnson further contributed to American put options by providing an analytical valuation method, offering precise solutions under certain conditions [10]. These developments illustrate the diverse approaches for addressing the complexities associated with American options, from approximations to simulation techniques, catering to different computational needs and accuracy requirements.

3 Methodology

To simplify the problem, this work assumes that the product of the downside probability and the upside probability is 1. Then, it does the following work to get the formulas for the theoretical price of American options and European options and takes the difference between them as a premium.

Step 1: Calculate the American option price. According to the exercise time of European options, this work first divides the conditions of American options by the value of $\boldsymbol{r}$ and then does a further classification based on the value of $\boldsymbol{K}$ to get the corresponding 2-period American option price using the binomial tree model.

Step 2: Calculate the European option price. According to the classification of $\boldsymbol{r}$ and $\boldsymbol{K}$ in **Step 1**, this work calculates the corresponding price in a 2-period European option using the binomial tree model and does further division if needed.

Step 3: Calculate the premium. After gaining the formulae of premium between two option prices by using the price of the American option, which is calculated in **Step 1,** subtracting the price of the European option, which is calculated in **Step 2**.

4 Results

In this section, we briefly discuss the results of American option prices and the early-exercise premium we get in our research. We start from the situation of American options in 2 periods that is without dividends and divide the situations according to the option type and value of r and K. Then we analyze the condition of 1-period American call options with dividends as additional content for our essay.

4.1 Options Without Dividends

4.1.1 Call Option

$r \geq 0$

In a 1-period binomial tree model, the following inequality always holds:

$$S_0 - K \leq S_0 - \frac{K}{1+r} \leq \left[S_0 - \frac{K}{1+r}\right]^+$$

Which means that the holding value is always larger than the exercise value at T_0. This conclusion could be expanded to the 2-period binomial tree model. Therefore, the investor would choose to hold the option until the maturity time, then the price of the American put option should be the same as the European put option, which is

$$\frac{1}{1+r}\left[q[X_1(S_0u)-K]^+\right]+(1-q)[X_1(S_0d)-K]^+\Big]$$

where

$$X_1(S_0u)=\frac{1}{1+r}\left[q\left(S_0u^2-K\right)^+ +(1-q)(S_0-K)^+\right]$$
$$X_1(S_0d)=\frac{1}{1+r}\left[q(S_0-K)^+ +(1-q)\left(S_0d^2-K\right)^+\right]$$

and r is the interest rate, q is the risk-neutral probability, K is the strike, u is the multiples of stock rises, d is the multiples of stock declines S_0 is the stock price at T_0.

Hence, the premium between the American option and the European option is 0.

$r < 0$

The classification under this condition is much more complicated. In the following formulae, K represents the strike, S_0 is the stock price at T_0, u is the multiples of stock rises, d represents the multiples of stock declines, T_N represents $T = N$.

(1) If $K < S_0d^2$, the investor would exercise at T_0 in the American option, then the price of the American option is $S_0 - K$. The price of its corresponding European option is $\frac{K}{(1+r)^2} - S_0$. Therefore, the premium is

$$\frac{K}{(1+r)^2}-K$$

(2) If $S_0\,d^2 < K < \frac{S_0\left[1-qu-q(1-q)\frac{1}{(1+r)^2}\right]}{1-q-q(1-q)\frac{1}{(1+r)^2}}$, the investor would exercise at T_0 and the American option price is$S_0 - K$. The European option price is $\frac{q(S_0u-K)}{1+r} + \frac{q(1-q)(S_0-K)}{(1+r)^2}$. Hence, the premium is

$$S_0-K-\frac{qS_0u}{1+r}+\frac{K[q(2-q)]+S_0\left(q^2-q\right)}{(1+r)^2}$$

(3) If$\frac{S_0\left[1-qu-q(1-q)\frac{1}{(1+r)^2}\right]}{1-q-q(1-q)\frac{1}{(1+r)^2}} < K < S_0$, the investor would choose to exercise atT_1, then the price of American option is$\frac{(1-q)(K-S_0d)}{1+r}+\frac{q(1-q)(K-S_0)}{(1+r)^2}$. Its corresponding European option price is $\frac{q(S_0u-K)}{1+r} + \frac{q(1-q)(S_0-K)}{(1+r)^2}$. Then, the premium is

$$\frac{-qKr}{(1+r)^2}=\frac{qK|r|}{(1+r)^2}$$

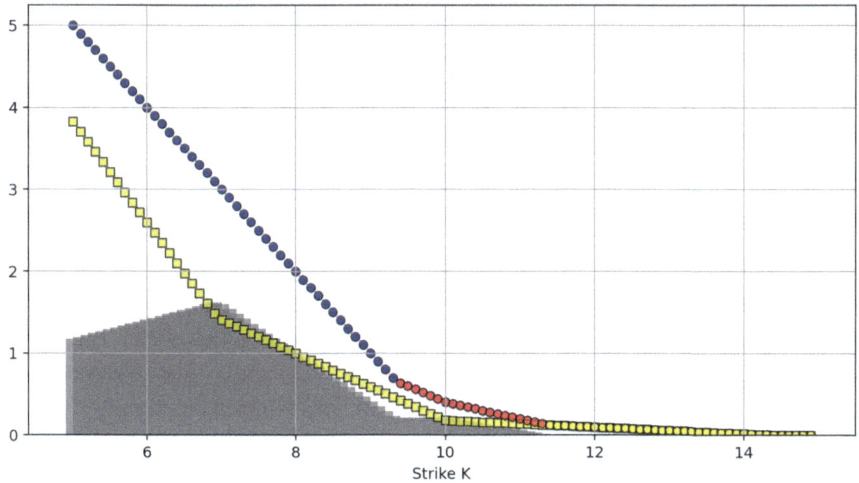

Fig. 1 The price of American and European options and the premium between the two options for $r < 0$

(4) If $S_0 < K < \frac{S_0 u(1+r) - qS_0 u^2}{(1+r)-q}$, in the American option, the investor would prefer to exercise at T_1, then the price of the American option is $\frac{q(S_0 u - K)}{1+r}$. And its corresponding European option price is $\frac{q^2(S_0 u^2 - K)}{(1+r)^2}$. So, the premium is

$$\frac{q(S_0 u - K)}{1+r} - \frac{q^2(S_0 u^2 - K)}{(1+r)^2}$$

(5) If $K > \frac{S_0 u(1+r) - qS_0 u^2}{(1+r)-q}$, the holding value would be larger than the exercise value at any point at T_1 and T_0. The investor would choose to hold the option until maturity time. Hence, the price of the American option and the European option would be the same, which are $\frac{q^2(S_0 u^2 - K)}{(1+r)^2}$. Therefore, the premium is 0.

In Fig. 1, the dot-line represents the price of American options, the square-line represents the price of European options, the shaded region in gray shows the premium between American option and European option for fixed r and different K. On both lines, blue dots mean the option price of the call option that investors exercise at T_0, red dots mean the option price of the call option that investors exercise at T_0, yellow dots and squares mean the option price of the call option that investors exercise at T_2.

4.1.2 Put Option

$r \leq 0$

In a 1-period binomial tree model, the following inequality always holds:

$$\mathrm{K} - \mathrm{S}_0 \leq \frac{K}{1+r} - \mathrm{S}_0 \leq \left[\frac{K}{1+r} - S_0\right]^+$$

Which means that the holding value is always larger than the exercise value at T_0.This conclusion could be expanded to the 2-period binomial tree model. Therefore, the investor would choose to hold the option until the maturity time, then the price of the American put option should be the same as the European put option, which is

$$\frac{1}{1+r}\left[q[K - X_1(S_0u)]^+ + (1-q)[K - X_1(S_0d)]^+\right]$$

where

$$X_1(S_0u) = \frac{1}{1+r}\left[q\left(K - S_0u^2\right)^+ + (1-q)(K - S_0)^+\right]$$

$$X_1(S_0d) = \frac{1}{1+r}\left[q(K - S_0)^+ + (1-q)\left(K - S_0d^2\right)^+\right]$$

and r is the interest rate, q is the risk-neutral probability, K is the strike, u is the multiples of stock rises, d is the multiples of stock declines S_0 is the stock price at T_0.

Hence, the premium between the American option and the European option is 0

$r > 0$

The classification under this condition is much more complicated. In the following formulae, K represents the strike, S_0 is the stock price at T_0, u is the multiples of stock rises, d represents the multiples of stock declines, T_N represents $T = N$.

(1) If $\mathrm{K} > \mathrm{S}_0\mathrm{u}^2$, the investor would exercise at T_0 in the American option, then the price of the American option is $K - S_0$. The price of its corresponding European option is $\frac{K}{(1+r)^2} - S_0$. Therefore, the premium is

$$K - \frac{\mathrm{K}}{(1+r)^2}$$

(2) If $\frac{S_0\left[(1+r)^2 - q(1-q) - (1-q)d(1+r)\right]}{(1+r)^2 - (1-q)(1+r) - q(1-q)} < \mathrm{K} < \mathrm{S}_0\mathrm{u}^2$, in American option, the investor would exercise at T_0 and its price is $K - S_0$. The corresponding European

option price is $\frac{(1-q)\left[K(1-q)+qS_0\right]}{(1+r)^2} - \frac{S_0d(1-q)}{1+r}$. Hence, the premium is

$$K - S_0 - \frac{(1-q)\left[K(1-q)+qS_0\right]}{(1+r)^2} + \frac{S_0d(1-q)}{1+r}$$

(3) If $S_0 < K < \frac{S_0\left[(1+r)^2-q(1-q)-(1-q)d(1+r)\right]}{(1+r)^2-(1-q)(1+r)-q(1-q)}$, the investor would choose to exercise atT_1, then the price of American option is $\frac{(1-q)(K-S_0d)}{1+r} + \frac{q(1-q)(K-S_0)}{(1+r)^2}$. Its corresponding European option price is $\frac{\left(\frac{K}{1+r}-S_0d\right)(1-q)}{1+r} + \frac{q(1-q)(K-S_0)}{(1+r)^2}$. Then, the premium is.

$$\frac{(1-q)Kr}{(1+r)^2}$$

(4) If $\frac{S_0d^2(1+r)-(1-q)S_0d}{r+q} < K < S_0$, in the American option, the investor would prefer to exercise at T_1, the price of the American option is $\frac{(1-q)(K-S_0d)}{K-S_0d}$. And its corresponding European option price is $\frac{(1-q)^2\left(K-S_0d^2\right)}{(1+r)^2}$. So, the premium is.

$$\frac{1-q}{K-S_0d}K - S_0d - \frac{(1-q)(K-S_0d)}{K-S_0d}$$

(5) If $K < \frac{S_0d^2(1+r)-(1-q)S_0d}{r+q}$, the holding value would be larger than the exercise value at any points at T_1 and T_0, then the investor would choose to hold the option until maturity time, hence the price of American option price would be the same as the European option price, which is $\frac{(1-q)^2\left(K-S_0d^2\right)}{(1+r)^2}$. Therefore, the premium is 0.

In Fig. 2, the upper dot-line represents the price of American options price, the lower square-line represents the price of European options, and the shaded region in gray shows the premium between American options and European options for fixed r and different K. Blue dots mean the option price of the call option that investors exercise at T_0, red dots mean the option price of the call option that investors exercise at T_1, yellow dots and squares mean the option price of the call option that investors exercise at T_2.

4.2 Option with Dividends

This work discussed the situation of a call option without dividends in the previous section. In the following section, it discusses the exercise and premium of a call option with dividends for a single period.

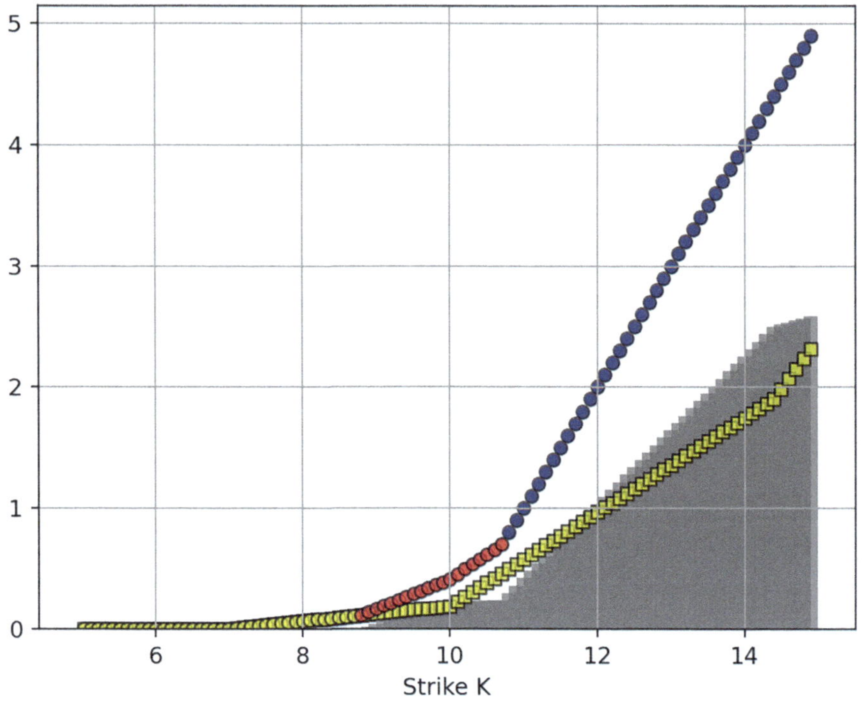

Fig. 2 The price of American and European options and premium between two options for $r > 0$

4.2.1 Risk-Neutral Probability

Under the assumption that the stock price is affected by dividends, the risk-neutral probability is given by the following equation

$$S_0 = \frac{q(S_0u + S_0D) + (1 - q)(S_0d + S_0D)}{1 + r}$$

which can be simplified as $q = \frac{1+r-d-D}{u-d}$

Without considering dividends, in order to prevent the existence of arbitrage opportunities, the interest rate on the bond must satisfy: $d < 1 + r < u$. This ensures that the expected return remains balanced. Similarly, in the condition considering the existence of dividends, the probability q should be a positive value, representing the likelihood of the stock price increasing. The following inequalities must hold: $d + D < 1 + r < u + D$. This inequality ensures that $1 + r$ is greater than the lower bound of the stock price movement plus the dividend and less than the upper bound of the stock price movement plus the dividend.

4.2.2 Exercise and Premium

In a one-period call option, the investor will choose to exercise early if the following condition is met.

$K < S_0 d$: In this case, the price at any points in 1-period binomial tree of European option is greater than 0,

$$S_0 - K + S_0 D > S_0 - \frac{K}{1+r}$$
$$D > \frac{rK}{(1+r)S_0}$$

Under this condition, the option will be exercised early at T_0; therefore, the premium between the American and European options is $S_0 D - \frac{Kr}{1+r}$.

$S_0 d$ < K < $S_0 u$: In this case, the price is greater than zero only when the stock price declines.

$$S_0 - K + S_0 D > \frac{q(S_0 u - K)}{1+r}$$
$$D > \frac{(S_0 u - S_0 d - Ku + Kd - K)(1+r) + Kd}{S_0 (u-d)(1+r) - S_0 u + K}$$

Under this condition, the option will be exercised early at T_0, therefore the premium between the American option and the European option is

$$S_0 - K + S_0 D - \frac{S_0 u(1 + r - d - D) - K(1 + r - d - D)}{(u - d)(1 + r)}$$

5 Conclusion

From an economic perspective, understanding the sensitivity of American option premiums to fluctuations in interest rates and strike prices is critical for helping investors and financial institutions manage their portfolios and providing insights into the broader impact of interest rates on investment strategies and risk management practices. In our study above, this work highlights the intricate relationship between interest rate, strike and American option premium, then get the conclusion that in a 2-period binomial-tree model of option without dividends, under the condition of $r > 0$ in call option and $r < 0$ in put option, the premium between American option and European option is 0. For $r < 0$ in the call option and $r > 0$ in the put option, the situations would be more complicated, and the formulae representing the premium between American options and European options would depend on the exercise time of the American option, which is affected by the value of K. Moreover, this work studies the situations with dividends in the call option when $r > 0$ in a 1-period binomial-tree model. By analyzing the price, researchers find that the dividend would affect the exercise time, thereby influencing the option price and premium between the American option and the European option for $r > 0$ in the American call option compared to the condition without dividends, which will never be exercised early for $r > 0$ in American call option. However, there are different patterns of dividends, and they would affect American option pricing, which is a topic researchers should have studied more carefully but needed further research. Furthermore, the interest, strike and premium would influence the pricing of more other options and financial instruments, which could be investigated in further studies.

Acknowledgements We would like to express our gratitude to Professor Johannes Ruf, who guided us and provided support and suggestions in our writing, and TA Andy Chen and Chole, who helped us greatly in our writing process.

References

1. Alghalith, M. (2020). Pricing the American options: A closed-form, simple formula. Physica A: Statistical Mechanics and its Applications, 548, 123873.
2. Azzalini, A. (2022). An overview on the progeny of the skew-normal family-A personal perspective. Journal of Multivariate Analysis, 188, 104851.
3. Cox, J. C., Ross, S. A., & Rubinstein, M. (1979). Option pricing: A simplified approach. Journal of Financial Economics, 7(3): 229-263.
4. Wang, S. (2024). Pricing European call options with interval-valued volatility and interest rate.Applied Mathematics and Computation, 474, 128698.
5. Black, F., & Scholes, M. (1973). The pricing of options and corporate liabilities. Journal of Political Economy, 81(3), 637-654.
6. Hull, J., & White, A. (1987). The pricing of options on assets with stochastic volatilities. Journal of Finance, 42(2), 281-300.
7. Beneder, R., & Vorst, T. (2011). Options on dividend-paying stocks. Journal of Derivatives, 19(2), 58-72.
8. Barone-Adesi, G., & Whaley, R. E. (1987). Efficient analytic approximation of American option values. Journal of Finance, 42(2), 301-320.
9. Longstaff, F. A., & Schwartz, E. S. (2001). Valuing American options by simulation: A simple least-squares approach. The Review of Financial Studies, 14(1), 113-147.
10. Geske, R., & Johnson, H. E. (1984). The American put option valued analytically. The Journal of Finance, 39(5), 1511-1524.